Staff Ride Handbook for the Battle of Chickamauga, 18—20 September 1863

by
Dr. William Glenn Robertson
Lieutenant Colonel Edward P. Shanahan
Lieutenant Colonel John I. Boxberger
Major George E. Knapp

Combat Studies Institute
U.S. Army Command and General Staff College
Fort Leavenworth, Kansas 66027-6900
1992

CONTENTS

CONTENTS

ILLUSTRATIONS
Figures

Maps

TABLES

INTRODUCTION

Ad bellum Pace Parati: prepared in peace for war. This sentiment was much on the mind of Captain Arthur L. Wagner as he contemplated the quality of military education at the Infantry and Cavalry School at Fort Leavenworth, Kansas, during the 1890s. Wagner believed that the school's curricula during the long years of peace had become too far removed from the reality of war, and he cast about for ways to make the study of conflict more real to officers who had no experience in combat. Eventually, he arrived at a concept he called the Staff Ride, which consisted of detailed classroom study of an actual campaign followed by a visit to the sites associated with that campaign. Although Wagner never lived to see the Staff Ride added to the Leavenworth curricula, an associate of his, Major Eben Swift, implemented the Staff Ride at the General Service and Staff School in 1906. In July of that year, Swift led a contingent of twelve students to Chattanooga, Tennessee, to begin a two-week study of the Atlanta campaign of 1864.

The Staff Ride concept pioneered at Leavenworth in the early years of the twentieth century remains a vital part of officer professional development today. At the U.S. Army Command and General Staff College, the Army War College, ROTC detachments, and units throughout the world, U.S. Army officers are studying war vicariously in peacetime through the Staff Ride methodology. That methodology (in-depth preliminary study, rigorous field study, and integration of the two) need not be tied to a formal schoolhouse environment. Units stationed near historic battlefields can experience the intellectual and emotional stimulation provided by standing on the hallowed ground where soldiers once contended for their respective causes. Yet units may find themselves without many of the sources of information on a particular campaign that are readily available in an academic environment. For that reason, the Combat Studies Institute has begun a series of handbooks on significant campaigns that will provide practical information to assist officers to conduct Staff Rides to these campaigns on their own. These handbooks are not intended to be used as a substitute for serious study by Staff Ride leaders or participants. Instead, they represent an effort to assist officers in locating sources, identifying teaching points, and designing meaningful field study phases. As such, they represent a starting point from which a more meaningful professional development experience may be crafted.

The campaign and Battle of Chickamauga, August—September 1863, is an excellent vehicle for a Staff Ride. Because of the size of the forces involved and the difficulty of the terrain encountered, it represents an opportunity to raise many challenging teaching points relevant to today's officer. Second, the nation has wisely preserved most of the primary battle area in the Chickamauga and Chattanooga National Military Park and has marked most unit positions for detailed study by visitors. These markers are linked by an extensive trail network that permits access to all significant areas of the field. Thus, the park is an excellent physical laboratory for the study of conflict at the tactical and human level. Finally, because of its proximity to the city of Chattanooga, Tennessee, the battle site is easily supportable logistically for Staff Ride groups of any size. In sum, this campaign offers a great opportunity for study by the professional officer, as generations of American soldiers have already discovered.

The *Staff Ride Handbook for the Battle of Chickamauga, 18—20 September 1863*, provides a systematic approach to the analysis of this great Civil War battle. Part I describes the organization of the Federal and Confederate Armies, detailing their weapons, tactics, and logistical, engineer, communications, and medical support.

In part II, the Chickamauga campaign is discussed, placing the battle in historical perspective and illustrating how the battle fits into the overall context of the Chickamauga campaign.

Part III furnishes a suggested route to follow in order to get a firsthand, concrete view of how the battle developed. By following this route, various phases of the battle can be discussed and significant points made concerning the evolving battle. Also in part III are various vignettes by participants in the battle that describe the fight and offer insights into the emotional disposition of the combatants.

Part IV furnishes current information on the Chickamauga site, sources of assistance, and logistical data for conducting a Staff Ride. In addition, appendixes give order of battle information for the two armies, meteorological data, and a list of Medal of Honor recipients in the battle . A bibliography is also provided.

I. CIVIL WAR ARMIES
Organization

The U.S. Army in 1861

The Regular Army of the United States on the eve of the Civil War was essentially a frontier constabulary whose 16,000 officers and men were organized into 198 companies scattered across the nation at 79 different posts. At the start of the war, 183 of these companies were either on frontier duty or in transit, while the remaining 15, mostly coastal artillery batteries, guarded the Canadian border and Atlantic coast or 1 of the 23 arsenals. In 1861, this Army was under the command of Lieutenant General Winfield Scott, the 75-year-old hero of the Mexican-American War. His position as general in chief was traditional, not statutory, because secretaries of war since 1821 had designated a general to be in charge of the field forces without formal congressional approval. The field forces themselves were controlled through a series of geographic departments, whose commanders reported directly to the general in chief. This department system, frequently modified, would be used by both sides throughout the Civil War for administering regions under Army control.

Army administration was handled by a system of bureaus whose senior officers were, by 1860, in the twilight of long careers in their technical fields. Six of the ten bureau chiefs were over seventy years old. These bureaus, modeled after the British system, answered directly to the War Department and were not subject to the orders of the general in chief. Predecessors of many of today's combat support and combat service support branches, the following bureaus had been established by 1861:

Quartermaster	Medical
Ordnance	Adjutant General
Subsistence	Paymaster
Engineer	Inspector General
Topographic Engineer*	Judge Advocate General

During the war, Congress elevated the Office of the Provost Marshal and the Signal Corps to bureau status and created a Cavalry Bureau. Note that no operational planning or intelligence staff existed: American commanders before the Civil War had never required such a structure.

This system provided suitable civilian control and administrative support to the small field army prior to 1861. Ultimately, the bureau

---

*Merged with the Engineer Bureau in 1863.

1

system would respond effectively, if not always efficiently, to the mass mobilization required over the next four years. Indeed, it would remain essentially intact until the early twentieth century. The Confederate government, forced to create an army and support organization from scratch, established a parallel structure to that of the U.S. Army. In fact, many important figures in Confederate bureaus had served in one of the prewar bureaus.

Raising the Armies

With the outbreak of war in April 1861, both sides faced the monumental task of organizing and equipping armies that far exceeded the prewar structure in size and complexity. The Federals maintained control of the Regular Army, and the Confederates initially created a regular force, mostly on paper. Almost immediately, the North lost many of its officers to the South, including some of exceptional quality. Of 1,108 Regular officers serving as of 1 January 1861, 270 ultimately resigned to join the South. Only a few hundred of 15,135 enlisted men, however, left the ranks.

The Federal government had two basic options for the use of the Regular Army. It could be divided into training and leadership cadre for newly formed volunteer regiments or be retained in units to provide a reliable nucleus for the Federal Army in coming battles. At the start, Scott envisioned a relatively small force to defeat the rebellion and therefore insisted that the Regulars fight as units. Although some Regular units fought well at the First Battle of Bull Run and in other battles, Scott's decision ultimately limited the impact of Regular units on the war. Battle losses and disease soon thinned the ranks of Regulars, and officials could never recruit sufficient replacements in the face of stiff competition from the states that were forming volunteer regiments. By November 1864, many Regular units had been so depleted that they were withdrawn from frontline service. The war, therefore, was fought primarily with volunteer officers and men, the vast majority of whom had no previous military training or experience.

Neither side had difficulty in recruiting the numbers initially required to fill the expanding ranks. In April 1861, President Abraham Lincoln called for 75,000 men from the states' militias for a 3-month period. This figure probably represented Lincoln's informed guess as to how many troops would be needed to quell the rebellion quickly. Almost 92,000 men responded, as the states recruited their "organized," but untrained, militia companies. At the First Battle of Bull Run in July 1861, these ill-trained and poorly equipped soldiers generally fought much better than they were led. Later, as the war began to require more manpower, the Federal government set enlistment quotas through various "calls," which local districts struggled to fill. Similarly, the Confederate Congress authorized the acceptance of 100,000 one-year volunteers in March 1861. One-third of these men were under arms within a month. The Southern spirit of voluntarism was so strong that possibly twice that number could have been enlisted, but sufficient arms and equipment were not then available.

As the war continued and casualty lists grew, the glory of volunteering faded, and both sides ultimately resorted to conscription to help fill the ranks. The Confederates enacted the first conscription law in American history in April 1862, followed by the Federal government's own law in March 1863. Throughout these first experiments in American conscription, both sides administered the programs in less than a fair and efficient way. Conscription laws tended to exempt wealthier citizens, and initially, draftees could hire substitutes or pay commutation fees. As a result, the health, capability, and morale of the average conscript was poor. Many eligible men, particularly in the South, enlisted to avoid the onus of being considered a conscript. Still, conscription or the threat of conscription ultimately helped provide a sufficient quantity of soldiers for both sides.

Conscription was never a popular program, and the North, in particular, tried several approaches to limit conscription requirements. These efforts included offering lucrative bounties, or fees paid to induce volunteers to fill required quotas. In addition, the Federals offered a series of reenlistment bonuses, including money, thirty-day furloughs, and the opportunity for veteran regiments to maintain their colors and be designated as "veteran" volunteer infantry regiments. The Federals also created an Invalid Corps (later renamed the Veteran Reserve Corps) of men unfit for frontline service who performed essential rear-area duties. The Union also recruited almost 179,000 blacks, mostly in federally organized volunteer regiments. By February 1864, blacks were being conscripted in the North as well. In the South, recruiting or conscripting slaves was so politically sensitive that it was not attempted until March 1865, far too late to influence the war.

Whatever the faults of the manpower mobilization, it was an impressive achievement, particularly as a first effort on that scale. Various enlistment figures exist, but the best estimates are that approximately 2 million men enlisted in the Federal Army during 1861—65. Of that number, 1 million were under arms at the end of the war. Because the Confederates' records are incomplete or lost, estimates of their enlistments vary from 600,000 to over 1.5 million. Most likely, between 750,000 and 800,000 men served the Confederacy during the war, with a peak strength never exceeding 460,000. Perhaps the greatest legacy of the manpower mobilization efforts of both sides was the improved Selective Service System that created the armies of World Wars I and II.

The unit structure into which the expanding armies were organized was generally the same for Federals and Confederates, reflecting the common roots for both armies. The Federals began the war with a Regular Army organized into an essentially Napoleonic, musket-equipped structure. Each of the 10 prewar infantry regiments consisted of ten 87-man companies with a maximum authorized strength of 878. At the beginning of the war, the Federals added nine Regular infantry regiments with a newer "French model" organizational structure. The new regiments contained 3 battalions, with a maximum authorized strength of 2,452. The new Regular battalion, with eight 100-man companies, was in effect equivalent to the prewar regiment. Essentially an effort to reduce staff officer slots, the new structure was unfamiliar to most leaders, and both sides used a variant of the old structure for newly formed volunteer regiments. The Federal War Department established a volunteer infantry regimental organization with a strength that could range from 866 to 1,046 (varying in authorized strength by up to 180 infantry privates). The Confederate Congress fixed its 10-company infantry regiment at 1,045 men. Combat strength in battle, however, was always much lower because of casualties, sickness, leaves, details, desertions, and straggling.

The battery remained the basic artillery unit, although battalion and larger formal groupings of artillery emerged later in the war in the eastern theater. Four understrength Regular regiments existed in the U.S. Army at the start of the war, and one Regular regiment was added in 1861, for a total of sixty batteries. Nevertheless, most batteries were volunteer organizations. A Federal battery usually consisted of 6 guns and had an authorized strength of 80 to 156 men. A battery of six 12-pounder Napoleons could include 130 horses. If organized as "horse" or flying artillery, cannoneers were provided individual mounts, and more horses than men could be assigned to the battery. Their Confederate counterparts, plagued by limited ordnance and available manpower, usually operated with a four-gun battery, often with guns of mixed types and calibers. Confederate batteries seldom reached their initially authorized manning level of eighty soldiers.

Prewar Federal mounted units were organized into five Regular regiments (two dragoon, two cavalry, and one mounted rifle), and one Regular cavalry regiment was added in May 1861. Originally, ten companies comprised a regiment, but congressional legislation in July 1862 officially reorganized the Regular mounted units into standard regiments of twelve "companies or troops" of seventy-nine to ninety-five men each. Although the term "troop" was officially introduced, most cavalrymen continued to use the more familiar term "company" to describe their units throughout the war. The Federals grouped two companies or troops into squadrons, with four to six squadrons comprising a regiment. Confederate cavalry units, organized on the prewar model, authorized ten 76-man companies per regiment. Some volunteer cavalry units on both sides also formed into smaller cavalry battalions. Later in the war, both sides began to merge their cavalry regiments and brigades into division and corps organizations.

For both sides, the unit structure above regimental level was similar to today's structure, with a brigade controlling three to five regiments and a division controlling two or more brigades. Federal brigades generally contained regiments from more than one state, while Confederate brigades often had several regiments from the same state. In the Confederate Army, a brigadier general usually commanded a brigade, and a major general commanded a division. The Federal Army, with no rank higher than major general until 1864, often had colonels commanding brigades and brigadier generals commanding divisions.

The large numbers of organizations formed, as shown in table 1, are a reflection of the politics of the time. The War Department in 1861 considered making recruitment a Federal responsibility, but this proposal seemed to be an unnecessary expense for the short war initially envisioned. Therefore, the responsibility for recruiting remained with the states, and on both sides, state governors continually encouraged local constituents to form new volunteer regiments. This practice served to strengthen support for local, state, and national politicians and provided an opportunity for glory and high rank for ambitious men. Although such local recruiting created regiments with strong bonds among the men, it also hindered filling the ranks of existing regiments with new replacements. As the war progressed, the Confederates attempted to funnel replacements into units from their same state or region, but the Federals continued to create new regiments. Existing Federal regiments detailed men back home to recruit replacements, but these efforts could never successfully compete for men joining new local regiments. The newly formed regiments thus had no seasoned veterans to train the recruits, and the battle-tested regiments lost men faster than they could recruit replacements. Many regiments on both sides were reduced to combat ineffectiveness as the war progressed. Seasoned regiments were often disbanded or consolidated, usually against the wishes of the men assigned.

Table 1. Federal and Confederate Organized Forces

	Federal		*Confederate*	
Infantry	19	regular regiments	642	regiments
	2,125	volunteer regiments	9	legions*
	60	volunteer battalions	163	separate battalions
	351	separate companies	62	separate companies
Artillery	5	regular regiments	16	regiments
	61	volunteer regiments	25	battalions
	17	volunteer battalions	227	batteries
	408	separate batteries		
Cavalry	6	regular regiments	137	regiments
	266	volunteer regiments	1	legion*
	45	battalions	143	separate battalions
	78	separate companies	101	separate companies

The Leaders

Because the organization, equipment, tactics, and training of the Confederate and Federal Armies were similar, the performance of units in battle often depended on the quality and performance of their individual leaders. General officers were appointed by their respective central governments. At the start of the war, most, but certainly not all, of the more senior officers had West Point or other military school experience. In 1861, Lincoln appointed 126 general officers, of which 82 were, or had been, professional officers. Jefferson Davis appointed eighty-nine, of which forty-four had received professional training. The remainder were political appointees, but of these, only sixteen Federal and seven Confederate generals had had no military experience.

Of the volunteer officers who comprised the bulk of the leadership for both armies, colonels (regimental commanders) were normally

---

*Legions were a form of combined arms team, with artillery, cavalry, and infantry. They were approximately the strength of a large regiment. Long before the end of the war, legions lost their combined arms organization.

appointed by state governors. Other field grade officers were appointed by their states, although many were initially elected within their units. Company grade officers were usually elected by their men. This long-established militia tradition, which seldom made military leadership and capability a primary consideration, was largely an extension of the states' rights philosophy and sustained political patronage in both the Union and the Confederacy.

Much has been made of the West Point backgrounds of the men who ultimately dominated the senior leadership positions of both armies, but the graduates of military colleges were not prepared by such institutions to command divisions, corps, or armies. Moreover, though many leaders had some combat experience from the Mexican War era, very few had experience above the company or battery level in the peacetime years prior to 1861. As a result, the war was not initially conducted at any level by "professional officers" in today's terminology. Leaders became more professional through experience and at the cost of thousands of lives. General William T. Sherman would later note that the war did not enter its "professional stage" until 1863.

Civil War Staffs

In the Civil War, as today, the success of large military organizations often depended on the effectiveness of the commanders' staffs. Modern staff procedures have evolved only gradually with the increasing complexity of military operations. This evolution was far from complete in 1861, and throughout the war, commanders personally handled many vital staff functions, most notably operations and intelligence. The nature of American warfare up to the midnineteenth century had not yet clearly overwhelmed the capabilities of single commanders.

Civil War staffs were divided into a "general staff" and a "staff corps." This terminology, defined by Winfield Scott in 1855, differs from modern definitions of the terms. Table 2 lists typical staff positions at army level, although key functions are represented down to regimental level. Except for the chief of staff and aides-de-camp, who were considered personal staff and would often depart when a commander was reassigned, staffs mainly contained representatives of the various bureaus, with logistical areas being best represented. Later in the war, some truly effective staffs began to emerge, but this was the result of the increased experience of the officers serving in those positions rather than a comprehensive development of standard staff procedures or guidelines.

Table 2. Typical Staffs

General Staff
  Chief of staff
  Aides
  Assistant adjutant general
  Assistant inspector general

Staff Corps
  Engineer
  Ordnance
  Quartermaster
  Subsistence
  Medical
  Pay
  Signal
  Provost marshal
  Chief of artillery

George B. McClellan, when he appointed his father-in-law as his chief of staff, was the first to officially use this title. Even though many senior commanders had a chief of staff, this position was not used in any uniform way and seldom did the man in this role achieve the central coordinating authority of the chief of staff in a modern headquarters. This position, along with most other staff positions, was used as an individual commander saw fit, making staff responsibilities somewhat different under each commander. This inadequate use of the chief of staff was among the most important shortcomings of staffs during the Civil War. An equally important weakness was the lack of any formal operations or intelligence staff. Liaison procedures were also ill-defined, and various staff officers or soldiers performed this function with little formal guidance. Miscommunication or lack of knowledge of friendly units proved disastrous time after time.

The Armies at Chickamauga

Major General William S. Rosecrans' Army of the Cumberland was organized into four infantry corps and a cavalry corps (see figure 1). Eleven infantry divisions would see action at Chickamauga. Rosecrans' effective strength was over 80,000 men, but only 62,000 would be available for the battle; most of the Reserve Corps and several additional units were securing the army's lines of communication, which stretched to Nashville. Although some recently

9

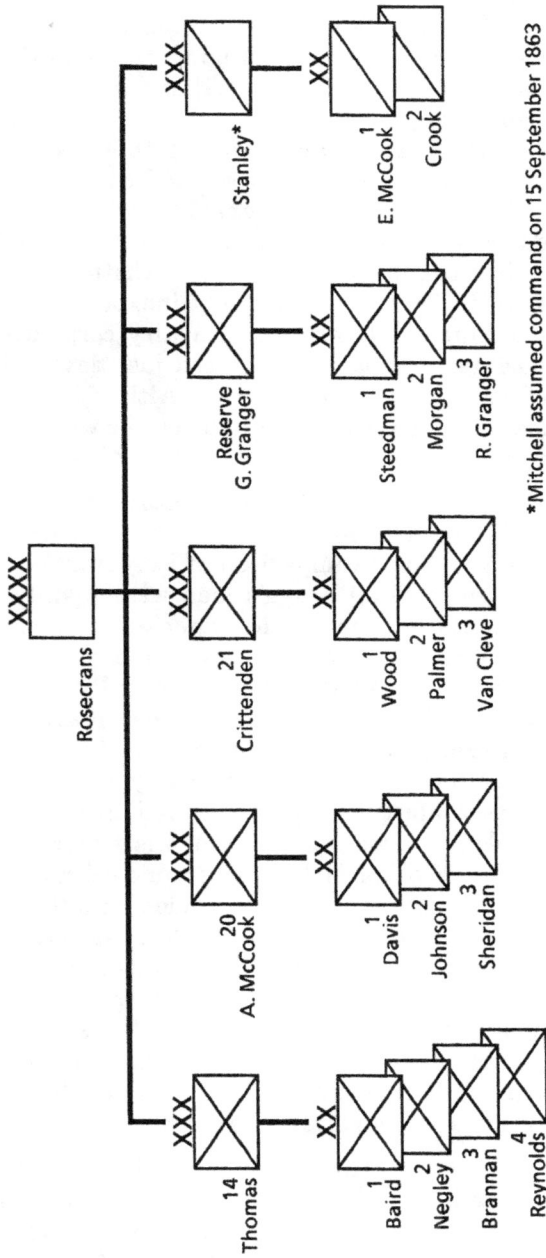

Figure 1. Organization of the Army of the Cumberland, 31 August—20 September 1863

*Mitchell assumed command on 15 September 1863

recruited green regiments were included, most of the Army of the Cumberland had considerable campaign and battle experience, with many units having fought at Shiloh, Perryville, and Stones River, as well as in many smaller skirmishes. Among these units was one Regular infantry brigade, comprised of battalions from the 15th, 16th, 18th, and 19th Infantry Regiments. Of Rosecrans' senior subordinates, George H. Thomas, a most capable and loyal Virginian, was clearly the best. He, Gordon Granger, and Alexander M. McCook (a member of the famous "fighting McCook family") were West Point graduates, although McCook was a young and immature corps commander. Rosecrans' other corps commander, Thomas L. Crittenden, though a veteran of the Mexican War, was relatively inexperienced at corps command. David S. Stanley, an excellent cavalry corps commander, became ill in midcampaign and was replaced just days prior to the battle by the ineffective Robert B. Mitchell. Although a few of his division commanders would prove inadequate, on the whole, Rosecrans was served by a better-than-average set of Civil War commanders.

On the Confederate side, General Braxton Bragg's Army of Tennessee grew to almost 60,000 men in the three weeks before the Battle of Chickamauga. (For a comparison of Rosecrans' and Bragg's effective strengths, see table 3.) Bragg's men were mainly veterans, though some regiments had no battle experience. Counting the reinforcements who would arrive by 20 September, Bragg's army contained eleven infantry divisions, organized initially into five corps. (For the organization of the Army of Tennessee, 1—19 September 1863, and its reorganization on 19—20 September 1863, see figures 2 and 3.) Bragg's senior subordinates were probably as capable as their Federal counterparts. Unfortunately, many had lost faith in their commander and tended to question many of his orders. Daniel H. Hill, Simon B. Buckner, William H. T. Walker, and John B. Hood were West Pointers, as was Episcopal Bishop Leonidas Polk. By the second day of battle, James Longstreet, a West Pointer with a strong reputation from service under Robert E. Lee in Virginia, joined Bragg along with 7,700 men. Joseph Wheeler and Nathan B. Forrest (the latter a particularly gifted soldier) commanded Bragg's two cavalry corps. The quality of some of Bragg's division commanders was exceptional: Alexander P. Stewart and Patrick R. Cleburne were among the best division commanders of the entire war.

Rosecrans' army staff was better organized than Bragg's. Although both men tended to handle too many details themselves, Rosecrans' logistical staff was more experienced, and he used his chief of staff, Brigadier General (later President) James A. Garfield, as an operational assistant during the battle. Bragg's headquarters was far

Table 3. Rosecrans' and Bragg's Effective Strengths

Rosecrans			Bragg		
31 Aug	80,400		21 Aug	43,600	
	−13,700	Reserve Corps divisions (Morgan's and Granger's on lines of communication duty)	28 Aug	+8,500	Walker's and Breckinridge's Divisions
			1 Sep	+4,800	Preston's Division
4 Sep	−1,100	Engineers on lines of communication duty	16 Sep	+2,700	McNair's and Gregg's Brigades
9 Sep	−1,300	Post's (Davis') brigade guarding trains	18 Sep	+4,000	Law's Division
			19—20 Sep	+3,700	Kershaw's and Humphreys' Brigades
10 Sep	−2,100	Wagner's (Wood's) brigade garrison in Chattanooga			
19 Sep	62,200		19—20 Sep	67,300	

more loosely run and employed lax procedures. Bragg also tended to use his staff more haphazardly, sending whoever seemed closest on liaison missions, including his chief of staff who never effectively coordinated staff activities. Much of Bragg's personal time was devoted to logistical details. Atrocious staff procedures in Leonidas Polk's corps headquarters contributed to the confusion and delays surrounding the initiation of the Confederate attack on 20 September.

Rosecrans' army was in excellent fighting trim. His delays after the Stones River and Tullahoma campaigns had allowed him to refit, and his soldiers had the high morale that only a series of victories can bring. In addition, he carried only 4 percent of his men on the sick rolls, a remarkably low figure for the Civil War. Morale and logistical support in Bragg's army could not match that of the Federals. Nevertheless, his soldiers possessed a stubborn pride born of adversity, and they were defending their home regions. In addition, Bragg's men knew of the coming reinforcements from Virginia.

Weapons

Infantry

During the 1850s, in a technological revolution of major proportions, the rifle-musket began to replace the relatively inaccurate smoothbore musket in ever-increasing numbers, both in Europe and America. This process, accelerated by the Civil War,

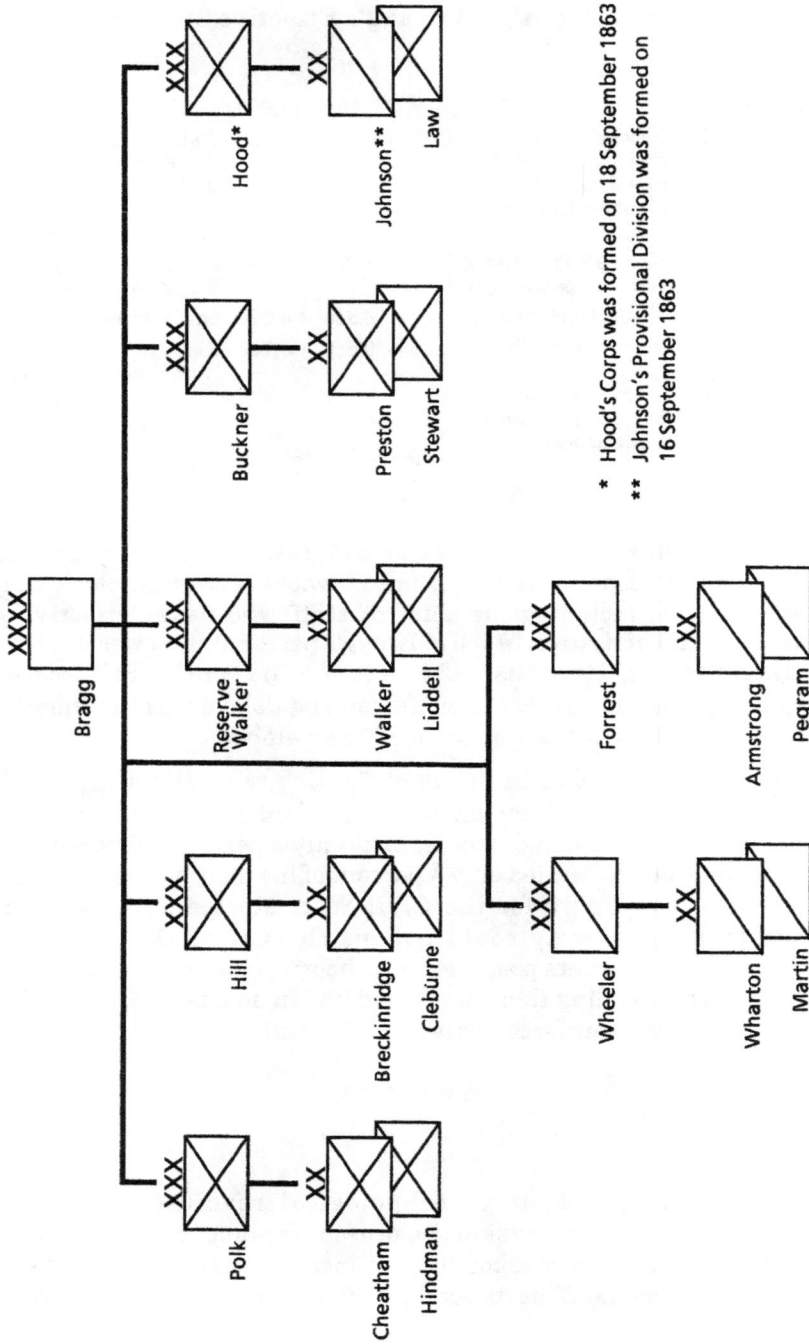

Figure 2. Organization of the Army of Tennessee, 1—19 September 1863

Bragg

Reserve
Walker

Walker
Liddell

Hood*

Johnson**
Law

Buckner

Preston
Stewart

Polk

Cheatham
Hindman

Hill

Breckinridge
Cleburne

Forrest

Armstrong
Pegram

Wheeler

Wharton
Martin

* Hood's Corps was formed on 18 September 1863

** Johnson's Provisional Division was formed on 16 September 1863

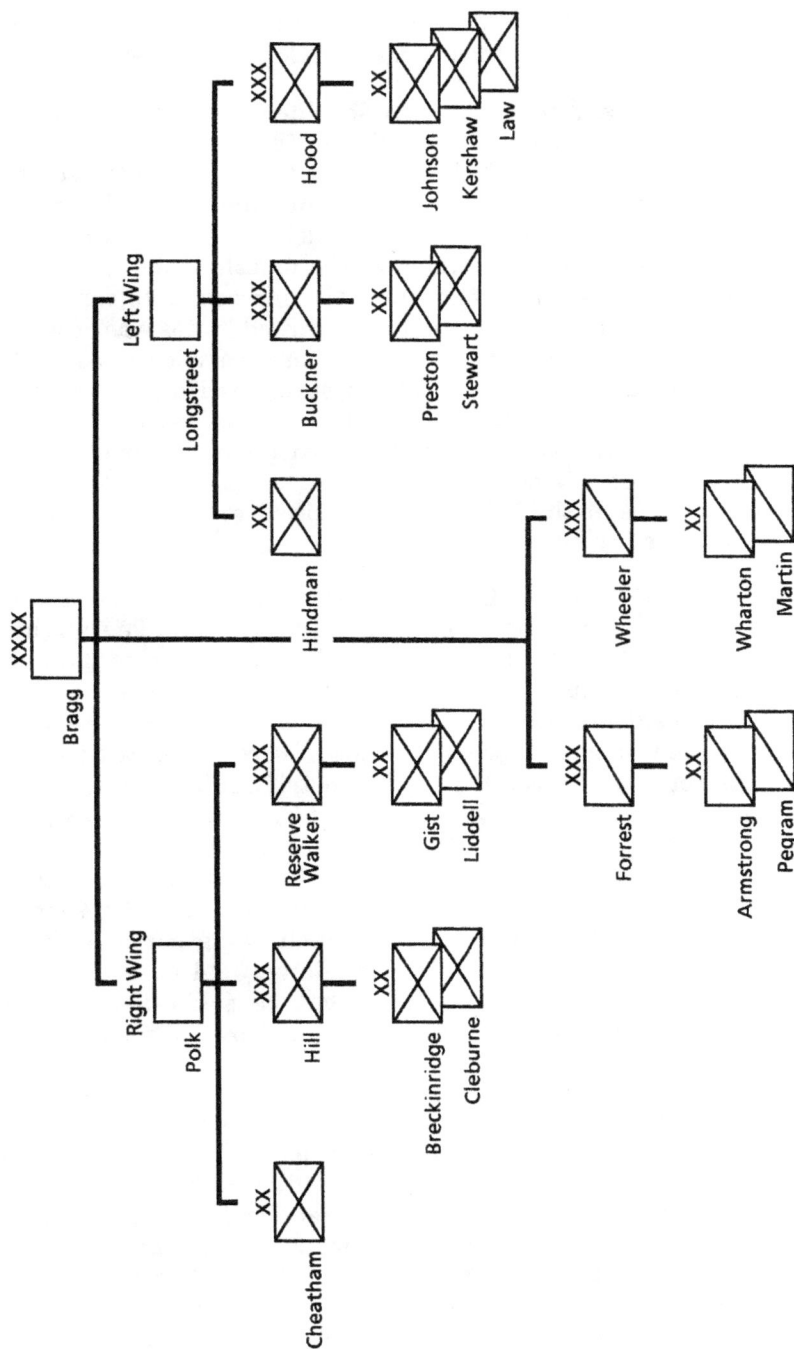

Figure 3. Reorganization of the Army of Tennessee, 19—20 September 1863

ensured that the rifled shoulder weapon would be the basic weapon used by infantrymen in both the Federal and Confederate Armies.

The standard and most common shoulder weapon used in the American Civil War was the Springfield .58-caliber rifle-musket, Models 1855, 1861, and 1863. In 1855, the U.S. Army adopted this weapon to replace the .69-caliber smoothbore musket and the .54-caliber rifle. In appearance, the rifle-musket was similar to the smoothbore musket. Both were single-shot muzzle-loaders, but the rifled bore of the new weapon substantially increased its range and accuracy. The rifling system chosen by the United States was designed by Claude Minié, a French Army officer. Whereas earlier rifles fired a round, nonexpanding ball, the Minié system used a hollow-based cylindro-conoidal projectile slightly smaller than the bore that could be dropped easily into the barrel. When the powder charge was ignited by a fulminate of mercury percussion cap, the released powder gases expanded the base of the bullet into the rifled grooves, giving the projectile a ballistic spin.

The Model 1855 Springfield rifle-musket was the first regulation arm to use the hollow-base, .58-caliber Minié bullet. The slightly modified Model 1861 was the principal infantry weapon of the Civil War, although two subsequent models in 1863 were produced in about equal quantities. The Model 1861 was 56 inches long overall, had a 40-inch barrel, and weighed 9 pounds 2 ounces. It could be fitted with a 21-inch socket bayonet (with an 18-inch triangular blade, 3-inch socket) and had a rear sight graduated to 500 yards. The maximum effective range of the Springfield rifle-musket was approximately 500 yards, although it had killing power at 1,000 yards. The round could penetrate 11 inches of white-pine board at 200 yards and 3 1/4 inches at 1,000 yards, with a penetration of 1 inch being considered the equivalent of disabling a human being. Range and accuracy were increased by the use of the new weapon, but the soldiers' vision was still obscured by the clouds of smoke produced by its black powder propellant.

To load a muzzle-loading rifle, the soldier took a paper cartridge in hand and tore the end of the paper with his teeth. Next, he poured the powder down the barrel and placed the bullet in the muzzle. Then, using a metal ramrod, he pushed the bullet firmly down the barrel until seated. He then cocked the hammer and placed the percussion cap on the cone or nipple, which, when struck by the hammer, ignited the gunpowder. The average rate of fire was three rounds per minute. A well-trained soldier could possibly load and fire four times per minute, but in the confusion of battle, the rate of fire was probably slower, two to three rounds per minute.

In addition to the Springfields, over 100 types of muskets, rifles, rifle-muskets, and rifled muskets—ranging up to .79 caliber—were used during the American Civil War. The numerous American-made weapons were supplemented early in the conflict by a wide variety of imported models. The best, most popular, and most numerous of the foreign weapons was the British .577-caliber Enfield rifle, Model 1853, which was 54 inches long (with a 39-inch barrel), weighed 8.7 pounds (9.2 with the bayonet), could be fitted with a socket bayonet with an 18-inch blade, and had a rear sight graduated to a range of 800 yards. The Enfield design was produced in a variety of forms, both long and short barreled, by several British manufacturers and at least one American company. Of all the foreign designs, the Enfield most closely resembled the Springfield in characteristics and capabilities. The United States purchased over 436,000 Enfield-pattern weapons during the war. Statistics on Confederate purchases are more difficult to ascertain, but a report dated February 1863 indicates that 70,980 long Enfields and 9,715 short Enfields had been delivered by that time, with another 23,000 awaiting delivery.

While the quality of imported weapons varied, experts considered the Enfields and the Austrian Lorenz rifle-muskets very good. Some foreign governments and manufacturers took advantage of the huge initial demand for weapons by dumping their obsolete weapons on the American market. This practice was especially prevalent with some of the older smoothbore muskets and converted flintlocks. The greatest challenge, however, lay in maintaining these weapons and supplying ammunition and replacement parts for calibers ranging from .44 to .79. The quality of the imported weapons eventually improved as the procedures, standards, and astuteness of the purchasers improved. For the most part, the European suppliers provided needed weapons, and the newer foreign weapons were highly regarded.

All told, the United States purchased about 1,165,000 European rifles and muskets during the war, nearly all within the first two years. Of these, 110,853 were smoothbores. The remainder were primarily the French Minié rifles (44,250), Austrian Model 1854s (226,294), Prussian rifles (59,918), Austrian Jagers (29,850), and Austrian Bokers (187,533). Estimates of total Confederate purchases range from 340,000 to 400,000. In addition to the Enfields delivered to the Confederacy (mentioned above), 27,000 Austrian rifles, 21,040 British muskets, and 2,020 Brunswick rifles were also purchased, with 30,000 Austrian rifles awaiting shipment.

Breech-loaders and repeating rifles were available by 1861 and were initially purchased in limited quantities, often by individual soldiers. Generally, however, rifles were not issued to troops in large numbers because of technical problems (poor breech seals, faulty ammunition), fear by the Ordnance Department that the troops would waste ammunition, and the cost of rifle production. The most famous of the breech-loaders was the single-shot Sharps, produced in both carbine and rifle models. The Model 1859 rifle was .52 caliber, was 47 1/8 inches long, and weighed 8 3/4 pounds, while the carbine was .52 caliber, 39 1/8 inches long, and weighed 7 3/4 pounds. Both weapons used a linen cartridge and a pellet primer feed mechanism. Most Sharps carbines were issued to Federal cavalry units.

The best known of the repeaters was probably the seven-shot Spencer, .52 caliber, which also came in both rifle and carbine models. The rifle was 47 inches long and weighed 10 pounds, while the carbine was 39 inches long and weighed 8 1/4 pounds. The first mounted infantry unit to use Spencer repeating rifles in combat was Colonel John T. Wilder's "Lightning Brigade" on 24 June 1863 at Hoover's Gap, Tennessee. The Spencer was also the first weapon adopted by the U.S. Army that fired a metallic rimfire, self-contained cartridge. Soldiers loaded rounds through an opening in the butt of the stock, which fed into the chamber through a tubular magazine by the action of the trigger guard. The hammer still had to be cocked manually before each shot.

Better than either the Sharps or the Spencer was the Henry rifle. Never adopted by the U.S. Army in large quantity, it was purchased privately by soldiers during the war. The Henry was a sixteen-shot, .44-caliber rimfire cartridge repeater. It was 43 1/2 inches long and weighed 9 1/4 pounds. The tubular magazine located directly beneath the barrel had a fifteen-round capacity with an additional round in the chamber. Of the approximately 13,500 Henrys produced, probably 10,000 saw limited service. The government purchased only 1,731.

The Colt repeating rifle (or revolving carbine), Model 1855, also was available to Civil War soldiers in limited numbers. The weapon was produced in several lengths and calibers, the lengths varying from 32 inches to 42 1/2 inches, while its calibers were .36, .44, and .56. The .36 and .44 calibers were made to chamber six shots, while the .56 caliber had five chambers. The Colt Firearms Company was also the primary supplier of revolvers, the .44-caliber Army revolver and the .36-caliber Navy revolver being the most popular (over 146,000 purchased). This was because they were simple, sturdy, and reliable.

Cavalry

Initially armed with sabers and pistols (and in one case, lances), Federal cavalry troopers quickly added the breech-loading carbine to their inventory of weapons. However, one Federal regiment, the 6th Pennsylvania Cavalry, carried lances until 1863. Troopers preferred the easier-handling carbines to rifles and the breech-loaders to awkward muzzle-loaders. Of the single-shot breech-loading carbines that saw extensive use during the Civil War, the Hall .52 caliber accounted for approximately 20,000 in 1861. The Hall was quickly replaced by a variety of carbines, including the Merrill .54 caliber (14,495), Maynard .52 caliber (20,002), Gallager .53 caliber (22,728), Smith .52 caliber (30,062), Burnside .56 caliber (55,567), and Sharps .54 caliber (80,512). The next step in the evolutionary process was the repeating carbine, the favorite by 1865 being the Spencer .52-caliber seven-shot repeater (94,194). Because of the South's limited industrial capacity, Confederate cavalrymen had a more difficult time arming themselves. Nevertheless, they too embraced the firepower revolution, choosing shotguns and muzzle-loading carbines as their primary weapons. In addition, Confederate cavalrymen made extensive use of battlefield salvage by recovering Federal weapons. However, the South's difficulties in producing the metallic-rimmed cartridges required by many of these recovered weapons limited their usefulness.

Field Artillery

In 1841, the U.S. Army selected bronze as the standard material for fieldpieces and at the same time adopted a new system of field artillery. The 1841 field artillery system consisted entirely of smoothbore muzzle-loaders: 6- and 12-pounder guns; 12-, 24-, and 32-pounder howitzers; and 12-pounder mountain howitzers. A pre-Civil War battery usually consisted of six fieldpieces—four guns and two howitzers. A 6-pounder battery contained four 6-pounder guns and two 12-pounder howitzers, while a 12-pounder battery had four 12-pounder guns and two 24-pounder howitzers. The guns fired solid shot, shell, spherical case, grapeshot, and canister rounds, while howitzers fired shell, spherical case, grapeshot, and canister rounds.

The 6-pounder gun (effective range 1,523 yards) was the primary fieldpiece used from the time of the Mexican War until the Civil War. By 1861, however, the 1841 artillery system based on the 6-pounder was obsolete. In 1857, a new and more versatile fieldpiece, the 12-pounder gun-howitzer (Napoleon), Model 1857, appeared on the scene. Designed as a multipurpose piece to replace existing guns and howitzers, the Napoleon fired canister and shell, like the 12-pounder howitzer, and solid shot comparable in range to the 12-pounder gun. The Napoleon was a bronze, muzzle-loading smoothbore with an effective range of 1,619 yards (see table 4 for a comparison of artillery data). Served by a nine-man crew, the piece could fire at a sustained rate of two aimed shots per minute. With less than fifty Napoleons initially available in 1861, obsolete 6-pounders remained in the inventories of both armies for some time, especially in the western theater.

Table 4. Types of Artillery Available at the Battle of Chickamauga

Type	Bore Diameter (inches)	Tube Weight (pounds)	Tube Length (inches)	Carriage Weight (pounds)	Range at 5° elevation (yards)	Army of the Cumberland	Army of Tennessee
Smoothbores							
6- pounder gun	3.67	884	60	900	1,523	14	29
12- pounder howitzer	4.62	788	53	900	1,072	16	37
12- pounder mountain howitzer	4.62	220	32.91	277	1,005	4	2
12- pounder gun-howitzer (Napoleon)	4.62	1,227	66	1,128	1,619	62	48
24- pounder howitzer	5.82	1,318	65	1,128	1,322	2	2
Rifles							
6- pounder James	3.8	880	60	900	1,700	36	3
10- pounder Parrott, 1863	3.0	890	74	900	1,850	28	8
3- inch ordnance rifle (Rodman)	3.0	816	69	900	1,830	38	16

Another new development in field artillery was the introduction of rifling. Although rifled guns provided greater range and accuracy, smoothbores were generally more reliable and faster to load. Rifled ammunition was semifixed, so the charge and the projectile had to be loaded separately. In addition, the canister load of the rifle did not perform as well as that of the smoothbore. Initially, some smoothbores were rifled on the James pattern, but they soon proved unsatisfactory because the bronze rifling eroded too easily. Therefore, most rifled artillery was either wrought iron or cast iron with a wrought-iron reinforcing band.

The most commonly used rifled guns were the 10-pounder Parrott and the Rodman, or 3-inch ordnance rifle. The Parrott rifle was a cast-iron piece, easily identified by the wrought-iron band reinforcing the breech. The 10-pounder Parrott was made in two models: the Model 1861 had a 2.9-inch rifled bore with three lands and grooves and a slight muzzle swell, while the Model 1863 version had a 3-inch bore and no muzzle swell. The Rodman or ordnance rifle was a long-tubed, wrought-iron piece that had a 3-inch bore with seven lands and grooves. Ordnance rifles were sturdier and considered superior in accuracy and reliability to the 10-pounder Parrott.

By 1860, the ammunition for field artillery consisted of four general types for both smoothbores and rifles: solid shot, shell, case, and canister. Solid shot was a round cast-iron projectile for smoothbores and an elongated projectile, known as a bolt, for rifled guns. Solid shot, with its smashing or battering effect, was used in a counterbattery role or against buildings and massed formations. The conical-shaped bolt lacked the effectiveness of the cannonball because it tended to bury itself on impact instead of bounding along the ground like a bowling ball.

Shell, also known as common or explosive shell, whether spherical or conical, was a hollow projectile filled with an explosive charge of black powder that was detonated by a time fuse. Shell was designed to break into jagged pieces, producing an antipersonnel effect, but the low-order detonation seldom produced more than three to five fragments. In addition to its casualty-producing effects, shell had a psychological impact when it exploded over the heads of troops. It was also used against field fortifications and in a counterbattery role. Case or case shot for both smoothbore and rifled guns was a hollow projectile with thinner walls than shell. The projectile was filled with round lead or iron balls set in a matrix of sulphur that surrounded a small bursting charge. Case was primarily used in an antipersonnel role. This type of round had been invented by Henry Shrapnel, a British artillery officer, hence the term "shrapnel."

Lastly, there was canister, probably the most effective round and the round of choice at close range (400 yards or less) against massed troops. Canister was essentially a tin can filled with iron balls packed in sawdust with no internal bursting charge. When fired, the can disintegrated, and the balls followed their own paths to the target. The canister round for the 12-pounder Napoleon consisted of twenty-seven 1 1/2-inch iron balls packed inside an elongated tin cylinder. At extremely close ranges, men often loaded double charges of canister. By 1861, canister had replaced grapeshot in the ammunition chests of field batteries.

Weapons at Chickamauga

The variety of weapons available to both armies during the Civil War is reflected at Chickamauga. A 5 June 1863 inspection report from the Army of the Cumberland listed the following: 20,603 Springfields; 29,277 Enfields; 4,352 Austrian rifles; 2,033 Spencers;

1,031 smoothbores; 980 Austrian muskets; 725 Belgian muskets; 633 Henry and French rifles; 504 Colt revolving rifles; 327 Whitney rifles; and 54 Minié rifles. On the Confederate side, Lieutenant Colonel Hypolite Oladowski, chief of ordnance for the Army of Tennessee, reported on 13 August 1863 that the following small arms were available: 10,500 Enfields (.577 caliber); 3,600 .58-caliber weapons (probably Springfields); 12,000 .69 caliber (mostly smoothbores); 2,000 .54 caliber (Mississippi and Austrian rifles); 3,000 .52-/.53-caliber Hall rifles; and 900 .70-caliber Brunswick rifles, M1835/51, and Austrian Bokers. The remainder probably belonged to the Confederate cavalry, and Oladowski reported those as Sharps, Maynard, Hall, and Smith models, as well as shotguns and musketoons.

The tremendous variety of weapons and calibers of ammunition required on the battlefield by each army presented enormous sustainment problems that ranged from production and procurement to supplying soldiers in the field. Amazingly, operations were seldom affected by the lack of ammunition, although the lack of standardization extended down to regimental level. For example, table 5 shows the variety of weapons even within Wilder's brigade.

Table 5. Variety of Weapons in Wilder's Brigade, 30 September 1863

Regiment	Spencers	Enfields	Colts	Springfields	Total
92d Illinois	172	280			452
98th Illinois	354		9		363
123d Illinois	262				262
17th Indiana	454			2	456
72d Indiana	127	43	—	38	208
Total	1,369	323	9	40	1,741

The Army of the Cumberland at Chickamauga had 35 1/3 batteries of artillery assigned, but during the battle, two of those batteries were not present on the field. One was with Colonel P. Sidney Post's brigade guarding the trains, the other with Brigadier General George D. Wagner's brigade in Chattanooga. The 33 1/3 batteries that were available supported their respective brigades with about 201 tubes; of those, 103 were rifled and 98 were smoothbores. All the Federal batteries consisted of six guns except Battery I, 4th United States, with four; Battery M, 4th United States, with four; the 18th Indiana with ten, and the Chicago Board of Trade with seven.

The Army of Tennessee had 40 1/2 batteries of artillery, although the total number of tubes is more difficult to determine because of numerous missing and incomplete reports. Published estimates range from 200 pieces (which appears excessive) to 150 (which is definitely too low). Of the 150 guns that can be identified by type and model, only 32 were rifled and 118 were smoothbores. Most of the Confederate batteries were four-gun units except Slocomb's Louisiana with six, Martin's Georgia with six, Jeffress' Virginia with five, Robertson's Florida with six, Baxter's Tennessee with two, Culpepper's South Carolina with three, Havis' Georgia with three, and Massenburg's Georgia with two. Refer again to table 4 for the major types of artillery available to the two armies during the Battle of Chickamauga.

The effectiveness of artillery at Chickamauga was limited because of the rugged terrain and the dense vegetation. Specifically, the Federals' advantage in numbers of longer-range rifled guns was negated by the lack of good fields of fire. For the most part, batteries on both sides simply followed the brigades to which they were assigned. Certainly on 19 September, they spent most of their time moving, unlimbering, and limbering weapons. As the victors, the Confederates acquired the spoils of the battle, including the artillery. Rosecrans' report after the battle acknowledged the loss of thirty-nine fieldpieces by the Army of the Cumberland. Because the captured guns were usually an improvement over their own pieces, many Confederate batteries incorporated the Federal weapons into their own commands shortly after the close of the battle.

Tactics

Tactical Doctrine in 1861

The Napoleonic Wars and the Mexican War were the major influences on American military thinking at the beginning of the Civil War. The campaigns of Napoleon and Wellington provided ample lessons in battle strategy, weapons employment, and logistics, while American tactical doctrine reflected the lessons learned in Mexico (1846—48). However, these tactical lessons were misleading because in Mexico relatively small armies fought only seven pitched battles. Because these battles were so small, almost all the tactical lessons learned during the war focused at the regimental, battery, and squadron levels. Future Civil War leaders had learned very little about brigade, division, and corps maneuver in Mexico, yet these units were the basic fighting elements of both armies in 1861—65.

The U.S. Army's experience in Mexico validated Napoleonic principles—particularly that of the offensive. In Mexico, tactics did not differ greatly from those of the early nineteenth century. Infantry marched in column and deployed into line to fight. Once deployed, an infantry regiment might send one or two companies forward as skirmishers, as security against surprise, or to soften the enemy's line. After identifying the enemy's position, a regiment advanced in closely ordered lines to within 100 yards. There, it delivered a devastating volley, followed by a charge with bayonets. Both sides used this basic tactic in the first battles of the Civil War.

In Mexico, American armies employed artillery and cavalry in both offensive and defensive battle situations. In the offense, artillery moved as near to the enemy lines as possible—normally just outside musket range—in order to blow gaps in the enemy's line that the infantry might exploit with a determined charge. In the defense, artillery blasted advancing enemy lines with canister and withdrew if the enemy attack got within musket range. Cavalry guarded the army's flanks and rear but held itself ready to charge if enemy infantry became disorganized or began to withdraw.

These tactics worked perfectly well with the weapons technology of the Napoleonic and Mexican Wars. The infantry musket was accurate up to 100 yards but ineffective against even massed targets beyond that range. Rifles were specialized weapons with excellent accuracy and range but slow to load and therefore not usually issued to line troops. Smoothbore cannon had a range up to 1 mile with solid shot but were most effective against infantry when firing canister at ranges under 400 yards. Artillerists worked their guns without much fear of infantry muskets, which had a limited range. Cavalry continued to use sabers and lances as shock weapons.

American troops took the tactical offensive in most Mexican War battles with great success, and they suffered fairly light losses. Unfortunately, similar tactics proved to be obsolete in the Civil War because of a major technological innovation fielded in the 1850s—the rifle-musket. This new weapon greatly increased the infantry's range and accuracy and loaded as fast as a musket. The U.S. Army adopted a version of the rifle-musket in 1855, and by the beginning of the Civil War, rifle-muskets were available in moderate numbers. It was the weapon of choice in both the Union and Confederate Armies during the war, and by 1862, large numbers of troops on both sides had rifle-muskets of good quality.

Official tactical doctrine prior to the beginning of the Civil War did not clearly recognize the potential of the new rifle-musket. Prior to 1855, the most influential tactical guide was General Winfield Scott's three-volume work, *Infantry Tactics* (1835), based on French tactical models of the Napoleonic Wars. It stressed close-order, linear formations in two or three ranks advancing at "quick time" of 110 steps (86 yards) per minute. In 1855, to accompany the introduction of the new rifle-musket, Major William J. Hardee published a two-volume tactical manual, *Rifle and Light Infantry Tactics*. Hardee's work contained few significant revisions of Scott's manual. His major innovation was to increase the speed of the advance to a "double-quick time" of 165 steps (151 yards) per minute. If, as suggested, Hardee introduced his manual as a response to the rifle-musket, then he failed to appreciate the weapon's impact on combined arms tactics and the essential shift the rifle-musket made in favor of the defense. Hardee's *Tactics* was the standard infantry manual used by both sides at the outbreak of war in 1861.

If Scott's and Hardee's works lagged behind technological innovations, at least the infantry had manuals to establish a doctrinal basis for training. Cavalry and artillery fell even further behind in recognizing the potential tactical shift in favor of rifle-armed infantry. The cavalry's manual, published in 1841, was based on French sources that focused on close-order offensive tactics. It favored the traditional cavalry attack in two ranks of horsemen armed with sabers or lances. The manual took no notice of the rifle-musket's potential, nor did it give much attention to dismounted operations. Similarly, the artillery had a basic drill book delineating individual crew actions, but it had no tactical manual. Like cavalrymen, artillerymen showed no concern for the potential tactical changes that the rifle-musket implied.

Regular Army infantry, cavalry, and artillery practiced and became proficient in the tactics that brought success in Mexico. As the first volunteers drilled and readied themselves for the battles of 1861, officers and noncommissioned officers taught the lessons learned from the Napoleonic Wars and validated in Mexico. Thus, the two armies entered the Civil War with a good understanding of the tactics that had worked in the Mexican War but with little understanding of how the rifle-musket might upset their carefully practiced lessons.

Early War Tactics

In the battles of 1861 and 1862, both sides employed the tactics proven in Mexico and found that the tactical offensive could still be successful—but only at a great cost in casualties. Men wielding rifled weapons in the defense generally ripped frontal assaults to shreds, and if the attackers paused to exchange fire, the slaughter was even greater. Rifles also increased the relative number of defenders, since flanking units now engaged assaulting troops with a murderous enfilading fire. Defenders usually crippled the first assault line before a second line of attackers could come forward in support. This caused successive attacking lines to intermingle with survivors to their front, thereby destroying formations, command, and control. Although both sides favored the bayonet throughout the war, they quickly discovered that rifle-musket fire made successful bayonet attacks almost impossible.

As the infantry found the bayonet charge to be of little value against rifle-muskets, cavalry and artillery made troubling discoveries of their own. Cavalry learned that the old-style saber charge did not work against infantry armed with rifle-muskets. Cavalry, however, continued its traditional intelligence gathering and screening roles and found its place as the "eyes and ears" of the army. Artillery, on its part, found that it could not maneuver freely to canister range as it had in Mexico, because the rifle-musket was accurate beyond that distance. Worse yet, at ranges where gunners were safe from rifle fire, artillery shot and shell were far less effective than canister. Ironically, rifled cannon did not give the equivalent boost to artillery effectiveness that the rifle-musket gave to the infantry. The increased range of cannons proved no real advantage in the broken and wooded terrain over which so many Civil War battles were fought.

There are several possible reasons why Civil War commanders continued to employ the tactical offensive long after it was clear that the defensive was superior. Most commanders believed the offensive was the decisive form of battle. This lesson came straight from the Napoleonic Wars and the Mexican-American War. Commanders who chose the tactical offensive usually retained the initiative over defenders. Similarly, the tactical defensive depended heavily on the enemy choosing to attack at a point convenient to the defender and continuing to attack until badly defeated. Although this situation occurred often in the Civil War, a prudent commander could hardly count on it for victory. Consequently, few commanders chose to exploit the defensive form of battle if they had the option to attack.

The offensive may have been the decisive form of battle, but it was very hard to coordinate and even harder to control. The better generals often tried to attack the enemy's flanks and rear but seldom achieved success because of the difficulty involved. Not only did the commander have to identify the enemy's flank or rear correctly, he also had to move his force into position to attack and then do so in conjunction with attacks made by other friendly units. (For the procedure in moving a regiment into line of battle from march column, see figure 4.) Command and control of the type required to conduct these attacks was quite beyond the ability of most Civil War commanders. Therefore, Civil War armies repeatedly attacked each other frontally,

Enemy direction →

① The route of march by companies in columns.

Regiments were the basic maneuver units at the beginning of the Civil War. The regimental line of battle was two men deep, with officers and file closers immediately behind. A regiment carried its own and the national colors near its center to mark its direction and alignment. One or more companies deployed well to the front as skirmishers.

Regiments attacked in this formation, either alone or in concert with other regiments to the right, left, and rear. Command and control was most critical at this level of battle. Normally, a regiment attacked either on its own commander's initiative or at the direction of a higher-level commander. A regimental attack might enjoy great success, however temporary, but when several regiments attacked simultaneously under the firm control of a brigade or division commander, results could be decisive. Most often, however, Civil War battles quickly devolved into a confusing blur of regimental attacks and withdrawals completely beyond the control of higher-level commanders.

② Companies march by their flanks until near the position the regiment will occupy. One company deploys as skirmishers.

SKIRMISHERS

③ Companies wheel into line of battle. One company deploys as skirmishers.

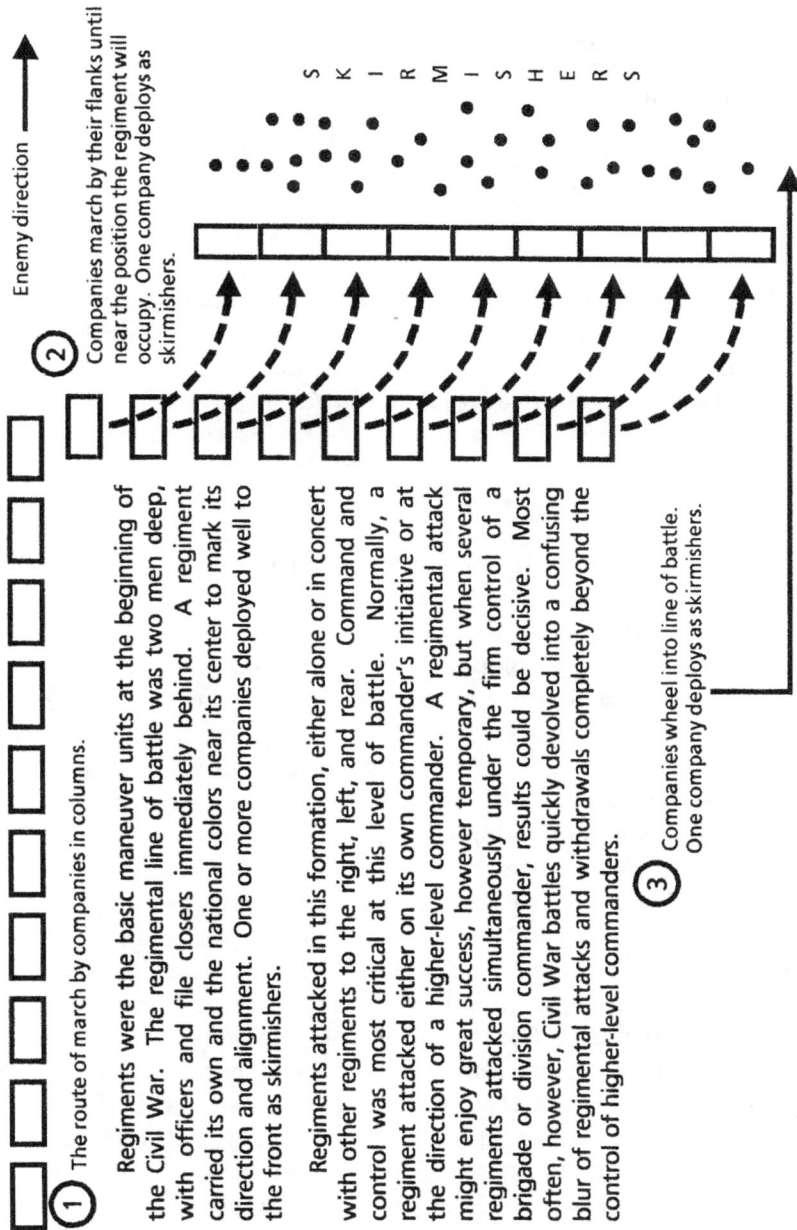

Figure 4. Regimental line of battle from march column

with resulting high casualties, because that was the easiest way to conduct offensive operations. When attacking frontally, a commander had to choose between attacking on a broad front or a narrow front. Attacking on a broad front rarely succeeded except against weak and scattered defenders. Attacking on a narrow front promised greater success but required immediate reinforcement and continued attack to achieve decisive results. As the war dragged on, attacking on narrow fronts against specific objectives became a standard tactic and fed the ever-growing casualty lists.

Later War Tactics

Poor training may have contributed to high casualty rates early in the war, but casualties remained high and even increased long after the armies became experienced. Continued high casualty rates resulted because tactical developments failed to adapt to the new weapons technology. Few commanders understood how the rifle-musket strengthened the tactical defensive. However, some commanders made offensive innovations that met with varying success. When an increase in the pace of advance did not overcome defending firepower (as Hardee suggested it would), some units tried advancing in more open order. But this sort of formation lacked the appropriate mass to assault and carry prepared positions and created command and control problems beyond the ability of Civil War leaders to resolve. Late in the war, when the difficulty of attacking field fortifications under heavy fire became apparent, other tactical expedients were employed. Attacking solidly entrenched defenders often required whole brigades and divisions moving in dense masses to rapidly cover intervening ground, seize the objective, and prepare for the inevitable counterattack. Seldom successful against alert and prepared defenses, these attacks were generally accompanied by tremendous casualties and foreshadowed the massed infantry assaults of World War I. Sometimes, large formations attempted mass charges over short distances without halting to fire. This tactic enjoyed limited success at Spotsylvania Court House in May 1864. At Spotsylvania, a Union division attacked and captured an exposed portion of the Confederate line. The attack succeeded because the Union troops crossed the intervening ground very quickly without artillery preparation and without stopping to fire their rifles. Once inside the Confederate defenses, the Union troops attempted to exploit their success by continuing their advance, but loss of command and control made them little better than a mob. Counterattacking Confederate units, in conventional formations, eventually forced the Federals to relinquish much of the ground gained.

As the war dragged on, tactical maneuver focused more on larger formations: brigade, division, and corps. In most of the major battles fought after 1861, brigades were employed as the primary maneuver formations. But brigade maneuver was at the upper limit of command and control for most Civil War commanders. Brigades might be able to retain coherent formations if the terrain were suitably open, but most often, brigade attacks degenerated into a series of poorly coordinated regimental lunges through broken and wooded terrain. Thus, brigade commanders were often on the main battle line trying to influence regimental fights. Typically, defending brigades stood in line of battle and blazed away at attackers as rapidly as possible. Volley fire usually did not continue beyond the first round. Most of the time, soldiers fired as soon as they were ready, and it was common for two soldiers to work together, one loading for the other to fire. Brigades were generally invulnerable to attacks on their front and flanks if units to the left and right held their ground or if reinforcements came up to defeat the threat.

An example of this sort of brigade maneuver occurred at Chickamauga on the morning of 20 September 1863 when the Confederates attacked the extreme left of the Union line. Major General John C. Breckinridge's Division attempted to turn the Union left, while Major General Patrick R. Cleburne's Division attacked frontally. Two of Breckinridge's brigades, led by Brigadier General Daniel W. Adams and Brigadier General Marcellus A. Stovall, turned the Union flank and threatened its rear, but Brigadier General Benjamin H. Helm's brigade ran into Major General George H. Thomas' main line and made no gains. Meanwhile, Cleburne's three brigades, under Brigadier Generals Lucius E. Polk, James Deshler, and S. A. M. Wood attacked into the strength of the Union line. Union reinforcements, however, drove off Adams and Stovall while the main line easily defeated the frontal attacks (see figure 5).

Two or more brigades comprised a division. When a division attacked, its brigades often advanced in sequence, from left to right or vice versa—depending on terrain, suspected enemy location, and number of brigades available to attack. At times, divisions attacked with two or more brigades leading, followed by one or more brigades ready to reinforce the lead brigades or maneuver to the flanks. Two or more divisions comprised a corps that might conduct an attack as part of a larger plan controlled by the army commander. More often, groups of divisions attacked under the control of a corps-level commander.

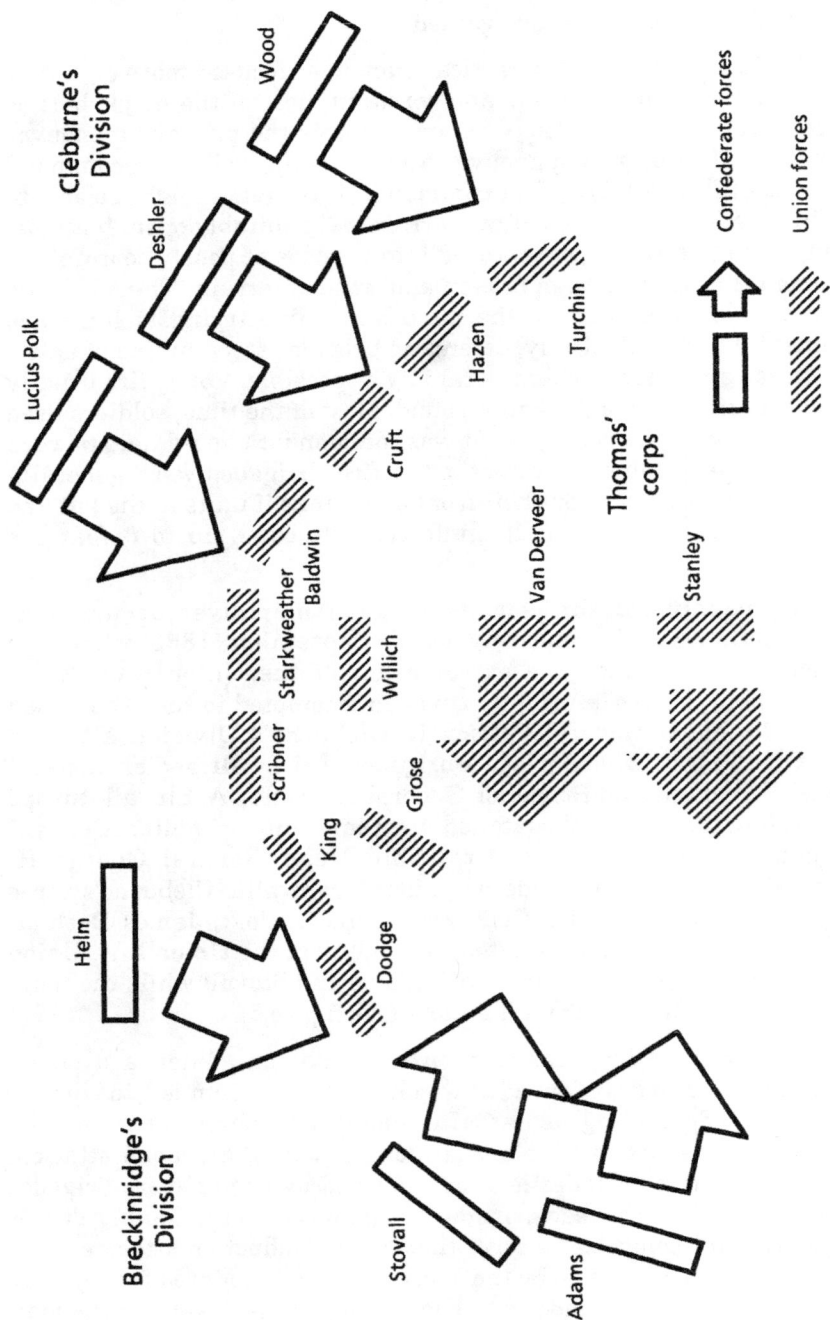

Figure 5. Maneuvering brigades at Chickamauga, 20 September 1863

Division and corps commanders generally took a position to the rear of the main line in order to control the flow of reinforcements into the battle, but they often rode forward into the battle lines to influence the action personally.

Of the three basic branches, cavalry made the greatest adaptation during the war. It learned to use its horses for mobility, then dismount and fight on foot like infantry. Cavalry regained a useful battlefield role by employing this tactic, especially after repeating and breech-loading rifles gave it the firepower to contend with enemy infantry. In contrast, artillery found that it could add its firepower to the rifle-musket and tip the balance even more in favor of the tactical defensive, but artillery never regained the importance to offensive maneuver that it held in Mexico. If artillery had developed an indirect firing system, as it did prior to World War I, it might have been able to contribute more to offensive tactics. Still, both sides employed artillery decisively in defensive situations throughout the war.

The most significant tactical innovation in the Civil War was the widespread use of field fortifications after armies realized the tactical offensive's heavy cost. It did not take long for the deadly firepower of the rifle-musket to convince soldiers to entrench every time they halted. Eventually, armies dug complete trenches within an hour of halting in a position. Within twenty-four hours, armies could create defensive works that were nearly impregnable to frontal assaults. In this respect, this development during the American Civil War was a clear forerunner of the kind of warfare that came to dominate World War I.

Summary

In the Civil War, the tactical defense dominated the tactical offense because assault formations proved inferior to the defender's firepower. The rifle-musket, in its many forms, provided this firepower and caused the following specific alterations in tactics during the war:

• It required the attacker, in his initial dispositions, to deploy farther away from the defender, thereby increasing the distance over which the attacker had to pass.

• It increased the number of defenders who could engage attackers (with the addition of effective enfilading fire).

• It reduced the density of both attacking and defending formations.

• It created a shift of emphasis in infantry battles toward firefights rather than shock attacks.

• It caused battles to last longer, because units could not close with each other for decisive shock action.

• It encouraged the widespread use of field fortifications. The habitual use of field fortifications by armies was a major American innovation in nineteenth-century warfare.

• It forced cavalry to the battlefield's fringes until cavalrymen acquired equivalent weapons and tactics.

• It forced artillery to abandon its basic offensive maneuver: that of moving forward to within canister range of defending infantry.

Tactics at Chickamauga

By September 1863, Civil War battle tactics had evolved to the point that brigades were the basic maneuver units. Thus, both sides fought the Battle of Chickamauga by maneuvering brigades and attacking or defending along brigade lines of battle. Usually, a division commander controlled attacks made by two or more brigades under his command. This required tremendous coordination and synchronization, which the Civil War command system generally failed to provide. Further, the Chickamauga battlefield was heavily wooded, which made brigade and divisional maneuver even more difficult. Much of the tactical confusion at Chickamauga resulted from the difficulty of maneuvering large bodies of troops through difficult terrain with a command system that depended mainly on voice commands.

At Chickamauga, the armies exhibited basic differences in the way they employed their divisions and brigades. Confederate brigades most often advanced with all regiments on line simultaneously. Union brigades generally advanced with two regiments forward and two following in a second line. Use of these formations at Chickamauga usually meant that a Confederate brigade would overlap a Federal brigade of similar size, giving Confederate divisions the advantage of a wider front. There was less uniformity within each army at division level, but Union divisions tended to defend with two brigades forward and one brigade to the rear in support. Did these formations reflect evolving doctrinal ideas? Were they responses to the restrictive nature of the terrain? Did commanders choose these methods to improve their ability to control their units? Perhaps the answers lie in the personalities, experiences, and abilities of the commanders on both sides. Essentially, the Army of the Cumberland fought a defensive battle. Major General William S. Rosecrans concentrated his army as rapidly as possible in a position from which he could either resume the operational offensive or fall back on Chattanooga and develop a new campaign. On 18, 19, and 20 September, General Braxton Bragg intended to isolate Rosecrans from Chattanooga, but most of his attacks were frontal assaults against increasingly well-prepared and alert defenses. In the main, the battle devolved into a series of poorly coordinated brigade and division assaults. A notable exception was Breckinridge's divisional attack on the extreme left of Thomas' XIV Corps on the morning of the 20th. In this fight, two of Breckinridge's brigades, Adams' and Stovall's, reached the Union rear and were in position to cooperate with attacks against Thomas' front. The complications of coordinating this maneuver, however, defeated it as surely as the rifle-musket fire from Union reinforcements that rushed to the spot. Merely turning Thomas' flank was not damaging enough to cause the Union line to crumble. Thomas' men stayed behind their fortifications, defeated Confederate attacks to their front, and let reinforcements turn back the threat to their flank and rear.

Lieutenant General James Longstreet's assault on 20 September, the stroke that routed Rosecrans' center, was a fluke. Longstreet's center, a column of three divisions organized in five lines, seems to have been more an adaptation to space than a conscious design. Although it was well organized and gallantly led, the grand column had the singular advantage of striking a vacant stretch of Union line. Had that line been properly held, Longstreet's attack might have failed or, at best, achieved only local success at a heavy cost. As it was, the confused breakthrough once again demonstrated the difficulty of Civil War tactical maneuvers, even in a case where the enemy was broken and routed. Although the Confederates held a huge advantage for over an hour, they could not exploit it because the command and control to do so did not exist. Later, Longstreet's attacks against the Snodgrass Hill position were typical frontal assaults that were poorly coordinated and culminated in heavy losses.

At Chickamauga, both armies employed shortsighted tactics and seldom achieved long-range, coordinated objectives. A few units, however, profitably deviated from the norm. One Confederate unit, Major General Alexander P. Stewart's Division, effectively employed a unique battle drill. Stewart moved his brigades forward in a column of brigades, and when a brigade ran short of ammunition, he rotated another into its place. This had the effect of keeping a continuous pressure of firepower against the Union defenders, who fell back from Stewart's attack. Another unit that had great tactical success at Chickamauga was Union Colonel John T. Wilder's mounted infantry brigade. Its five mounted infantry regiments, mostly armed with Spencer repeating rifles, fought dismounted and were supported by an oversized battery of artillery. In two important firefights, Wilder's brigade shattered Confederate infantry attacks. The firepower of the Spencers, coupled with that of the artillery battery, and the mobility of horses made Wilder's brigade unbeatable at Chickamauga. On the northern end of the battlefield, a Confederate unit, Major General Nathan B. Forrest's Cavalry Corps, employed tactics similar to Wilder's. Forrest's men also used horses for mobility and fought on foot as infantry. Although not armed with repeating rifles, they employed a more open formation in the advance, and they had good success on the northern flank at Chickamauga.

In sum, Chickamauga was like most other Civil War battles in terms of tactics. Attacks were piecemeal, frontal, and uncoordinated, and they generally failed to dislodge defenders. However, some tactical innovations, such as the rotation maneuver used by Stewart's Division and the open order employed by Forrest's cavalry, gave attackers a better chance of success. Employed defensively, Wilder's brigade clearly showed how repeating rifles could dramatically influence battle. Unfortunately, these innovations were the exception rather than the rule. The same tactics that failed at Shiloh, Antietam, Fredericksburg, and Murfreesboro failed again at Chickamauga.

Logistical Support

Victory on Civil War battlefields seldom hinged on the quality or quantity of tactical logistics. On the operational and strategic level, however, logistical capabilities and concerns always shaped the plans and sometimes the outcomes of campaigns. And as the war lengthened, the logistical advantage shifted inexorably to the North. The Federals controlled the majority of the financial and industrial resources of the nation, and with their ability to import any needed materials, they ultimately created the best-supplied army the world had yet seen. Despite suffering from shortages of raw materials, the Confederates generated adequate ordnance, but they faltered gradually in their ability to acquire other war materiel. The food supply for Southern armies was often on the verge of collapse, largely because limitations of the transportation network were compounded by political-military mismanagement. Still, the state of supply within field armies on both sides depended more on the caliber of the people managing resources than on the constraints of available materiel.

One of the most pressing needs at the start of the war was for sufficient infantry and artillery weapons. Large quantities of outmoded muskets were on hand for both sides, either in arsenals or private hands, but the Federals initially had only 35,000 modern rifle-muskets, while the Confederates had seized about 10,000. Purchasing agents rushed to Europe to buy existing stocks or contract for future production. This led to an influx of outmoded weapons, which resulted in many soldiers going into battle with Mexican War-era smoothbore muskets. As late as the fall of 1863, soldiers on both sides in the western theater were armed with muskets: several of Grant's regiments in the Vicksburg campaign noted exchanging their muskets for captured Confederate Enfields, and in the Battle of Chickamauga, up to one-third of the Confederates were still armed with muskets. Modern artillery pieces were generally available in adequate quantities, though the Confederates usually were outgunned. Although breech-loading technology was available and the Confederates had imported some Whitworths from England, muzzle-loading smoothbore or rifled cannon were the standard pieces used by both armies.

With most of the government arsenals and private manufacturing capability located in the North, the Federals ultimately produced sufficient modern firearms for their armies, but the Confederates also accumulated adequate quantities—either from battlefield captures or through the blockade. In addition, exceptional management within the Confederate Ordnance Bureau led to the creation of a series of arsenals throughout the South that produced large quantities of munitions and weapons.

The Northern manufacturing capability permitted the Federals eventually to produce and outfit their forces with repeating arms, the best of which had been patented before 1861. Initially, however, the North's conservative Ordnance Bureau would not risk switching to a new, unproven standard weapon that could lead to soldiers wasting huge quantities of ammunition in the midst of an expanding war. By 1864, after the retirement of Chief of Ordnance James Ripley and with President Lincoln's urging, Federal cavalry received seven-shot Spencer repeating carbines, which greatly increased battle capabilities.

Both sides initially relied on the states and local districts to provide some equipment, supplies, animals, and foodstuffs. As the war progressed, more centralized control over production and purchasing emerged under both governments. Still, embezzlement and fraud were common problems for both sides throughout the war. The North, with its preponderance of railroads and developed waterways, had ample supply and adequate distribution systems. The South's major supply problem was subsistence. Arguably, the South produced enough food during the war to provide for both military and civilian needs, but mismanagement, parochial local interests, and the relatively underdeveloped transportation network often created havoc with distribution.

In both armies, the Quartermaster, Ordnance, Subsistence, and Medical Bureaus procured and distributed equipment, food, and supplies. The items for which these bureaus were responsible are not dissimilar to the classes of supply used today. Some needs overlapped, such as the Quartermaster Bureau's procurement of wagons for medical ambulances, but conflicts of interest usually were manageable. Department and army commanders requested needed resources directly from the bureaus, and bureau chiefs wielded considerable power as they parceled out occasionally limited resources.

When essential equipment and supplies could not be obtained through normal channels, some commanders used their own resources to procure them. One example of this practice was Colonel John T. Wilder, who personally contracted for Spencer rifles for his mounted brigade in the Army of the Cumberland. Wilder obtained an unsecured personal loan to purchase the weapons, and his men reimbursed him from their pay. The Federal government picked up the cost after the rifles' worth was demonstrated in the Tullahoma and Chickamauga campaigns.

Typically, materiel flowed from the factory to base depots as directed by the responsible bureaus. Supplies were then shipped to advanced depots, generally a city on a major transportation artery safely within the rear area of a department. During campaigns, the armies established temporary advance depots served by rail or river transportation. From these points, wagons carried the supplies forward to the field units. This principle is somewhat similar to the modern theater sustainment organization.

The management of this logistical system was complex and crucial. A corps wagon train, if drawn by standard six-mule teams, would be spread out from five to eight miles, based on the difficulty of terrain, weather, and road conditions. The wagons, which were capable of hauling 4,000 pounds in optimal conditions, could carry only half that load in mountainous terrain. Sustenance for the animals was a major restriction, because each animal required up to twenty-six pounds of hay and grain a day to stay healthy and productive. Bulky and hard to handle, this forage was a major consideration in campaign planning. Wagons delivering supplies more than one day's distance from the depot could be forced to carry excessive amounts of animal forage. If full animal forage was to be carried, the required numbers of wagons to support a corps increased dramatically with each subsequent day's distance from the forward depot. Another problem was created by herds of beef that often accompanied the trains or were appropriated en route. This provided fresh (though tough) meat for the troops but slowed and complicated movement.

The bulk-supply problems were alleviated somewhat by the practice of foraging, which, in the proper season, supplied much of the food for animals and men on both sides. Foraging was practiced with and without command sanction wherever an army went, and it became command policy during Ulysses S. Grant's Vicksburg campaign and William T. Sherman's Atlanta campaign. Rosecrans' decision to endure pressure from Washington and wait for the corn to ripen before starting his campaign in August 1863 was an example of the crucial impact of animal forage on operations and also an illustration of a commander who understood some of the complexities of logistics for a major campaign.

Logistics at Chickamauga

Supplies for Rosecrans' Chickamauga campaign flowed from Louisville (a base depot) to Nashville (an advanced depot) to temporary depots established near the Tennessee River at Stevenson and Tracy City. Bragg's supply system, however, was more politically complicated. Because Virginia could not produce enough food to sustain Robert E. Lee's army continuously, the Confederate government designated Georgia as the sustainment area for the Army of Northern Virginia, with Atlanta as the primary depot. This meant that Bragg could not draw supplies from Atlanta even though it was barely 100 miles away. Although Bragg was ultimately allowed to use the Atlanta depot, such policies created bureaucratic headaches for Confederate Army commanders throughout the war. Bragg established advance depots along the Western and Atlantic Railroad at Resaca, Dalton, and Catoosa Station (near Ringgold) as the campaign progressed.

Once Rosecrans left his rail lines by crossing the Tennessee River, wagons became even more crucial. Major General Alexander M. McCook's XX Corps, which contained three divisions during the Chickamauga campaign, used over 850 wagons and ambulances pulled by over 4,700 mules and horses. These wagons, in addition to hauling routine daily supplies, tools, tentage, and personal baggage, initially carried three weeks' rations and enough ammunition to fight two major battles, as well as three days' forage for the animals (for a sample of logistical data, see table 6). During movement, ammunition wagons received priority, followed by food, medical items, and other supplies. Sutlers (private businessmen selling "luxuries," who were

Table 6. Sample of Federal Logistical Data

Item	Packing	Weight (lbs.)
Bulk ammunition:		
.58 caliber, expanding ball (500-grain bullet)	1,000 rounds per case	98
12-pounder Napoleon canister (14.8 lbs. per round)	8 rounds per box	161
"Marching" ration (per man per day):		2
1 lb. hard bread (hartack)		
3/4 lb. salt pork or 1/4 lb. fresh meat		
1 oz. coffee		
3 oz. sugar and salt		
Forage (per horse per day):		26
14 lbs. hay and 12 lbs. grain		
Personal equipment:		50—60
Includes rifle, bayonet, 60 rounds of ammunition, haversack, 3 days' rations, blanket, shelter half, canteen, personal items		

precursors of the present-day post exchanges) followed these army wagons. Logisticians had learned early to push supplies as far forward as possible, so this train followed its units on the march and closed to within a few miles of the forward units when battle was imminent. At the start of the Battle of Chickamauga, the bulk of these trains moved to Chattanooga and relative safety, but ammunition wagons remained with the divisions.

Units at Chickamauga used two techniques of ammunition resupply during the battle. Either small groups of men were detailed to move back to the wagons to hand-carry the 98- to 135-pound boxes of ammunition forward or regiments withdrew to the ammunition wagons to refit. Artillery batteries usually sent empty caissons to the rear to replenish their stocks. Although no written doctrine existed on the subject, many units on both sides had established simple and remarkably effective methods to handle resupply operations. In any number of battle reports, descriptions of resupply techniques resemble some of the standard operating procedures that are taught in branch schools today.

Engineer Support

Engineers on both sides performed many tasks essential to every campaign. Engineers trained at West Point were at a premium; thus, many civil engineers, commissioned as volunteers, supplemented the work being done by engineer officers. The Confederates, in particular, relied on civilian expertise because many of their trained engineer officers sought line duties. State or even local civil engineers planned and supervised much of the work done on local fortifications.

In the prewar U.S. Army, the Corps of Engineers contained a handful of staff officers and one company of trained engineer troops. This cadre expanded to a four-company Regular engineer battalion. Congress also created a single company of topographic engineers, which joined the Regular battalion when the engineer bureaus merged in 1863. In addition, several volunteer pioneer regiments, some containing up to 2,000 men, supported the various field armies. The Corps of Engineers also initially controlled the fledgling Balloon Corps, which provided aerial reconnaissance. The Confederate Corps of Engineers, formed as a small staff and one company of sappers, miners, and pontoniers in 1861, grew more slowly and generally relied on details and contract labor rather than established units with trained engineers and craftsmen.

Engineer missions for both sides included construction of fortifications; repair and construction of roads, bridges, and, in some cases, railroads; demolition; limited construction of obstacles; and construction or reduction of siege works. The Federal Topographic Engineers, a separate prewar bureau, performed reconnaissance and produced maps. The Confederates, however, never separated these functions in creating their Corps of Engineers. Experience during the first year of the war convinced the Federals that all engineer functions should be merged under a single corps because qualified engineer officers tended to perform all related functions. As a result, the Federals also merged the Topographic Engineers into their Corps of Engineers in March 1863.

Bridging assets included wagon-mounted pontoon trains that carried either wooden or canvas-covered pontoon boats. Using this equipment, trained engineer troops could bridge even large rivers in a matter of hours. The most remarkable pontoon bridge of the war was the 2,200-foot bridge built by Army of the Potomac engineers in 1864 over the James River—one of over three dozen pontoon bridges built in support of campaigns in the east that year. In 1862, the Confederates began developing pontoon trains after they had observed their effectiveness. In fact, during the Atlanta campaign of 1864, General Joseph Johnston had four pontoon trains available to support his army.

Both armies in every campaign of the war traveled over roads and bridges built or repaired by their engineers. Federal engineers also helped clear waterways by dredging, removing trees, or digging canals. Fixed fortifications laid out under engineer supervision played critical roles in the Vicksburg campaign and in actions around Richmond and Petersburg. Engineers also supervised the siege works to reduce those fortifications.

While the Federal engineer effort expanded in both men and materiel as the war progressed, the Confederate efforts continued to be hampered by major problems. The relatively small number of organized engineer units available forced Confederate engineers to rely heavily on details or contract labor. Finding adequate manpower, however, was often difficult because of competing demands for it. Local slave owners were reluctant to provide labor details when labor was crucial to their economic survival. Despite congressional authorization to conscript 20,000 slaves as a labor force, state and local opposition continually hindered efforts to draft slave labor. Another related problem concerned the value of Confederate currency. Engineer efforts required huge sums for men and materiel, yet initial authorizations were small, and although congressional appropriations grew later in the war, inflation greatly reduced effective purchasing power. A final problem was the simple shortage of iron resources, which severely limited the Confederates' ability to increase railroad mileage or even produce iron tools.

In 1861, maps for both sides were also in short supply; for many areas in the interior, they were nonexistent. As the war progressed, the Federals developed a highly sophisticated mapping capability. Federal topographic engineers performed personal reconnaissance to develop base maps, reproduced them by several processes, and distributed them to field commanders. Photography, lithographic presses, and eventually photochemical processes gave the Federals the ability to reproduce maps quickly. Western armies, which usually operated far from base cities, carried equipment to reproduce maps on campaigns with their army headquarters. By 1864, annual map production exceeded 21,000 copies. Confederate topographic work never approached the Federal effort in quantity or quality. Confederate topographers initially used tracing paper to reproduce maps. Not until 1864 did the use of photographic methods become widespread in the South.

Engineers at Chickamauga

Engineers in neither the Army of the Cumberland nor the Army of Tennessee had a tactical role in the Battle of Chickamauga, although the Federal engineers performed essential missions in upgrading roads, railroads, and supply depots, as well as bridging the Tennessee River. Rosecrans' organic engineer assets included two special units: the 1st Michigan Engineers and Mechanics and the Pioneer Brigade. The former was a regiment of 1,000 men who were specially recruited for their engineering skills. The latter, formed at Rosecrans' direction, had men detailed from virtually every company in his army. In mid-September 1863, the Pioneer Brigade contained nearly 950 men. The technical expertise and construction talents of these men were supplemented by infantry detailed to perform manual labor, such as cutting trees and demolishing buildings for bridging material.

During the Chickamauga campaign, the 1st Michigan built a trestle bridge across the Tennessee River at Bridgeport that was used by two Federal divisions. The Pioneer Brigade was spread along the railway southward from Nashville, building bridges and fortifications as well as constructing platforms at the temporary depot at Stevenson, Alabama. A company from this brigade built the pontoon bridge across the Tennessee River at Caperton's Ferry. Although trained as infantry, neither unit was involved in combat during this campaign, although elements of the 1st Michigan had fought with distinction at Stones River ten months earlier.

Bragg's engineers consisted of 4 companies with a combined effective strength of just over 300 men. These companies, formed by details of infantrymen, were supervised by Bragg's chief engineer, Captain S. W. Presstman. Limited information about their activities exists, although one of the companies built and maintained a pontoon bridge across the Tennessee River at Chattanooga until Bragg evacuated the city in early September.

The engineer staff officers at the army headquarters of both armies created maps. The Army of the Cumberland had refined a portable photochemical process for reproducing maps in the field and therefore created, updated, and distributed maps to at least brigade level. Federal maps depicted the gross terrain features, major roads, and existing towns, including the locations of various isolated houses, but at best, these maps were only general guides. As units moved through areas, commanders noted new roads and other features on their maps and forwarded that information to the army engineers so updated maps could be made and issued. Despite the Confederates' long-term control over the area, their maps were hardly more specific or more available than the Federal maps. Bragg's chief engineer was personally tasked with reconnaissance and mapping only after the army evacuated Chattanooga.

Ultimately, commanders on both sides used local citizens to provide additional information about local terrain. Longstreet's "living map" during the grand assault of 20 September was Thomas Brotherton, a soldier whose cabin was in the center of the line of attack. Rosecrans and some of his subordinate commanders also used local citizens—the McDonalds, Dyers, and Glenns—to provide information about the area during the battle.

Communications Support

Communications systems used during the Civil War consisted of line-of-sight signaling, telegraphic systems, and various forms of the time-honored courier methods. The telegraph mainly offered viable strategic and operational communications, line-of-sight signaling provided operational and limited tactical possibilities, and couriers were most heavily used for tactical communications.

The Federal Signal Corps was in its infancy during the Civil War, Major Albert C. Myer having been appointed the first signal chief in 1860. His organization grew slowly and became officially recognized as the Signal Corps in March 1863 and achieved bureau status by November of that year. Throughout the war, the Signal Corps remained small, its maximum strength reaching just 1,500 officers and men, most of whom were on detached service with the corps. Myer also indirectly influenced the formation of the Confederate Signal Service. Among the men who assisted Myer in prewar testing of his wigwag signaling system* was Lieutenant E. P. Alexander. Alexander used wigwag signals to the Confederates' advantage during the First Battle of Bull Run and later organized the Confederate Signal Corps. Officially established in April 1862, the Confederate Signal Corps was attached to the Adjutant and Inspector General Department. It attained the same size as its Federal counterpart, with nearly 1,500 men ultimately being detailed for service.

Myer also fought hard to develop a Federal field telegraph service. This field service utilized the Beardslee device, a magneto-powered machine operated by turning a wheel to a specific point, which sent an electrical impulse that keyed the machine at the other end to the same letter. Although less reliable than the standard Morse code telegraph key, the Beardslee could be used by an operator with only several hours' training and did not require bulky batteries for a power source.

---

*Myer's wigwag system, patented in 1858, used five separate numbered movements of a single flag. Four number groups represented letters of the alphabet and a few simple words and phrases. The system could also be employed at night by using kerosene torches.

Myer's field telegraph units carried equipment on wagons that enabled its operators to establish lines between field headquarters. The insulated wire could also be hooked into existing trunk lines, thus offering the potential to extend the reach of the civilian telegraph network. Control over the existing fixed telegraph system, however, remained with the U.S. Military Telegraph Service. Myer lost his struggle to keep the field telegraph service under the Signal Corps when Secretary of War Edwin M. Stanton relieved Myer as the signal chief in November 1863 and placed all telegraph activity under the Military Telegraph Service.

Although the Confederate Signal Corps' visual communications capabilities were roughly equal to those of the Federals', Confederate field telegraph operations remained too limited to be of operational significance. The Confederates' existing telegraph lines provided strategic communications capabilities similar to those of the Federals, but the lack of resources and factories in the South for producing wire precluded their extending the prewar telegraph networks.

Communications at Chickamauga

The Chickamauga campaign presents, particularly from the Federal side, a view of the complexities of the early development and integration of different communications systems. The fixed telegraph system operated by the U.S. Military Telegraph Service provided strategic communications. Thus, army commanders could send and receive messages from Washington on the same day. The Army of the Cumberland's chief signal officer, Captain Jesse Merrill, expanded the capabilities of this fixed network by developing "trains" that carried over 100 miles of uninsulated wire and poles on wagons which could extend the telegraph lines to the advancing army. Using these assets, Merrill's trained civilian operators established a number of field stations east of the Tennessee River in early September 1863. On 17 September, Rosecrans ordered Merrill to link the army's field headquarters with Chattanooga. By the morning of 19 September, Merrill had established stations at Crawfish Spring and the Widow Glenn's cabin, along the Dry Valley Road west of Thomas' headquarters, and at Major General Gordon Granger's Reserve Corps headquarters at Rossville.

The Signal Corps detachment of the Army of the Cumberland, under Captain John C. Van Duzer, contained five field units with Beardslee devices. These "flying trains," operated by 1 officer and 16 men, carried some 400 slender poles and 10 miles of insulated telegraph wire on wagons. Although this system could not network directly with the Military Telegraph Service, it did link Thomas' and

McCook's corps headquarters near Pond Spring on 17 September. This tactical communications capability remained unused during the actual battle, though some of the insulated wire helped Merrill's telegraph operation.

Both sides also used small signal corps detachments, which set up signal stations on Lookout Mountain and other high ground. These stations sent messages by flag (or lantern at night) as far as line-of-sight and weather conditions permitted. While the Confederates employed semaphore techniques, the Federal signalers used Myer's wigwag system. Both sides used simple codes. The Federals used sets of two concentric rotating disks, one containing the groups of wigwag numbers and the second containing the letters of the alphabet. By prearranging the set of the wheels, the Federals could encode messages and change the set if necessary. This system proved secure, for no evidence exists that the Confederates broke the Federal codes. The Confederates used a sheet with rows of letters, not dissimilar to a page from a modern communications code book, and used prearranged code words to modify the encoding sequence. Confederate encoding procedures were often sloppy, and entries in Federal records show that this code was frequently broken. Although these signal systems were of some use in transmitting orders, they usually proved more helpful in providing information about enemy activities, because movements of both armies were often visible from suitable vantage points. Still, limited capabilities and the commanders' lack of appreciation for telegraph and signal flag systems precluded any real influence on the battle itself.

The courier system, using mounted staff officers or detailed soldiers to deliver orders and messages, was the most viable tactical communications option short of commanders meeting face to face. Although often effective, this system was fraught with difficulties, as couriers were captured, killed, or delayed en route to their destinations; commanders misinterpreted or ignored messages; and situations changed by the time a message was delivered. The weaknesses of the courier system, though not critical in themselves, did tend to compound other errors or misjudgments during the campaign. For instance, Bragg, using couriers, could not convince his subordinates to attack Major General James S. Negley's isolated division in McLemore's Cove on 10 September, and the young private sent to notify Lieutenant General Daniel H. Hill that he was to initiate the attack on the morning of 20 September could not locate that general in the dark woods. The Federals, too, had problems: information offered by one of Thomas' couriers prompted Rosecrans to issue (by courier) the order that moved Brigadier General Thomas J.

Wood's division out of line minutes before Longstreet's assault on 20 September.

The effectiveness of communications systems during the battle and campaign was hindered by the number of different systems employed, as well as the senior commanders' inexperience in utilizing the systems. The Federal Army had five different modes of communications: the existing civilian telegraph network, the extended lines provided by Merrill's military telegraph trains, the Signal Corps' "flying trains" (with Beardslee devices), the Signal Corps' wigwag flag stations, and the numerous couriers provided by each headquarters. Most of these systems were not compatible, thereby requiring a transfer of the form of message at each node. Moreover, most of the systems were under the control of different men, none of whom, including the army commander, fully understood the potential capabilities or problems of the overall system.

Medical Support

Federal and Confederate medical systems followed a similar pattern. Surgeons general and medical directors for both sides had served many years in the prewar Medical Department but were hindered by an initial lack of administrative experience in handling large numbers of casualties, as well as the state of medical science in the midnineteenth century. Administrative procedures improved with experience, but throughout the war, the simple lack of knowledge about the true causes of disease and infection led to many more deaths than direct battlefield action.

After the disaster at the Battle of First Bull Run, the Federal Medical Department established an evacuation and treatment system developed by Surgeon Jonathan Letterman. At the heart of the system were three precepts: consolidation of field hospitals at division level, decentralization of medical supplies down to regimental level, and centralization of medical control of ambulances at all levels. A battle casualty evacuated from the front line normally received treatment at a regimental holding area immediately to the rear. From this point, wagons or ambulances carried wounded men to a division field hospital, normally within a mile of the battle lines. Seriously wounded men could then be further evacuated by wagon, rail, or watercraft to general hospitals located usually in towns along lines of communication in the armies' rear areas.

Although the Confederate system followed the same general principles, Confederate field hospitals were often consolidated at brigade rather than division level. A second difference lay in the established span of control of medical activities. Unlike their Federal counterparts, who had control over all medical activities within an army area, a Confederate army medical director had no control of activities beyond his own brigade or division field hospitals. A separate medical director for general hospitals was responsible for evacuation and control. In practice, both sets of medical directors resolved potential problems through close cooperation. By 1863, the Confederacy had also introduced rear area "wayside hospitals," which were intended to handle convalescents en route home on furloughs.

Procedures, medical techniques, and medical problems for both sides were virtually identical. Commanders discouraged soldiers from leaving the battle lines to escort wounded back to the rear, but such practice was common, especially in less-disciplined units. The established technique for casualty evacuation was to detail men for litter and ambulance duty. Both armies used bandsmen, among others, for this task. Casualties would move or be assisted back from the battle line, where litter bearers evacuated them to field hospitals using ambulances or supply wagons. Ambulances were specially designed two- or four-wheel carts with springs to limit jolts, but rough roads made even short trips agonizing for wounded men. Brigade and division surgeons staffed consolidated field hospitals. Hospital site considerations were the availability of water, potential buildings to supplement the hospital tents, and security from enemy cannon and rifle fire. The majority of operations performed at field hospitals in the aftermath of battle were amputations. Approximately 70 percent of Civil War wounds occurred in the extremities, and the soft Minié ball shattered any bones that it hit. Amputation was the best technique then available to limit the chance of serious infection. The Federals were generally well supplied with chloroform, morphine, and other drugs, though shortages did occur on the battlefield. Confederate surgeons often lacked critical drugs and medical supplies.

Medical Support at Chickamauga

Although the Letterman system had been adopted by Grant's Army of the Tennessee by mid-1863, the Army of the Cumberland's medical system was then still in transition. In February 1863, Medical Director Glover Perin, a veteran of sixteen years of Army medical service, had inherited an evacuation system in disarray. As an interim measure, he convinced Rosecrans to give quartermasters control of ambulances, but they were to respond to their respective medical directors or surgeons. This transitional system lasted until January 1864, when Perin finally was able to implement the Letterman system more fully.

The hospital system, however, corresponded with the Letterman model. General hospitals established at cities like Nashville, Memphis, Louisville, and Cincinnati made over 12,000 beds available for Rosecrans' army. In addition, Perin established interim general hospitals at Stevenson, Bridgeport, and Chattanooga as the Chickamauga campaign progressed.

The Confederate medical structure for Bragg's army followed the standard pattern, except for its unique general hospital system. Surgeon Samuel Stout, Bragg's general hospital director, required general hospitals to be mobile. Thus, general hospitals established in Chattanooga and the surrounding towns evacuated and reestablished themselves closer to Atlanta in as little as seventy-two hours as Bragg withdrew from Chattanooga. In a series of general hospitals established between Dalton and Marietta, Bragg's Medical Department had nearly 7,500 available hospital beds.

During the Battle of Chickamauga, seven Federal division hospitals gathered around Crawfish Spring, two miles south of the battlefield, and one was established around the Cloud house just north of the battlefield. Two division hospitals were formed in the rear of the battle lines in Dyer Field and near Snodgrass Hill until enemy attacks forced them to displace rearward. On 20 September, as the Federal battle line collapsed, the hospitals at Crawfish Spring packed up and evacuated to Chattanooga but were forced to leave about 2,500 seriously wounded and 52 surgeons to be captured by the Confederates. The Confederates used a mix of consolidated division and brigade hospitals, which were set up generally along Chickamauga Creek for most of the battle.

The greatest challenge for medical staffs occurred after the battle. The Confederates, already short of doctors and with medical supply stockage levels barely adequate for their own needs, had to treat large numbers of wounded Federal troops in addition to their own. The 2,500 Federal wounded captured at hospitals and the thousands of Federal wounded on the battlefield—added to the almost 15,000 Confederate battle injuries—initially overwhelmed the Confederate surgeons. It took the Confederates almost two weeks to finish policing the battlefield, and many soldiers lay for six to ten days before receiving any medical attention. On 30 September, the Confederates transferred 1,740 of the most seriously wounded Federals to Chattanooga under a flag of truce. The Federal challenge after the battle was less severe because of the smaller numbers of wounded under their control. Just over 4,000 Federal casualties initially made their way or were brought to Chattanooga, where the surgeons made every effort to evacuate

Table 7. Casualties of the Battle

	Federal	Confederate
Killed	1,657	2,312
Wounded	9,756	14,674
Missing	4,757	1,468
Totals	16,170	18,454

them to the safer hospitals across the river. By 23 September, only 800 of these wounded remained in medical facilities in Chattanooga. (For Federal and Confederate casualties, see table 7.)

II. CHICKAMAUGA CAMPAIGN OVERVIEW

The Chickamauga campaign took place in the summer and fall of 1863—a period of catastrophic Confederate defeats in the eastern and western theaters of the Civil War. In July, Robert E. Lee's Army of Northern Virginia suffered 25,000 casualties and turned back from its second invasion of the North after the Battle of Gettysburg. Never again would that Southern army seriously threaten Northern territory. Also in July, John C. Pemberton's Army of Mississippi surrendered 30,000 men at Vicksburg. Thus, in mid-1863, middle Tennessee was the only theater in which the Confederacy had not suffered a major reversal. The last Confederate army of real significance, General Braxton Bragg's Army of Tennessee defended middle Tennessee and Chattanooga against Major General William S. Rosecrans' Army of the Cumberland. They faced each other near Murfreesboro, where they had fought a great battle at the end of 1862.

Although western Tennessee had fallen to the Union in early 1862, much of middle and eastern Tennessee remained under Confederate control in the summer of 1863. The area was important to both sides for many reasons. President Abraham Lincoln was particularly interested in liberating eastern Tennessee because so many loyal Unionists lived there. The most direct rail connection between Virginia and the western part of the Confederacy also passed through Knoxville. In the apportionment of commissary resources, Confederate armies in the east depended on this region for subsistence. Middle and eastern Tennessee contributed essential pork and corn to the Confederate commissary, as well as copper and saltpeter for percussion caps and gunpowder.

Chattanooga was an important military objective for the North because of its position as a gateway through the Appalachian Mountains into the South's heartland. A city of approximately 2,500 people, it was a central rail junction. The Memphis and Charleston Railroad ran west to the Mississippi River. The Nashville and Chattanooga Railroad entered Chattanooga from middle Tennessee. The Western and Atlantic Railroad ran to the southeast toward Atlanta. To the northeast ran the East Tennessee Railroad to Knoxville, Bristol, and Lynchburg, Virginia, with connections to Richmond. Furthermore, the South had valuable commissary, quartermaster, and ordnance depots in Chattanooga. Also, several Confederate hospitals were located in and near the city. The rail connection through Atlanta linked Chattanooga with munitions and iron production centers in Georgia and Alabama. Most important,

Chattanooga was a key place from which the Union could sustain a further advance on its next objective—Atlanta.

The terrain between Murfreesboro and Chattanooga offered many challenges to armies attempting to traverse it or conduct operations there. Approximately twenty miles southeast of Murfreesboro lay a range of hills, almost mountainous in height, broken by several defiles—Hoover's, Liberty, Bellbuckle, and Guy's Gaps. Through these gaps ran several roads as well as the railroad between Nashville and Chattanooga. Behind the hills about forty miles southeast of Murfreesboro lay the Duck River, a deep, narrow stream with few fords. Beyond the Duck, the country was rough, with rocky ranges of hills rising to a high, rolling plateau called the barrens. The porous topsoil of that desolate area barely covered a layer of clay that temporarily held rain, creating massive quagmires after a storm. Fifteen miles beyond the Duck River, another stream, the Elk River, flowed westward out of the barrens. In turn, the barrens gave way to the range of mountains known as the Cumberland Plateau. The Tullahoma campaign, a preliminary phase of the Chickamauga campaign, would occur in the area between Murfreesboro and the Cumberland Plateau.

East of the high plateaus and gorges of the Cumberland Mountains, and generally parallel to them, lay the broad Tennessee River. Rising in east Tennessee and flowing generally southwest until it entered northeast Alabama, the Tennessee cut through the mountains west of Chattanooga in a canyon of massive proportions. South of the river, the land rose sharply to the Sand and Raccoon Mountains, then dropped almost as sharply into the valley of Lookout Creek before rising again to Lookout Mountain, the largest of the ridges that slant southwest across the Tennessee-Georgia-Alabama border. The northern end of Lookout Mountain was crossed by only three significant roads in 1863. The main road west from Chattanooga followed the Tennessee River valley along a narrow shelf under the northern promontory of the mountain where the river swept around Moccasin Bend. The next crossing was fourteen miles southwest of Chattanooga at Stevens Gap. Last was a rough road over the mountain more than twenty miles farther south at Winston's Gap in Alabama. Beyond Lookout Mountain lay Missionary Ridge, which guarded Chattanooga's eastern flank. East of Missionary Ridge, several branches of Chickamauga Creek watered a series of valleys between gently rolling hills. After a three-week campaign beginning on the banks of the Tennessee River and traversing two mountain barriers, the two armies found themselves confronting each other on opposite sides of West Chickamauga Creek.

By the summer of 1863, the Union drive to secure Tennessee had stalled. Union armies had done well in western Tennessee, beginning in early 1862 in the Fort Henry and Fort Donelson campaign that led to the capture of Nashville—the first Confederate state capital taken in the war. Thereafter, Union forces had used the Tennessee River to move deeper into Tennessee, Alabama, and Mississippi, but the Confederacy had countered with offensives of its own. This ebb and flow resulted in a stalemate in middle Tennessee, following the Battle of Stones River in January 1863. After that bloody battle, Bragg withdrew to the Duck River and assumed the defensive. He put one corps at Shelbyville and another at Wartrace, both in strong positions. His cavalry screened both flanks, and infantry controlled the four mountain gaps to his north through which he expected the Union Army to advance. Rosecrans occupied Murfreesboro and seemed content to remain there in spite of repeated urging by the Lincoln administration to move forward.

Both Rosecrans and Bragg thought their positions inferior. Rosecrans had about 80,000 men to Bragg's 50,000, but as much as 20 percent of the Union Army had to guard supply lines against Confederate raids. Rosecrans' cavalry force was weak, and he used this argument repeatedly in delaying his advance. Bragg's most pressing problems were that Vicksburg had priority in the west for troops and Lee's army in the east drew much of its subsistence from the region in which Bragg's army operated. Bragg had to detach troops from his army to aid Vicksburg, and this eliminated, at least in his mind, the idea that he should take the offensive against Rosecrans. Fortunately for Bragg, Rosecrans declined to advance. Soon, events in the east and west concluded with Confederate defeats at Gettysburg and Vicksburg. Both sides shifted their focus to middle Tennessee.

Under severe pressure from Washington, Rosecrans finally moved forward on 24 June 1863. He used his cavalry and reserve infantry corps as a diversion toward Shelbyville, then moved with his main body to turn the Confederate right flank between Wartrace and Manchester. Despite a pouring rain, bottomless roads, and some small fights for the gaps through rough country south of Murfreesboro, Rosecrans successfully outflanked the Confederates, and Bragg withdrew to Tullahoma after less than a week of maneuver. Rosecrans next sought to cross the Elk River and seize control of Bragg's supply line. Again, Bragg narrowly escaped the trap and withdrew all the way to Chattanooga, which he occupied on 4 July. In nine days of skillful maneuvering, Rosecrans forced Bragg out of Tennessee at a cost of less than 600 casualties. This brilliant and relatively bloodless operation is known as the Tullahoma campaign.

In early July, Rosecrans halted the Army of the Cumberland along the Fayetteville-Decherd-Manchester-McMinnville line, in sight of the formidable barrier of the Cumberland Mountains. In preparation for further advances, he sent Major General Philip H. Sheridan's division beyond the Cumberland Plateau to Stevenson, Alabama, and worked to repair the railroad from that point back to Murfreesboro. Unsatisfied, the War Department again demanded that Rosecrans advance. In response, on 16 August, after six weeks of preparation and rest, Rosecrans sent the Army of the Cumberland over the Cumberland Mountains toward the Tennessee River on a broad front. In less than a week, his army closed to the river with corps-size forces near Stevenson and Bridgeport, Alabama, and Shellmound, Tennessee. The next forward movement would take the Federals across the Tennessee River, where Bragg's veterans waited.

When Rosecrans pushed the Army of the Cumberland across the wide Tennessee River in early September 1863, his primary goal was to capture Chattanooga, Tennessee. Delaying his final advance until the end of the summer when the corn ripened and the railroad from Nashville was repaired, in late August, he mounted a masterful deception operation to mislead the Confederate defenders. While four brigades demonstrated opposite Chattanooga and upstream, the bulk of the Army of the Cumberland quietly gathered at four crossing sites far below the city shielded by Sand and Lookout Mountains. Bragg, who had kept his infantry force concentrated near Chattanooga, was badly served by Major General Joseph Wheeler's Cavalry Corps, which screened the river line below Chattanooga. Concentrating on resting and refitting after the arduous Tullahoma campaign, Wheeler and his men were mainly located far back from the river and did not contest any of the crossings. Nor did they provide Bragg with timely information of Federal activity. Blinded by a belief that Rosecrans would have to cross the Tennessee River north of Chattanooga in order to support Major General Ambrose E. Burnside's force in east Tennessee, Bragg and his principal subordinates eventually learned of the Federal crossings from a civilian.

In early September, Rosecrans divided his army into three segments and began a wide-front advance that he hoped would flank Bragg's army out of Chattanooga without a major battle. Major General Thomas L. Crittenden's XXI Corps advanced directly toward Chattanooga along the railroad that passed through a canyon in Sand Mountain. Major General George H. Thomas' XIV Corps crossed Sand and Lookout Mountains and entered McLemore's Cove en route to LaFayette, Georgia. Major General Alexander M. McCook's XX Corps followed Major General David S. Stanley's Cavalry Corps across Sand

and Lookout Mountains to the vicinity of Alpine, Georgia. Although the columns were not within mutual supporting distance because of the mountainous terrain, Rosecrans believed the threat posed to Bragg's line of communication by Thomas, McCook, and Stanley would force the evacuation of Chattanooga.

As Rosecrans expected, Bragg evacuated Chattanooga on 8 September. Rather than retreat beyond the mountains along the railroad to his base at Atlanta, however, Bragg elected to keep his army concentrated near LaFayette, Georgia. There, shielded by Pigeon Mountain, a spur of Lookout, the Army of Tennessee could await the arrival of reinforcements and seize any opportunity to defeat the scattered elements of the Army of the Cumberland in detail. Joined by Major General Simon B. Buckner's forces from east Tennessee, Bragg felt confident enough to strike the leading division of Thomas' XIV Corps with overwhelming force in McLemore's Cove. Unfortunately for Bragg, the leader of the expedition, Major General Thomas C. Hindman, took counsel of his fears and dallied for two days without making a serious attack. Failing in McLemore's Cove, Bragg next turned northward to destroy a portion of Crittenden's XXI Corps near Lee and Gordon's Mill on West Chickamauga Creek. This mission was entrusted to Lieutenant General Leonidas Polk, who also was unable to engage the Federals as Bragg proposed. Frustrated by these failures, Bragg paused at LaFayette for several days while waiting for additional troops from Mississippi and Virginia to appear.

On discovering that Bragg's army was not in flight toward Atlanta and recognizing the dangerous position his army was in, Rosecrans hastily began to concentrate his scattered units and move them northward to cover Chattanooga. Because of the distances and the rough terrain, McCook's XX Corps was the slowest to move. Delayed by faulty information, inadequate reconnaissance, and the sheer difficulty of moving thousands of men and animals over 2,000-foot mountains, McCook did not join Thomas' XIV Corps in McLemore's Cove until 17 September. Together, the two corps then continued northward toward Crittenden's position around Lee and Gordon's Mill. Their route generally followed the west bank of West Chickamauga Creek, with Missionary Ridge on their left. Fearing that Bragg would attempt to cut him off from Chattanooga, Rosecrans ordered Thomas on 18 September to make a night march northward beyond Crittenden's position at the mill.

His spirits raised by the continued arrival of reinforcements, Bragg devised a new battle plan. Believing that Crittenden's XXI Corps was the northernmost unit of Rosecrans' army, Bragg ordered most of his forces to move northward east of the Chickamauga and cross the creek downstream of the Federals holding Lee and Gordon's Mill. From north to south, Brigadier General Bushrod R. Johnson's Division (a provisional organization) would seize Reed's Bridge; Major General William H. T. Walker's Reserve Corps would seize Alexander's Bridge; and Buckner's Corps would utilize Thedford's Ford. After crossing, these units would sweep south, crushing the left of the Federal Army and driving the entire force south into McLemore's Cove and away from Chattanooga. While the flanking forces seized the crossings, Polk's Corps and Hill's Corps would fix the Federals along Chickamauga Creek.

By the evening of 18 September, Bushrod Johnson, joined by Major General John B. Hood and leading elements of Lieutenant General James Longstreet's Corps from Virginia, had captured Reed's Bridge and had advanced southward into the forest toward LaFayette Road. Walker and Buckner had also gained the west bank of Chickamauga Creek, although Walker's men had paid heavily in casualties for Alexander's Bridge. They, too, bivouacked for the night in the woods north of what they believed to be the Federal left flank. Because they had not gained the main north-south highway between LaFayette and Rossville, however, they were unaware of Thomas' XIV Corps as it marched northward through the night and took up position on LaFayette Road at the Kelly farm. The only night contact occurred when a brigade of Major General Gordon Granger's Reserve Corps, attempting to regain Reed's Bridge, bumped into rear-echelon elements of Johnson's Confederates at a road junction near Jay's Mill.

Believing that they had destroyed Reed's Bridge and trapped a single Confederate brigade west of the creek, Granger's men withdrew early on the morning of 19 September. On their way north, they informed Thomas, who resolved to destroy the lone Confederate unit. Thomas sent Brigadier General John M. Brannan's division eastward into the forest toward Reed's Bridge. Near Jay's Mill, Brannan's men met one of Brigadier General Nathan B. Forrest's cavalry brigades covering the Confederate army's right rear, and the battle was joined. For the remainder of the day, both Rosecrans and Bragg could do little more than feed reinforcements northward to extend the battle line and attempt to stabilize the situation. Their efforts were hindered by the terrain, which consisted primarily of a thick forest broken only occasionally by a few small fields. Neither commander had wanted to fight a battle in the thickets between Chickamauga Creek and LaFayette Road; Bragg had hoped to fight in the more open country to the south, while Rosecrans had hoped to reach a more defensible position closer to Chattanooga. Nevertheless, when the forces collided around Jay's Mill, the battle assumed a momentum of its own.

When Forrest saw that his cavalry faced Federal infantry, he brought up part of Walker's Reserve Corps and began to drive Brannan's men back. In turn, Thomas reinforced Brannan with more of the XIV Corps. When Walker was subsequently supported by part of Polk's Corps, Rosecrans responded with divisions from both McCook and Crittenden to assist Thomas. As the day progressed, a division of Buckner's Corps joined Polk and extended the Confederate line southward. Pressing forward with great spirit, Buckner's men shattered one of Crittenden's divisions, gained LaFayette Road, and threatened to split the Federal army in the vicinity of the Brotherton farm. Federal reinforcements from both north and south of the penetration finally forced the Confederates to relinquish the road and withdraw eastward into the forest. Hood's Corps then mounted another threat to the vital road in the vicinity of the Viniard farm but was finally fought to a bloody standstill by elements of all three Federal corps. When darkness closed the fighting, the Federals still held LaFayette Road, but Thomas' men had been pressed back a mile to a defensive position around Kelly Field.

During the night, the Army of the Cumberland prepared for a coordinated defense on the following day. Thomas strengthened his position on the army's left with log breastworks, McCook withdrew slightly to refuse the army's right flank, and Crittenden assumed a reserve position behind the army's center. Within the Confederate lines, Bragg brought forward several divisions that had not been engaged and devised an offensive plan. This plan called for a coordinated attack, beginning on the Confederate right and rolling southward, that would again attempt to flank the Federal army and drive it southward away from Chattanooga. Longstreet's arrival during the night permitted Bragg to reorganize his five infantry corps into two wings, with Longstreet commanding the Left Wing of six divisions and Polk the Right Wing of five divisions. Lieutenant General Daniel H. Hill's Corps, now under Polk's Right Wing, was to begin the attack at sunrise. Unfortunately, a combination of poor staff work and the lack of initiative by senior commanders prevented Hill from learning of his critical mission until the day was well advanced.

When the Confederate attack finally began—four hours late—one of Hill's divisions actually got around Thomas' flank and advanced several hundred yards into the Federal rear before being ejected by the timely arrival of Federal reinforcements. The success was unsupported, because Hill had used Walker's Corps to close a gap farther south in his lines. Elsewhere, units of the Confederate Right Wing futilely battered themselves against Thomas' unyielding defense. On the Confederate left, one of Longstreet's divisions attacked soon after Hill's men and also made no impression on the Federal line. Just to the south along Brotherton Road, Hood's Corps of three divisions—formed in column of divisions—was withheld by Longstreet until just after 1100. On Longstreet's signal, the grand column swept forward and was joined by the remainder of the Left Wing. Fortuitously, Hood's column struck a segment of the Federal line that was momentarily devoid of troops and crashed through.

The opening in the Federal line was the result of a complicated series of events and misperceptions that had been building all morning. Even before the action began on the Federal left, Thomas had been calling for reinforcements, and he continued to do so in the face of the Confederate attacks. Both Rosecrans and Thomas ordered units from the army's center and right toward the left. As a result of these movements, Rosecrans came to believe that a gap existed in the Federal right-center, and he responded by ordering Brigadier General Thomas J. Wood's division, already in line, to move north to close the gap. Again, because of a combination of circumstances, there was actually no gap in the Federal line until Wood's departure created one. McCook agreed to fill Wood's space, but Hood's Corps entered the gap before Wood could act, and the Federal line was irreparably split.

As Longstreet's troops burst into Dyer Field, Federal units on both sides of the break failed to reestablish a continuous line. Rosecrans, McCook, and Crittenden, along with elements of several Federal divisions, were all swept from the field, and the senior commanders finished the day in Chattanooga. Two intact Federal brigades and fragments of several others rallied northwest of the break on high ground known as Horseshoe Ridge or Snodgrass Hill. Separated from the remainder of the Federal army, which was still holding the Kelly Field enclave, the units on Snodgrass Hill prepared to make a last stand. Just as they were about to be outflanked by Bushrod Johnson's Confederates, they were reinforced by Brigadier General James B. Steedman's division of Granger's Reserve Corps. Although Confederate units continued to attack the Snodgrass Hill defenders throughout the remainder of the afternoon, they were unable to drive the Federals from the ridge. Finally, not long before sundown, Thomas received a message from Rosecrans to withdraw the surviving Federal units to Rossville. Much of the withdrawal was conducted cleanly, although the last units to leave Kelly Field suffered heavily and several regiments were left behind on Snodgrass Hill. Nevertheless, Thomas successfully gathered most of the Army of the

Cumberland at Rossville. There was no immediate Confederate pursuit.

In the days immediately following the battle, the Federals withdrew into Chattanooga and prepared to withstand a siege. Hampered by transportation weaknesses and crippled by massive casualties, Bragg's Army of Tennessee slowly followed and attempted to starve Rosecrans' army out of the city. Both armies had suffered heavily at Chickamauga. Rosecrans had lost 16,170 killed, wounded, and missing out of about 62,000 engaged, while Bragg had suffered a total of 18,454 casualties out of approximately 67,000 engaged. Such losses meant that neither army could do much until the casualties in men and materiel had been replenished. While Bragg gained the remainder of Longstreet's command en route from Virginia and the exchanged prisoners from the Vicksburg campaign, the Army of the Cumberland received far more massive reinforcements from both the Army of the Potomac and the Army of the Tennessee. Those Federal reinforcements would ultimately join the Army of the Cumberland in sweeping Bragg's army from Tennessee.

Because his victory at Chickamauga was not exploited in any meaningful way, Bragg's triumph was short-lived. As the last Confederate victory in the western theater, the battle served mainly to buy a little more time for the Southern cause. Federal troops in both Virginia and Mississippi were diverted from their primary missions to rescue the Army of the Cumberland, thereby affecting the timetable for Federal victory in those areas. Otherwise, the great expenditure of lives by both sides had little effect. Because they had left the field while others stayed, Rosecrans, McCook, and Crittenden all had their military careers blighted as a result of the battle. Nor did the victors, Bragg and Longstreet, gain much from their success. Honorably distinguished were George Thomas (thereafter known as the Rock of Chickamauga) and the thousands of soldiers who contended for their respective causes in the woods bordering the"River of Death"—the largest battle in the western theater.

III. SUGGESTED ROUTE AND VIGNETTES
Introduction

In September 1863, in the Battle of Chickamauga, approximately 130,000 soldiers fought on a battlefield less than 4 miles square. Most of the critical battle terrain, over 5,000 acres, is now within the boundaries of the Chickamauga and Chattanooga National Military Park. More than 1,000 monuments, plaques, and artillery pieces in the park assist the visitor in interpreting the actions of the battle. Virtually all of these markers are connected by a series of trails that permit access to all important parts of the battlefield. This combination of markers and trails makes the battlefield portion of the park an excellent site for studying a major Civil War battle. Many of the insights to be derived from such a study remain relevant to soldiers of any era in studying their profession. Indeed, such study was formally acknowledged in the enabling legislation as a major reason for the creation of the park in 1890.

Because the battlefield is so vast and the interpretive markers so numerous, military visitors may find it difficult to cover all major aspects of the battle in any meaningful way. Some may elect to survey the field quickly in its totality; others may choose to concentrate on a particular unit, branch, or phase of the action.

This section of the handbook contains a series of maps, stands, and vignettes for a Staff Ride of the Battle of Chickamauga that covers the full two days. As presented, the route for each day encompasses nearly eleven miles of walking and can require ten hours per day to complete. Each stand contains a description of the actions occurring in its vicinity, a vignette highlighting those events, and some potential teaching points that can be used to stimulate discussion about the current military relevance of the historical action. These stands should be used selectively to tailor a Staff Ride to an individual group's objectives and the time available.

The ten route maps in this handbook are adapted from a topographical map of the Chickamauga and Chattanooga National Military Park that is available for purchase at the Visitor Center. The most expeditious way to travel to the numbered stands is to follow the Staff Ride route arrows on maps 2 through 5 and 7 through 10. These routes usually follow the nearest available trail or road between the stands. Maps 1 and 6 provide an overview of the complete battlefield showing the position of the various maps in relation to each other. The underbrush and gently rolling terrain make it easy to miss a specific stand or monument while walking cross-country. If a stand is missed, it is usually faster to backtrack along the existing trails rather than to move in a straight line between stands, unless the group leader is very familiar with the terrain.

All trails and roads in the park are open to foot traffic. Although cars or vans can move easily along any open route, large buses will have problems in certain areas. If using cars or buses to move between locations, check the routes in advance. Some park roads are one-way, and the entrances to some unimproved roads are blocked to vehicles. Visitors need to pay particular attention to finding suitable bus turn-arounds and parking only in authorized areas, not along the sides of the roads.

LEGEND

Park boundary

Map outlines

Scale

0   .5   1 miles

McFarland-Gap Road

McDonald crossroads

MAP 2

Reed's Bridge Road

Creek

West Chickamauga

Park Visitor Center

McDonald Field

Reed's Bridge

Snodgrass Field

Snodgrass cabin

Kelly Field

MAP 3

Winfrey Field

Jay's Mill

Alexander Bridge Road

Kelly house

Horseshoe Ridge

Vittetoe Road

Poe Road

Battle Line Rd

Poe Field

Brotherton Road

Brock Field

Jay's Mill Road

Dyer Field

Dyer cabin site

Dyer Road

Brotherton cabin

Brotherton Field

Lytle Hill

Glenn-Kelly Road

LaFayette Road

Alexander house site

West Chickamauga Creek

Alexander's Bridge

Wilder Tower

Widow Glenn cabin site

Glenn Field

Viniard-Alexander Road

MAP 5

Glenn-Viniard Road

Viniard Field

Thedford's Ford

MAP 4

Dalton's Ford

West Chickamauga Creek

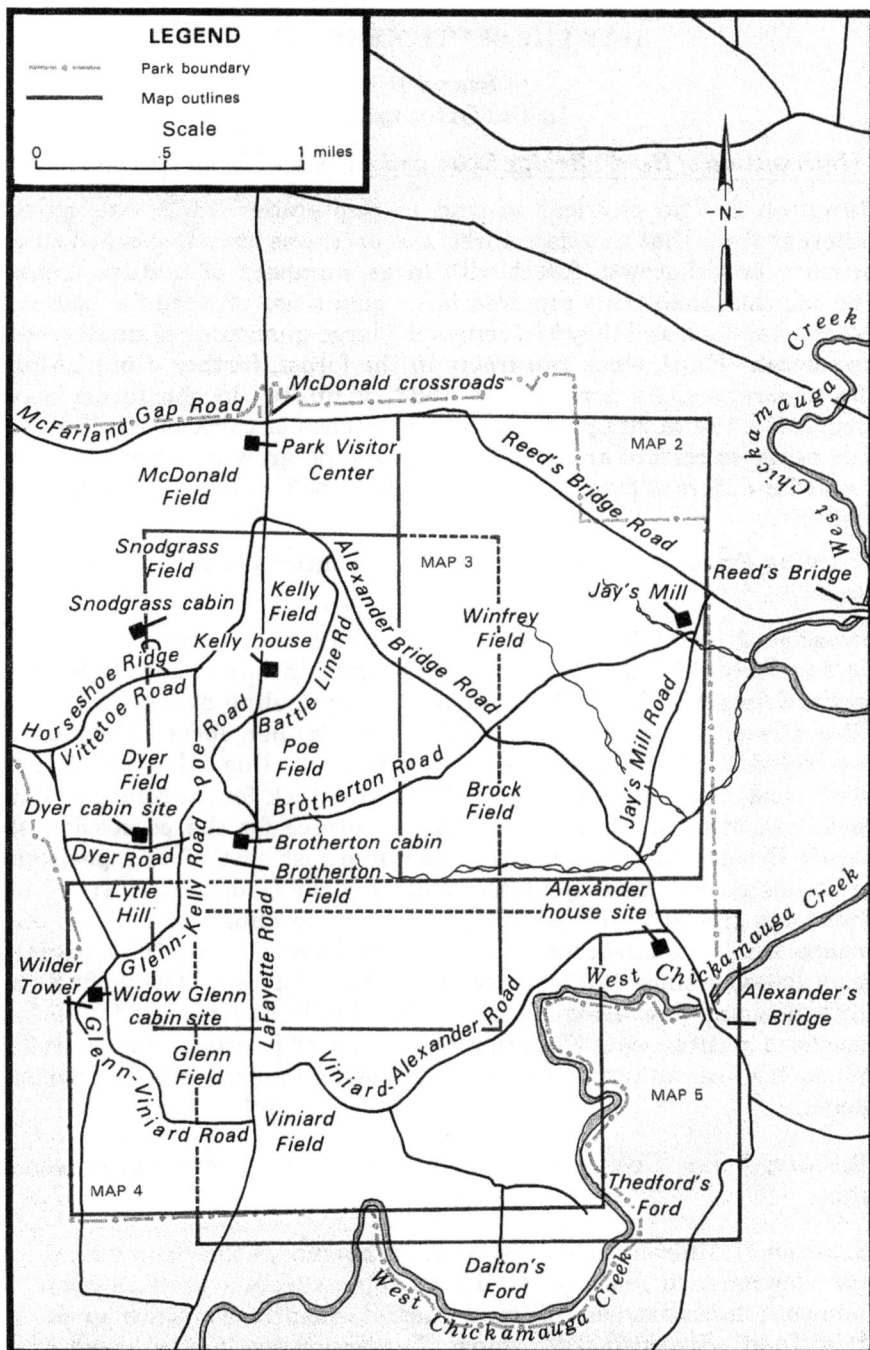

Map 1. Sites of maps 2 through 5 in relation to the Chickamauga and Chattanooga National Military Park for day 1

DAY 1 (19 SEPTEMBER 1863)

Stand 1
Initial Orientation

(Intersection of Reed's Bridge Road and Jay's Mill Road [see map 2])

Situation 1: The physical setting in September 1863 was quite different from that of today. First, the area was mostly clothed in a primary or old-growth forest with large numbers of mature trees. Second, the inhabitants required large quantities of wood for houses, fences, and fuel, and they had consumed large quantities of small trees and brush. Third, stock ran freely in the forest, further diminishing the understory. As a result, in 1863, visibility in the forest was frequently 150 to 200 yards, although patches of thick brush limited this range in certain areas. Today, succeeding growth has produced a forest far different from that of September 1863, with greatly reduced visibility.

Teaching Points: Tactical doctrine and formations of 1863, vegetative cover.

Situation 2: Minty's final delay position, 18 September 1863, p.m. Colonel Robert H. G. Minty's cavalry brigade initially chose to screen forward (east) of Reed's Bridge along the ridgeline overlooking Pea Vine Creek. Fighting dismounted, Minty's men forced Brigadier General Bushrod R. Johnson's four brigades into line of battle. After a short time, the weight of the Confederate attack forced Minty to fall back, and his orderly delay became a footrace for the possession of Reed's Bridge. Minty formed his new line just east of this position while his cavalrymen attempted to destroy the bridge. The arrival of Johnson's troops forced Minty to abandon the efforts to destroy the bridge, and the Confederates crossed it between 1500 and 1600, having been delayed since 1200. Minty withdrew his forces slowly, first to Jay's Mill and then down Brotherton Road to LaFayette Road until he reached a position near Viniard Field. There, he joined Colonel John T. Wilder's forces in forming a blocking position adjacent to LaFayette Road.

Teaching Points: Covering force operations, delay, defense of a crossing site.

Situation 3: After crossing the West Chickamauga Creek at a fording site downstream and at Reed's Bridge, which was still intact, Johnson's force reached this road junction, then turned south on Jay's Mill Road. By nightfall, most Confederates had passed the intersection, except for some rear-echelon troops and stragglers. That

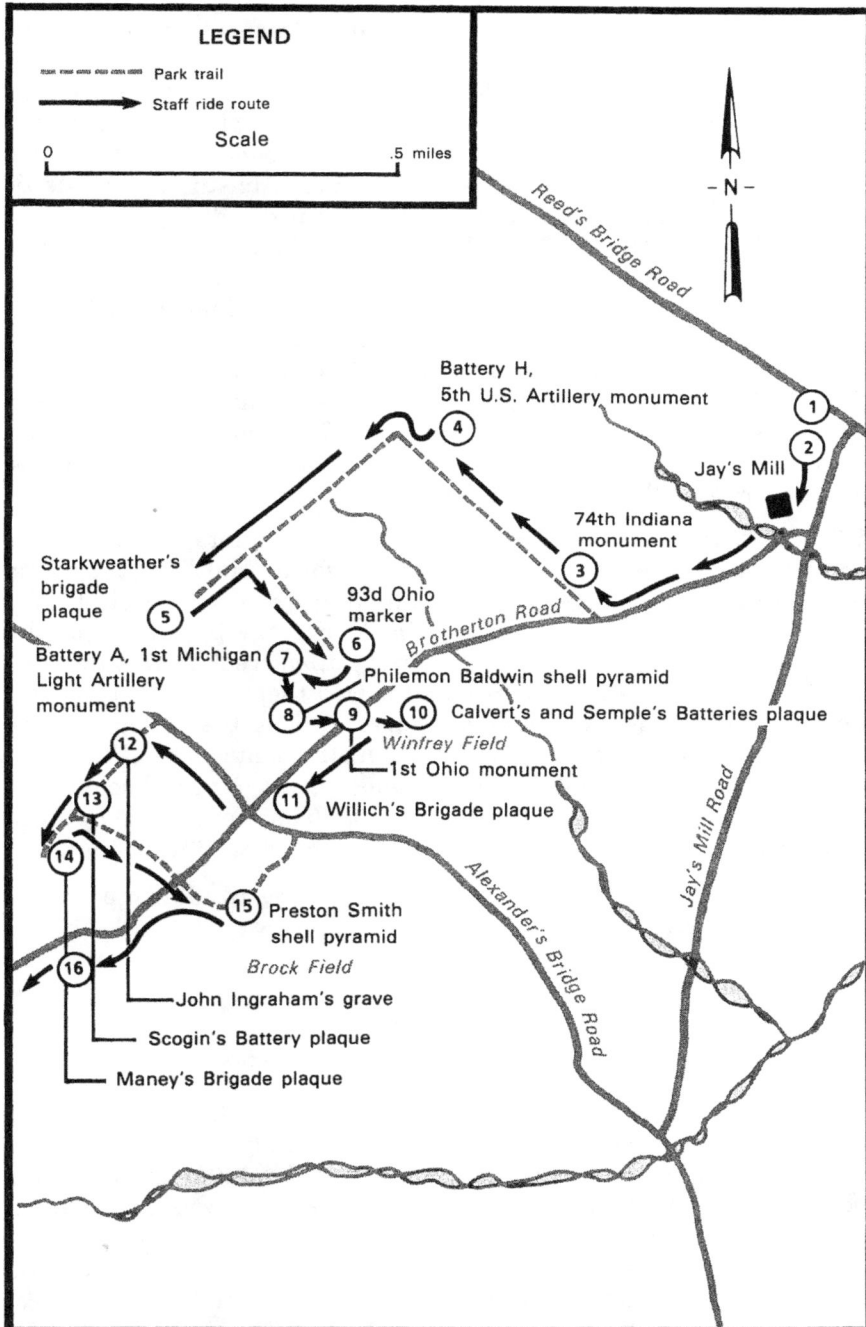

LEGEND

Park trail

Staff ride route

Scale

0 .5 miles

- N -

Reed's Bridge Road

Battery H, 5th U.S. Artillery monument

1

Jay's Mill

2

74th Indiana monument

3

4

Brotherton Road

Starkweather's brigade plaque

5

93d Ohio marker

6

Battery A, 1st Michigan Light Artillery monument

7

Philemon Baldwin shell pyramid

8

9

10 Calvert's and Semple's Batteries plaque

Winfrey Field

1st Ohio monument

11 Willich's Brigade plaque

12

13

14

Jay's Mill Road

15 Preston Smith shell pyramid

Brock Field

16

John Ingraham's grave

Scogin's Battery plaque

Maney's Brigade plaque

Alexander's Bridge Road

Map 2. Day 1, stands 1 through 16

evening, Colonel Daniel McCook's brigade of Major General Gordon Granger's Reserve Corps arrived to support Minty's defense of the bridge. McCook halted about 400 yards west of the intersection and sent scouts forward. During the night, the scouts captured a number of Confederate prisoners. Interrogation of the prisoners revealed that they were from Brigadier General Evander McNair's Brigade of Johnson's Division. In response, McCook formed a defensive line for the night, supported by Colonel John G. Mitchell's brigade of the Reserve Corps. Meanwhile, Federal pickets advanced to this spot. Around 0300, 19 September, McCook sent the attached 69th Ohio Infantry Regiment forward to destroy Reed's Bridge. This regiment set fire to the bridge but failed to destroy it before returning to the Federal line. Back at the line, the regiment found McCook under attack and preparing to retreat. Leaving the area, McCook reported that he had isolated McNair's Brigade west of the Chickamauga, thereby setting events in motion that triggered the battle.

Vignette: "Eli Shields was in the lead when we ran into the rebel army and had the nerve to sing out in a clear voice, 'Halt!' To this some thoughtful Johnny replied, 'Keep your dam [*sic*] mouth shut!' We pulled Shields off and pushed him back into the brush out of the immediate sight and hearing of the enemy, then crept back to the road and picked up one after another, and placed them with Eli to guard, until we had taken twenty-two prisoners. Among the prisoners were several belonging to a band, and their instruments were taken with them. There was also a rebel major, whose horse, a very fine one, we gave to Colonel McCook." (Henry J. Aten, *History of the Eighty-Fifth Regiment Illinois Volunteer Infantry*, Hiawatha, KS, 1901, 103.)

Teaching Points: Effect of false assumptions, random nature of significant events.

Stand 2
Jay's Mill

(Intersection of Jay's Mill Road and Brotherton Road [see map 2])

Situation: 18 September 1863, p.m. Late in the afternoon, Bushrod Johnson's Division reached this road junction. Johnson favored a right turn onto Brotherton Road, but Major General John B. Hood, at this point, took command of the column and directed it southward along Jay's Mill Road toward Alexander's Bridge. Around midnight, Confederate cavalry arrived from the south to screen Hood's right and rear and established a picket line not far south of Jay's Mill.

19 September 1863, a.m. Before sunrise, a scout from the 1st Georgia Cavalry approached the mill and found several of McCook's

soldiers warming themselves around a fire after filling their canteens at a spring. The Confederates opened fire, and the Federals retreated to their picket line. As the exchange of fire grew, Brigadier General H. B. Davidson ordered the 1st Georgia forward, followed by the whole brigade. By this time (0700), McCook had been ordered to withdraw, and the Confederate cavalry pursued him for only a short distance and then returned to the vicinity of Jay's Mill. About this time, Brigadier General Nathan B. Forrest and Brigadier General John Pegram arrived and ordered elements of Davidson's Brigade to scout westward. These units encountered Colonel John T. Croxton's Federal brigade and fled in panic back to the mill. Momentarily, the entire Confederate brigade was thrown into confusion, but finally, Forrest, Pegram, and Davidson rallied the brigade and formed it into line. Forrest rode off for reinforcements. For the next hour, Davidson's Brigade faced the lead brigade (Croxton's) of Brannan's 3d Division, XIV Corps.

Vignette: "Before the bugle could sound the mount, half of the Brigade was in the saddle—we had dismounted in column—and there was no need to form . . . the notes of the bugle had not died away when came the order Face Right! Head of column to left! Forward! Trot! and away we went for the crest of the hill. The 6th had just about got into the form of an inverted L when the demoralized and panic stricken troopers came down upon us over the crest with a rush that threatened to swamp us in the wildest confusion. . . . Wild eyed, hatless, horseless, without guns many of them wounded and bleeding, two on one horse, riderless horses by the score, some frenzied by wounds and pain, some on three legs leaping painfully, men yelling at the top of their voice, 'Git boys! The woods are full of yankees.'" (J. W. Minnich to H. V. Boynton, 8 December 1900, Unit Files, Chickamauga and Chattanooga National Military Park, Fort Oglethorpe, GA.)

Teaching Points: Meeting engagement, reconnaissance, security.

Stand 3
Croxton's Brigade

(74th Indiana monument [see map 2])

Situation: 19 September 1863, a.m. Brigadier General John M. Brannan's division had marched through the night and by early morning was stretched out along LaFayette Road in the vicinity of Kelly Field. In the meantime, Major General George H. Thomas had received word from McCook about the Confederate brigade trapped on the west side of Chickamauga Creek. In response, Thomas ordered Brannan to deploy his brigades in line of battle and to advance toward Reed's Bridge to locate and destroy this "lone" brigade. Brannan, in turn, ordered Colonel Ferdinand Van Derveer's brigade to advance eastward generally along Reed's Bridge Road. Next, he ordered Croxton's brigade to advance eastward into the woods bordering the southern end of Kelly Field. Colonel John M. Connell's brigade followed behind to support the two leading brigades.

Croxton advanced with three regiments forward and two behind in support, covering his advance with skirmishers. After an advance of about one mile, the Federal skirmishers made contact with the advance elements of Davidson's Brigade, and the battle opened in the woods west of Jay's Mill. Although neither commander had planned to fight in the woods bordering Chickamauga Creek, both began to feed additional units into the fight as they arrived.

Vignette: "At sunrise we halted by the road long enough to make a cup of coffee. On we went again and by 9 a.m. our skirmishers ran against the enemy—Soon the 2nd Brigade were [*sic*] in line of battle—We halted in the edge of a wood, very soon our skirmishers came back on the run and a troop of Rebel Cavalry came rushing over the hill close on to our skirmishers—Steady boys, wait for the word, was heard from our Col—on came the cavalry, the advance had raced 150 yds without seeing us. One tremendous volley rang along the whole line, at first all was smoke, then dust from struggling steeds, a few riderless horses, were running here and there, save which nothing was seen of that cavalry troop. Thus began the battle of Chickamauga—I have read of cavalry charges and seen them in print but this was the first reality of the kind I had witnessed and truly it was a grand sight." (Peter B. Kellenberger, Corporal, Company I, 10th Indiana, Croxton's brigade, to a friend, 15 November 1863, Unit Files, Chickamauga and Chattanooga National Military Park, Fort Oglethorpe, GA.)

Teaching Points: Meeting engagement, command and control.

Stand 4
King's Brigade

(Battery H, 5th U.S. Artillery monument [see map 2])

Situation 1: 19 September 1863, a.m. When Forrest rode off to find help for Davidson's troops, he met General Braxton Bragg and Major General William H. T. Walker, the Reserve Corps commander, in the vicinity of Alexander's Bridge. In response to Forrest's request for support, Walker directed Colonel Claudius C. Wilson to move his brigade northward. Beginning his advance at about 0900, Wilson came into action on Davidson's left, flanking Croxton's position. In response to this new threat, Croxton faced south with several of his regiments.

This change of front caused considerable confusion, and the Federals were forced to give up ground before the situation was stabilized. By 1000, Croxton's ammunition was almost exhausted, and he called for reinforcements.

After Thomas sent Brannan after the "lone" brigade, he ordered Brigadier General Absalom Baird to follow with his division. Baird advanced the 1st Division with Brigadier General John H. King's brigade on the left, Colonel Benjamin F. Scribner's brigade on the right, and Brigadier General John C. Starkweather's brigade in support. Scribner came up on Croxton's right, which permitted Croxton to withdraw and resupply. King's brigade, composed of Regular units, entered the position vacated by Croxton and faced southeast, the direction in which Wilson had retired. Warned of Confederates on his right flank, King began to orient his brigade toward the new threat but was hit by Brigadier General St. John R. Liddell's Confederate division. Caught in a vulnerable position, the brigade broke and could not be rallied until it passed beyond Van Derveer's position on Reed's Bridge Road.

Vignette: "I pushed everything to the front, my first line driving the enemy before them for a mile, and meeting General A. Baird, division commander, at about 10 a.m., was ordered to make a new front at right angles with the other. I only had time, however to get the Sixteenth Infantry and battery in position before being assailed by an overwhelming force. At this time the troops on my right were giving ground to the enemy in confusion. I immediately gave orders for the battery to limber up but it could not be done as the horses as they were brought up to the guns were shot down.

"The officers and men, finding it impossible to retire, remained with their pieces (firing) until they were forcibly taken from them by the enemy. It was at this time that I lost the First Battalion Sixteenth Infantry (made prisoners), with the exception of 5 commissioned officers and 62 men." (Brigadier General John H. King, in *The War of the Rebellion: A Compilation of the Official Records of the Union and Confederate Armies* [Washington, DC: U.S. Government Printing Office, 1899; reprint, Wilmington, NC: Broadfoot Publishing Co., 1985], vol. 30, pt. 1, 309. Hereafter referred to as *O.R.*)

Teaching Points: Nature of nonlinear battlefield, inflexible positions, unit cohesion, discipline, rallying a broken unit, resupply during battle.

Situation 2: 19 September 1863, a.m. First Lieutenant Howard M. Burnham's Battery H, 5th U.S. Artillery (four 12-pounder Napoleons and two 10-pounder Parrotts) supported King's brigade. Because of the change of front and the dense woods, the battery was only able to fire four rounds of canister before it was overrun. Burnham, in command only a month, was mortally wounded. This battery was eventually recaptured during a Federal counterattack led by Colonel Gustave Kammerling of the 9th Ohio Infantry Regiment, a German unit from Van Derveer's brigade.

Teaching Points: Difficulties of artillery operating in wooded terrain, limited fields of fire, infantry support of the guns and security, importance of battle drills.

Situation 3: 19 September 1863, a.m. On Reed's Bridge Road, Van Derveer's brigade had repulsed both Confederate cavalry probes and an attack by Brigadier General Matthew D. Ector's Brigade of Walker's Reserve Corps by the time King's routed troops came racing out of the woods. Chasing King's Regulars were Liddell's Confederates, who had already overrun another of Baird's brigades, that of Scribner. The pursuing Confederates were stopped by the unexpected appearance of Van Derveer's men in their front and shortly thereafter by the approach of Croxton's brigade on their flank. Overmatched, Liddell's Division withdrew eastward across Brotherton Road.

Vignette: "Then the firing broke out again . . .; first the scattering fire of skirmishers—then the terrific file firing of regiments, then the artillery, then the 'rebel yell,' and the firing gradually approached us. We stood attentive and expectant for a few minutes, then a straggling line of men in blue appeared coming toward us in wild retreat, their speed accelerated by the firing and yelling of the exultant Confederates who were close behind them. I do not remember any more appalling spectacle than this was for a few minutes; but our men took it with grim composure, lying down until the stampeded brigade had passed over our line, then rising and blazing a volley into the enemy's faces, which abruptly ended the yelling and the charge. They had not expected such a reception, and all efforts of their officers to get or hold their men in line for a fight, were in vain. They promptly retreated in their turn until out of range and out of sight. This was Walthall's Confederate Brigade of Liddell's Division." (Lieutenant Colonel J. W. Bishop, 2d Minnesota Infantry, "Van Derveer's Brigade at Chickamauga," *Glimpses of the Nation's Struggle* [Minneapolis, MN: Aug. Davis, Publisher, 1909] 6:7—8.)

Teaching Points: Command and control, discipline, rallying broken units.

Stand 5
Starkweather's Brigade

(Starkweather's brigade plaque,
northwest of Winfrey Field [see map 2])

Situation: 19 September 1863, a.m. Starkweather's brigade advanced from Kelly Field as the reserve of Baird's division. En route, Starkweather received orders to move to his left to relieve Croxton's brigade. Before he could change directions, Starkweather encountered Croxton's withdrawing troops. Next, Starkweather faced southeast toward the sounds of the fighting. As he attempted to refuse his flanks by tucking them back, his front and right were struck by Colonel Daniel C. Govan's Brigade of Liddell's Division. Disoriented, confused, and struck from an unexpected direction, Starkweather's unit collapsed and raced to the rear. The brigade eventually rallied three-quarters of a mile north of this position. Late in the afternoon, Starkweather's and Scribner's brigades moved back into this area in support of Brigadier General Richard W. Johnson's division.

Vignette: "We had marched thus but a short distance and were rising the slope of a hill when we were suddenly opened on by a body of the enemy's infantry lying concealed below its crest. . . . There is a buzz and confusion on the right of the regiment—it wavers, it breaks. . . . Our left companies now break and follow the right in confusion. The Twenty-fourth Illinois and Twenty-first Wisconsin are in line, kneeling to the rear of us. We pass over them and try to form our companies in their rear. But the companies have melted into a panic stricken mob, and even brave men, seeing the whole throng double-quicking to the rear, have but poor encouragement to face, single-handed, the storm of lead that is hurtling after them. I halt a moment in rear of the Twenty-fourth Illinois, and do all I can to check the retreating fugitives—but it is only for a moment. The rebels fiercely attack the second line in overwhelming numbers, and the old Twenty-fourth and Twenty-first, after a very few volleys, waver, break, run. The fight is ended, so far as our brigade is concerned. We are whipped, and move rapidly to the rear, disorganized and demoralized. The enemy, however, cannot follow us. Heavy firing on both flanks gives evidence that they still have their hands full. Our pace slackens. I keep near the colors, and try to gather the stragglers around them; but my heart's in my mouth. I feel more like crying than anything else. The 'Old Brigade' that we have all been boasting about is disgraced, and we, who never ran before, are completely broken up—not a regiment or a company left." (Lieutenant John M. Johnston, 79th Pennsylvania Infantry, *The New Era*, Lancaster, PA, 10 September 1892.)

Teaching Points: Unit panic, rallying broken units.

Stand 6
Scribner's Brigade

(93d Ohio marker, northwest edge of Winfrey Field [see map 2])

Situation: 19 September 1863, a.m. When Baird's division entered the forest in support of Brannan, Scribner's brigade was on the division's right. Scribner found the flank of Wilson's Brigade and forced Wilson to withdraw, relieving pressure on Croxton. Scribner continued to advance until he reached Winfrey Field, where he halted his brigade. Scribner had assumed that there were friendly forces on his right, but this proved to be false when reports from his skirmishers indicated that Confederates were on his right (Liddell's Division). In an effort to meet this threat, Scribner bent back his two right regiments, the 10th Wisconsin and 38th Indiana.

Vignette: "About this time I was informed by my skirmishers that the enemy was passing to our right. . . . I was immediately after informed that my right was being turned. Dr. Miller, my brigade surgeon, coming up, reported the enemy in my rear; that he had been in their hands. As information like this came in I dispatched the same to the general commanding division, and threw a company of skirmishers to my right and rear. Scarcely had their deployment been completed when the enemy opened upon them a destructive fire. To form a front to the right by causing the Thirty-eighth Indiana to change their front to the rear and to change the Tenth Wisconsin to the right of the Thirty-eighth Indiana and limber the battery to the rear, between the two regiments, employed but a few moments; this, too, under a heavy fire. The enemy charged down upon me along my whole line, pouring in canister and shell. I had now dispatched every staff officer and orderly with information of my position, asking for support, expressing my intention to hold my place with desperation until assistance arrived; for I felt that the safety of the forces on my left depended upon holding this position. I had observed a line of our forces in my rear passing to the left. I sent to the officer for assistance, but he had other orders." (Colonel Benjamin F. Scribner, in *O.R.*, vol. 30, pt. 1, 286.)

Teaching Points: Reconnaissance, security.

Stand 7
Van Pelt's Battery

(Battery A, 1st Michigan Light Artillery monument [see map 2])

Situation: 19 September 1863, a.m. Well known in the army because of its reputation gained at the Battle of Stones River, this battery consisted of six 10-pounder Parrotts. Now commanded by First

Lieutenant George W. Van Pelt, the battery belonged to Scribner's brigade. Worried about his right flank, Scribner turned Van Pelt's guns to the right and supported them with the 38th Indiana and 10th Wisconsin Infantry Regiments. Placed in front of the guns instead of the normal position in the rear, the supporting infantry was driven back in disorder by Govan's Brigade of Liddell's Division. The battery was overrun, Van Pelt and six of his men were killed, and five of the six guns were lost.

Vignette 1: August Bratnober of the supporting 10th Wisconsin Infantry: "Early in the morning of the 19th we were moved to the front again and directly behind a line of battle that was then in action. The bullets were whistling and shells were flying over us and we expected to be pushed into the fight any minute. Not a man had been hit yet. Soon our battery passed in front of us on the run and we were ordered to follow. . . . They drew up in line and we were ordered directly in front of it and ordered to lie down; this was called supporting the battery. We then had our knapsacks on and were lying down at full length on our faces with heads down hill. Every body felt that this was wrong as we could not roll over to reload in that condition. Soon the battery began firing; the concussion of the guns was terrific and we were fairly bumped against the guns at every discharge. Directly our skirmishers were driven in and we saw the enemy coming out of the timber across the ravine from us. Then the cannon began in earnest but we could see plainly that they were firing too high. On they came three double lines deep, then they charged, after the front line fired the next line passed through them, the first line reloading as they came on, and so on. We had orders to wait for the command before firing and we did. Our fire fairly stunned them but we could not reload without raising up. . . . The artillery horses were mostly shot early in the attack. We had to retreat and lost our battery right there. On they came firing in the same manner and we lost a lot of our men . . . and when we finally rallied what there was left, we found we had lost half of the regiment in killed and wounded." (August Bratnober Account, Unit Files, Chickamauga and Chattanooga National Military Park, Fort Oglethorpe, GA.)

Vignette 2: Gallant defense of the guns: "Lieutenant Van Pelt, in command of the Battery, in dying at his guns, has given to the history of the war an incident that will form one of the brightest pages. Men grow to be attached to their guns, the natural result of that feature of discipline which inculcates that it is a great dishonor to lose a Battery. Van Pelt was proud of his guns. They had grown to be a terror to the enemy. . . . The men, too, loved the guns, and they sealed the devotion on that day with their blood. The principal among them was Van Pelt. With his horses killed, his men dead, and his supports overwhelmed and driven back, the enemy rushed upon the battery. Van Pelt, as the last act of his young life, drew his sword and sprang to the front of his pieces, with that inexplicable frenzy which supplies with strength as with courage, he cried (so his men say) with a voice of thunder, 'Don't dare touch these guns.' On the inexorable wave of glistening bayonets surged, over and past him, burying him under his lost guns." (Charles E. Belknap, *History of the Michigan Organizations at Chickamauga, Chattanooga and Missionary Ridge* [Lansing, MI: Robert Smith Printing Company, 1899], 170—71.)

Teaching Points: Face of battle, infantry support and defense of a battery, leadership.

Stand 8
Colonel Philemon P. Baldwin

(Philemon Baldwin shell pyramid, Winfrey Field [see map 2])

Situation: 19 September 1863, a.m. Johnson's 2d Division, XX Corps, had left its bivouac site near Crawfish Spring around sunrise when it was ordered to report to Thomas. Around 1200, Johnson's division arrived in the Kelly Field area and was ordered to advance in support of Baird's division. Johnson deployed Colonel Philemon P. Baldwin's brigade on the left, Brigadier General August Willich's brigade on the right, and Colonel Joseph B. Dodge's brigade in reserve. Johnson's division soon made contact with Major General Benjamin F. Cheatham's Division and, after a fight of several hours, pushed the Confederates back to and beyond Winfrey Field. Baldwin's regiments moved into position at the northwest end of Winfrey Field, where they repulsed an assault by Liddell's Division before dark. A lull then occurred until sunset, when Major General Patrick R. Cleburne launched his division in a night attack against Johnson's division. When the attack began, Baldwin was with the 6th Indiana Infantry Regiment in his second line. As his first line crumbled, Baldwin raced forward, then back to the 6th Indiana. Ordering a charge, he was killed in the ensuing confusion.

Vignette: "His confidence in the old Sixth in a case of emergency, as I suppose, brought him back near it, and just on its right where he had left the moment before. But by this time the rebels were upon us, and he, as I suppose, concluded that a counter charge was the best way to meet the enemy, and immediately rode through our ranks and called on the Sixth Indiana to follow him. This, of course, placed him between the two fires, which were only a few yards apart, and both him and his horse were killed instantly. The regiment, very sensibly, did not obey an order which never should have been given. . . .

"I think the members of the old Sixth will all bear witness that Colonel Baldwin was a brave officer, of fine military bearing and 'a splendid disciplinarian, but it certainly was very rash in him to ride between the two firing lines just at this time, as by so doing he lost his life, and if the regiment had obeyed his command, in my opinion, it would have proved the certain death of many of its members as well as its utter route [sic], which would have resulted in a stampede. In my criticisms of Colonel Baldwin, I do not wish to be understood as trying to reflect upon his character and reputation as a brave, daring officer, but merely in this particular case, that under the excitement, his judgment was at fault. But the mistake cost the brave Colonel his life, as he died where he fell and he and his personal effects fell into the hands of the enemy." (C. C. Briant, *History of the Sixth Regiment Indiana Volunteer Infantry* [Indianapolis, IN: Wm. B. Burford, 1891], 233—34.)

Teaching Points: Command and control, chain of command, succession of command.

Stand 9
Baldwin's Brigade

(1st Ohio monument [see map 2])

Situation: 19 September 1863, p.m. Lieutenant Colonel Bassett Langdon's 1st Ohio Infantry Regiment was the right flank regiment of Baldwin's brigade of Johnson's division. Because the ground to his front permitted the enemy to approach his position in defilade, Langdon sent his skirmishers forward beyond the field. Around sunset, the skirmishers were pushed back by another Confederate advance. Still concerned about his front, Langdon sent out another company of skirmishers, but they were unable to stop the advance of the Confederate line and were recalled. Langdon's position was subsequently outflanked when the unit on his right was thrown back and the 1st Ohio had to withdraw hastily.

Vignette: "About sunset my skirmishers were pressed back with serious loss to within a few yards of the regiment, where they were exposed to so hot a fire from the enemy that I recalled them to tempt the enemy into the open field. . . . Finding the enemy not disposed to enter the open, and the firing having increased on my right, I sent Company A again into the field as skirmishers to prevent the enemy's getting too close to my front unobserved, the nature of the ground being such as to raise an apprehension of that character. This company was in the act of deploying when it found itself exposed to a very hot fire on its right flank, and immediately took position to meet it and opened fire warmly in return. At this instant General Willich's regiment [49th Ohio] on my immediate right, opened fire in line, and warned by all these indications where the real attack would come, I hastily recalled the skirmishers, intending to meet it by a volley at short range. Unfortunately the recall of the skirmishers, who fell back firing, and the heavy roll of musketry on our right, with the whistling of the enemy's bullets, set the guns of my right company going and an irregular file fire ran along my front from right to left, mainly directed to the enemy in my front. Meantime, I strove in vain to make myself heard to stop the firing and to call the regiment to attention. In thirty seconds the regiment on my right was broken and running to the rear in great confusion, and while I was striking my men (who were lying down) with the flat of my sword to get their attention, the rebel line was seen within 40 yards of my right flank moving rapidly up perpendicularly to it. I was barely able to get my men to their feet in time to see the rebel colors flaunted almost in their faces, and their guns being mostly unloaded I directed them to retire." (Lieutenant Colonel Bassett Langdon, in *O.R.*, vol. 30, pt. 1, 572.)

Teaching Points: Command and control, cohesion, withdrawal under pressure.

Stand 10
Cleburne's Night Attack
(Calvert's and Semple's Batteries plaque [see map 2])

Situation 1: Wood's Brigade, 19 September 1863, p.m. Late in the afternoon, Cleburne's Division of Lieutenant General Daniel H. Hill's Corps was brought from south of the battlefield to support the Confederate right. By 1800, Cleburne's three brigades were formed behind Cheatham's and Liddell's Divisions. Cleburne's front extended almost a mile with Brigadier General Lucius E. Polk's Brigade on the right, Brigadier General S. A. M. Wood's Brigade in the center, and Brigadier General James Deshler's Brigade on the left. After conferring with Bragg, Hill ordered Cleburne to attack through Cheatham's and Liddell's positions. On the right, Polk met little opposition and passed beyond Baldwin's flank. When Wood's Brigade advanced out of the woods into Winfrey Field, its right faced Baldwin, while the left made contact with Willich's brigade. As Wood's regiments neared the Federal front, the attack stalled, and the brigade became fragmented. In the darkness, the fight disintegrated into confusion.

Vignette: "About this time Major McGaughy gave the command to 'march in retreat,' which was obeyed in bad order, the regiment retreating in confusion.... I then asked Major McGaughy why he gave the order to retreat. He replied that the Forty-fifth Alabama Regiment, the battalion of direction, was falling back and that he had been ordered to be guided by the movements of that regiment. As soon as the men had been rallied and formed, Major McGaughy again gave the command to advance, when we moved forward. . . . I will here state that Companies E and G acted badly. . . . Captain Archer, Company G, while in my presence made no effort to rally his men when ordered to halt, but led them in the retreat. I attribute the confusion in our retreat to a want of the proper command over their men on the part of the officers of Companies E and G; to the darkness of the night; to the failure of the left wing to hear the command 'retreat,' they believing that the right wing was being driven back, and to the fact that just previous to receiving the order to retreat our line was fired into several times from the rear." (Captain Frederick A. Ashford, 16th Alabama Infantry Regiment, Wood's Brigade, in *O.R.*, vol. 30, pt. 2, 163.)

Teaching Points: Command and control in a night attack, amicicide.

Situation 2: Shortly after Wood's assault was stalled, Cleburne's chief of artillery, Major T. R. Hotchkiss, brought forward Calvert's Arkansas and Semple's Alabama Batteries. In daylight, this maneuver would have been suicidal, but in the darkness, the eight guns were relatively safe and put on a spectacular but relatively ineffective show. Nevertheless, the artillerymen claimed that their support was decisive.

Vignette: "General Wood's brigade had fallen back under the heavy fire from the enemy's guns, when I moved up at a trot and let fly the dogs of war into the Yankee ranks, and in a brief period the enemy fled in confusion. Night closed the bloody scene, and we slumbered on the victorious field." (First Lieutenant Thomas J. Key, commanding Calvert's Arkansas Battery, in *O.R.*, vol. 30, pt. 2, 186.)

Teaching Points: Face of battle, combined arms.

Stand 11
Willich's Brigade

(Willich's Brigade plaque, picnic area [see map 2])

Situation: 19 September 1863, p.m. By midafternoon, Willich's brigade, in the center of Johnson's division, had reached this point. That night, when Cleburne's Division attacked, Willich's brigade was still in place, although it was under orders to withdraw. Before those orders were implemented, the left of Wood's Brigade hit Willich's brigade and drove it back toward the Kelly Field line.

Vignette: "I received a written order from General Johnson to fall back at 6:30 p.m. to our general line of battle. With dusk the attack looked for took place. The enemy had succeeded in bringing his batteries and masses of infantry into position. A shower of canister and columns of infantry streamed at once into our front and both flanks. My two front regiments were swept back to the second line. This line for a moment came into disorder. Then they received the command, 'Dress on your colors'; repeated by many men and officers; and in no time the four regiments formed one solid line, sending death into the enemy's masses, who immediately fell back from the front, and there did not answer with a single round.

"On my left, the Third Brigade had also been successful; on my right, the Second Brigade appears to have lost ground, because, at once, a line of rebels poured from the right and rear a volley in my right flank. One regiment only, the Thirty-second Indiana, faced them, and the enemy soon disappeared. Then I fell slowly back in two lines, and coming to the general line of battle, I found General Johnson, who designated the place for the brigade to bivouac." (Brigadier General August Willich, in *O.R.*, vol. 30, pt. 1, 539.)

Teaching Points: Command and control at night, rallying units at night.

Stand 12
Battle Casualties

(John Ingraham's grave [see map 2])

Situation 1: 19 September 1863. Cheatham's Division met the Federal divisions of Johnson and Major General John M. Palmer on this ground and held its position for more than two hours before withdrawing. In Brigadier General John K. Jackson's Brigade, on Cheatham's right, were many local men. One of these men, John Ingraham, was killed, and his friends later buried him where he fell. Ingraham's grave is the only one marked on the battlefield. As such, his sacrifice represents all of the 34,624 casualties of the Battle of Chickamauga. Of that number, 24,430 were wounded, far more than the medical facilities of either side could handle. Because the Confederates held the field at the end of the battle, they were responsible for most of the wounded of both armies. The quality of medical training and treatment was marginal, but for the most part, the medical personnel did their best under the circumstances. After the battle, civilian nurses joined the medical teams.

Vignette: "It rained so hard that I found it impossible to visit the patients. I was gratified to see how much solicitude the surgeons exhibited for them. They were out in the rain nearly all the morning, trying to make the patients as comfortable as possible. They said that the rain was pouring down on some of them, but it could not be avoided. They informed me that from what they had heard of many of the other brigade hospitals, the men were in a much worse plight than theirs. . . . As we rode out of the yard I tried to look neither to the right or left, for I knew there were many pairs of eyes looking sadly at us from the sheds and tents. I could do nothing for them, and when that is the case I try to steel my heart against their sorrows. I saw men cooking in the rain; it seemed like hard work keeping the fire up. . . . As we rode out the tents of the different field hospitals came in view; when we thought of the inmates and their sufferings, it only served to add to the gloom." (Kate Cumming, civilian nurse, 30 September 1863, in *Kate: The Journal of a Confederate Nurse* [Baton Rouge: Louisiana State University Press, 1959], 152—53.)

Situation 2: A total of 3,969 men were killed at Chickamauga. Lacking a graves registration organization, the Confederates could spare few combat troops to care for the dead. Nevertheless, some individuals received special treatment.

Vignette: "It was about 10 o'clock when in line of battle, we were ordered to charge. Brother Rufus repeated his request to me not to go with them in the charge. He was in command of our company. I stopped but the regiment moved forward at double quick. . . . [After the battle, Private Douglas Cater eventually found his brother Rufus— dead, robbed, and shot in the head. He cradled the body in his arms throughout the night. The next day,] when the regiment was ready to move forward a detail of men was left to go to the wagons for spades and picks to bury our dead. Dr. Gus Hendrick, a private in our company, obtained a spade and pick and he and I dug two graves, one for his brother and one for mine. It took a long time and much hard work to get these graves ready. We wrapped blankets around the bodies of our brothers and placed them in these crude graves. There were no caskets, no flowers, but there were loving hands that filled in the earth on these blanket enshrouded forms and cut their names on the rough boards which marked the place where they were laid." (Douglas John Cater, Company I, 19th Louisiana Infantry Regiment, Adams' Brigade, in William D. Cater, *"As It Was," the Story of Douglas John Cater's Life*, 1981, 173—76.

Teaching Points: Mass casualties, graves registration, evacuation procedures, face of battle.

Stand 13
Obsolete Weapons

(Scogin's Battery plaque [see map 2])

Situation: This is a Model 1841, 12-pounder howitzer, an obsolete weapon in 1863. As such, it is representative of the mix of old and new weapons used by both armies at Chickamauga. At the far end of their respective logistics pipelines, Major General William S. Rosecrans and General Braxton Bragg faced the challenge of integrating obsolete and modern weapons into a winning combined arms team, a problem not unknown to other centuries.

Teaching Points: Force modernization.

Stand 14
Maney's Brigade

(Maney's Brigade plaque [see map 2])

Situation: 19 September 1863, p.m. Around 1400, Brigadier General George Maney's Brigade advanced to this position and relieved Jackson's Brigade. Maney's Brigade, in turn, was attacked in front and on its flanks and held its position for only forty-five minutes. No matter how serious the situation, however, the men in the ranks found something humorous to distract them from the serious business of war.

Vignette: "[Our] brave chaplain rode along with our brigade, on an old string-haltered horse, as we advanced to the attack at Chickamauga, exhorting the boys to be brave, to aim low, and to kill the Yankees as if they were wild beasts. He was eloquent and patriotic. He stated that if he only had a gun *he too would go* along as a private soldier. You could hear his voice echo and re-echo over the hills. He had worked up his patriotism to a pitch of genuine bravery and daring that I had never seen exhibited, when *fliff, fluff, fluff, fluff, FLUFF, FLUFF - a whiz, a BOOM and a shell screams through the air*. The reverend . . . stops to listen, like an old sow when she hears the wind, and says, 'Remember boys, that he who is killed will sup tonight in Paradise.' Some soldier hollered at the top of his voice, 'Well, parson, you come along and take supper with us.' *BOOM! whiz, a bomb burst*, and the parson at that moment put spurs to his horse and was seen to limber to the rear, and almost every soldier yelled out, 'The parson isn't hungry, and never eats supper.'" (Sam R. Watkins, *"Co. Aytch": A Side Show of the Big*

Show [Chattanooga, TN: Times Printing Company, 1900; reprint, New York: Collier Books, 1962], 103.)

Teaching Point: Role of the chaplain.

Stand 15
Cleburne's Night Attack

(Preston Smith shell pyramid [see map 2])

Situation: 19 September 1863, p.m. Dodge's brigade occupied this position on the right of Johnson's division when night fell. Dodge's brigade was the target of Deshler's Brigade, the left unit of Cleburne's Division. In the darkness, Deshler's Brigade veered to the left and uncovered Brigadier General Preston Smith's Brigade, which was advancing in Deshler's support. Believing himself to be in a second line, Smith had not covered his front with skirmishers. The resulting encounter was a shock to both sides.

Vignette 1 (Confederate perspective): "The enemy, finding it impossible to drive us from our position, sullenly retired out of range, and comparative quiet prevailed along our lines until 6 p.m., when General Smith, being informed a night attack was determined upon, was ordered that so soon as General Deshler's brigade . . . should advance to his front, to move his brigade forward as General Deshler's support. After having advanced in this order some 200 yards, the engagement was commenced on the right, and extended to Deshler's brigade, in our front. Advancing a short distance farther, it being quite dark, a portion of this brigade became somewhat confused and fell back on our line. General Smith ordered them to move forward, which order was obeyed, and we continued to advance but a short distance when they a second time fell back on our line and were again urged forward by General Smith. Instead of moving direct to the front, they obliqued to the left and uncovered the two right regiments of General Smith's brigade. In the darkness General Smith did not know this, and a third time coming upon troops at a halt in his immediate front, presuming them to belong to General Deshler's command, he and Captain Thomas H. King, volunteer aide, rode to the front to ascertain the delay. On riding up to the line (which proved to be the enemy) and asking who was in command of these troops, he was discovered to be a Confederate officer, and he and Captain King were both killed. I at the same time was in front of my regiment, accompanied by Captain Donelson, acting assistant adjutant-general to General Smith, to know the cause of the delay of what I supposed to be a portion of General Deshler's command. Riding up to a soldier, I asked him to what command he belonged. Discovering that I was a Confederate officer, he fired at me, missing me, but killing Captain Donelson who was by my side. I immediately ordered some files from the 12th Tennessee Regiment to shoot him, which they did, killing him instantly. The line in front, seeing their situation, cried out, 'Do not shoot; we surrender.' I then rode forward and found them in grounding their arms. Discovering a stand of colors in my front, I asked, 'Who has those colors?' The reply was, 'The color bearer.' I then said, 'Sir, to what command do you belong?' He replied, 'To the Seventy-seventh Pennsylvania Regiment.' I then took from him the stand of colors and handed them to Captain Carthel, Forty-seventh Tennessee Regiment, and ordered him to turn them, with the prisoners captured (about 300 in number), over to General Cheatham." (Colonel Alfred J. Vaughn Jr., 13th Tennessee Infantry Regiment, in *O.R.*, vol. 30, pt. 2, 107—8.)

Vignette 2 (Federal perspective): "The Seventy-seventh [Pennsylvania] was on the extreme right of the division, and had attained a position considerably in advance of the troops on its right. But as the enemy seemed thoroughly beaten, no immediate evil resulted. General Willick [*sic*], however, immediately ordered Colonel Rose to send out a detachment to the right to ascertain how wide was the gap between his troops and next of the line. Two companies, under Lieutenant Colonel Pyfer, were dispatched, who soon returned reporting the distance a mile and a quarter. General Willick ordered the position to be held, and said that troops would be sent to fill the gap. Just at dark a heavy rebel column of fresh troops attacked with great violence. That fatal gap was not filled, and the Seventy-seventh Pennsylvania, and Seventy-ninth Illinois, with flanks exposed, were left to battle alone with an overpowering hostile force. With a coolness and courage rarely paralleled, the men held their ground, and when at length outflanked, and the line enfiladed, there were signs of wavering, the officers seized the colors, and with unwonted heroism, and daring, inspired the men, by their example, with fresh enthusiasm to maintain the fight, and to hold the ground. The action became desperate, and hand to hand, and to distinguish friend from foe was difficult. In the midst of the fight the rebel general Preston Smith was shot down by Sergeant Bryson, the General having taken the Sergeant for one of his own men, and being in the act of striking him with his sword for some conceived offence. But the odds were too great, and that little band of heroes was forced to yield, all the field officers, seven line officers, and seventy men of the Seventy-seventh falling into the hands of the enemy. Those who escaped retired during the night. . . ." (Captain J. J. Lawson in George W. Skinner, ed., *Pennsylvania at Chickamauga and Chattanooga* [Harrisburg, PA: W. S. Ray, State Printer, 1897], 206—7.)

Teaching Points: Lack of security, failure to perform reconnaissance, confusion of night combat.

Stand 16
Hazen's and Turchin's Brigades

(North edge of Brock Field [see map 2])

Situation: 19 September 1863, p.m. Entering the battle in early afternoon on the right of Johnson's division was Palmer's 2d Division, XXI Corps. Palmer's division advanced in echelon of brigades, with Brigadier General William B. Hazen's brigade leading. They fought on the edge of the woods west of the field, first against Smith's Brigade, then against Brigadier General Otho F. Strahl's. Exhausting its ammunition, Hazen's brigade was relieved around 1500 by Brigadier General John B. Turchin's brigade of Major General Joseph J. Reynold's division, XIV Corps. Hazen withdrew to Poe Field where the ammunition trains were located. Turchin deployed to the left of Brigadier General Charles Cruft's brigade of Palmer's division. Around 1600, in response to a Confederate attack on Palmer's right, Turchin and Cruft attacked south and west into the Confederate flank, blunting the attack. Around 1700, Turchin and Cruft withdrew to a position near Kelly Field.

Vignette: "The enemy being repulsed on my front, the brigade of General Willich advanced to the front and left, and the brigade of General Hazen being withdrawn, my brigade was isolated from other troops. I decided to take to the right, and formed in two lines on the left of General Cruft's brigade, of Palmer's division.

"Shortly afterward, at about 4:30 p.m., the enemy came in heavy columns on our front; there was wavering and indecision, and I ordered a charge. The brigade yelled, rushed forward, and drove the enemy back in confusion, taking some prisoners. The brigade of General Cruft charged with us. After consulting General Cruft, we decided to fall back, to reform our line, on the original position. This being done, I received orders from the general commanding to join the Second Brigade, which I subsequently did, and that closed the day." (Brigadier General John B. Turchin, in *O.R.*, vol. 30, pt. 1, 474.)

Teaching Points: Ammunition resupply, local counterattack.

Stand 17
A. P. Stewart's Division

(Stewart's Division plaque,
woods south of Brotherton Road [see map 3])

Situation: 19 September 1863, p.m. When Cheatham's Division proved
to be overmatched, Bragg sent Major General Alexander P. Stewart's
Division to assist the Confederates around Brock Field. Given vague
instructions on where to enter the fight, Stewart elected to support
Cheatham's left and formed his division in column of brigades. Around
1400, Brigadier General Henry D. Clayton's Brigade, Stewart's
leading unit, engaged elements of Brigadier General Horatio P. Van
Cleve's and Palmer's divisions, which had forced Brigadier General
Marcus J. Wright's Brigade of Cheatham's Division to withdraw.
When Clayton's green troops exhausted their ammunition, Stewart
replaced them with Brigadier General John C. Brown's Brigade.
Clayton's Brigade then withdrew to resupply. In turn, Brown's Brigade
was replaced by Brigadier General William B. Bate's Brigade. By
1630, by rotating his brigades into the fight, Stewart drove Van
Cleve's units from their position on the high ground south of the
Brotherton cabin. Clayton's Brigade then reentered the fight and
penetrated to Dyer Field. Unfortunately, Stewart's attack was
unsupported, and his units west of LaFayette Road were eventually
forced back by the approach of Brannan's and Major General James S.
Negley's divisions. Stewart had achieved a limited penetration, but
without support, his tactical success could not be exploited.

Vignette: "About 11 o'clock we moved by the right flank 400 or 500
yards in rear of Johnson's division, and soon afterward 800 yards
farther, halting immediately in rear of the left of Cheatham's division,
which was then hotly engaged. His left brigade, being numerically
overpowered and repulsed, was relieved by Brigadier-General Clayton,
immediately in my front. I followed this movement closely, being so
near to Clayton's line that many of my command were wounded and a
few killed before I could return the fire. The front line advanced but
little under the combined fire of the enemy's artillery and small-arms
until General Clayton reported his ammunition exhausted.

"At about 2 p.m., in obedience to orders received in person from
the major-general commanding, I relieved him, and encountered the
enemy in an unbroken forest, rendered the more difficult of passage by
the dense undergrowth which for more than 200 yards extended along
my entire line; and the difficulties were still further enhanced by the
smoke of battle and the burning of the woods, rendering it impossible
to distinguish objects 20 paces in advance. My skirmishers

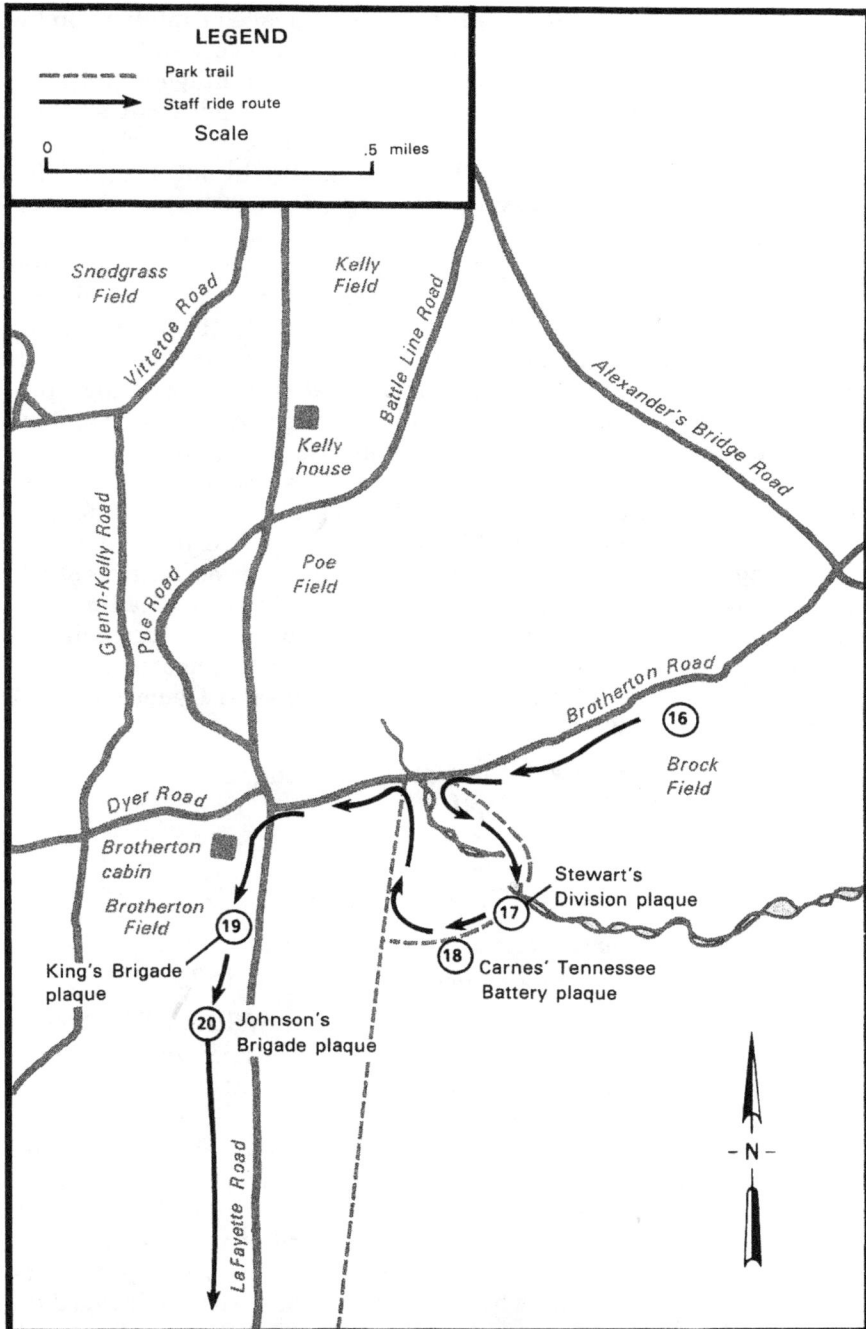

LEGEND

Park trail

Staff ride route

Scale

0 .5 miles

Snodgrass Field

Kelly Field

Vittetoe Road

Battle Line Road

Alexander's Bridge Road

Glenn-Kelly Road

Poe Road

Kelly house

Poe Field

Brotherton Road

Dyer Road

Brock Field

16

Brotherton cabin

Brotherton Field

Stewart's Division plaque

King's Brigade plaque

19

17

Carnes' Tennessee Battery plaque

18

20 Johnson's Brigade plaque

LaFayette Road

- N -

Map 3. Day 1, stands 17 through 20

encountering the enemy at 100 yards or less, I pushed rapidly upon his lines under a most terrific fire from all arms. There was no position from which my artillery could be served with advantage against the enemy, while two of his batteries immediately in my front and one almost on my right flank filled the air with grape, canister, shells, and solid shot, while volley after volley of musketry in quick succession swept my men by scores at every discharge. For 400 yards, however, my line steadily advanced without faltering at any point until the enemy had been driven beyond the tangled undergrowth and his first line completely routed. A stubborn resistance from the second line, supported by artillery posted upon a slight acclivity in our front and pouring showers of canister upon us for a few minutes, checked our progress; but again we advanced, driving back his second line up to and beyond the summit of the ridge, until my right rested upon and my center and left had passed the crest. Unfortunately, however, at the moment when the rout of the second line was about being made as complete as the disaster to the first a few minutes previous, a force of the enemy appeared on my right flank, and had well nigh turned it, compelling the Eighteenth and Forty-fifth Tennessee Regiments to retire rapidly and in some confusion under a heavy enfilading fire. This necessitated the withdrawal of the center and left, there being no support upon my right for a mile, and none in my rear nearer than 600 yards, and which was then not in motion." (Brigadier General John C. Brown, in *O.R.*, vol. 30, pt. 2, 370—71.)

Teaching Points: Leadership, initiative, training, cohesion, tactical formations, synchronization, depth.

Stand 18
Carnes' Tennessee Battery

*(Carnes' Tennessee Battery plaque,
woods south of Brotherton Road [see map 3])*

Situation: 19 September 1863, p.m. Captain William W. Carnes' Battery, consisting of two 6-pounder smoothbores and two 12-pounder howitzers, supported Wright's Brigade of Cheatham's Division. Around 1330, the battery went into action on the left of the division, firing canister because of the nearness of the enemy. The battery had no infantry support on its left, the direction from which Federal reinforcements approached the battlefield. Soon after it went into action, the battery was attacked on its left and rear by Van Cleve's division. After many of the men and most of the horses were killed, the remaining gunners withdrew hastily on foot. The Federals dragged the guns back to the road, where they were recaptured by Stewart's advancing infantry. From a complement of seventy-eight officers and men, one officer and eighteen men were killed, eighteen men wounded, and one captured. Only ten of the battery's fifty-nine horses survived.

Vignette: "The woods. . .were so dense with undergrowth that it was almost impossible to keep the battery up with the infantry line. The infantry struck the enemy first, and as soon as Carnes could clear the ground of undergrowth, which he had to do with a detail of men armed with axes, he put his battery in position, and opened on the advancing Federals with canister. In the heavy fighting which immediately followed, many of the men and horses were soon killed or disabled; and Carnes, seeing the impossibility of saving his guns if our line should be pressed back, sent his orderly to report the situation to the division commander and ask for help. Receiving reply to hold his ground as long as possible, Capt. Carnes dismounted his officers and sergeants and put them and the drivers of the disabled horses at the guns to replace the cannoneers as they were shot down, and, giving the enemy double charges of canister at close range, drove back the line in his front; but as he had no support on his left, the Federals swung around the battery until it was almost surrounded. Finding it impossible to hold out longer, Carnes sent his few surviving men to the rear and, with his sergeant, fired his left gun a few times as rapidly as possible to keep back the fast closing lines, and then he and his sergeant jumped to their horses, which were tied near by. The sergeant, mounting first, was riddled with bullets from a volley that passed over the Captain as he was in the act of mounting, wounding his horse. Making a dash for the now narrow opening to the rear, Capt. Carnes escaped capture by being well mounted and a good rider. His horse was struck a number of times, and could barely carry his rider till he reached the support coming from the rear, and fell just after he passed through the advancing Confederate line." (T. L. Massenburg, "Capt. W. W. Carnes's Battery at Chickamauga," *Confederate Veteran* 6 [November 1898]:518.

Teaching Points: Small-unit leadership, combined arms, face of battle.

Stand 19
E. A. King's Brigade

(King's brigade plaque, Brotherton Field [see map 3])

Situation: 19 September 1863, p.m. While advancing to support Palmer's division, Colonel Edward A. King's brigade of Reynolds' division was diverted to support Van Cleve's division. The 75th Indiana Regiment was left in this position to support the 19th and 7th Indiana Batteries along this ridge overlooking LaFayette Road. King's remaining regiments went into position on the right of Van Cleve's

84

line in the woods east of LaFayette Road. Both Van Cleve's and King's regiments were driven back to this ridge (1530—1600) by the left of Stewart's Division and the right of Bushrod Johnson's Division. By 1630, the Federals also evacuated this line despite the strength of the position. Several attached units, notably the 92d Illinois Regiment and four mountain howitzers of the 18th Indiana Battery (from Wilder's brigade), were also caught in the rout.

Vignette: "My four mountain howitzers were with the Ninety-second Illinois Volunteers detached from the brigade on Saturday, and under Sergeant Anderson, Seventy-second Indiana Volunteers, did good fighting. Sergeant Anderson was wounded severely, and Sergeant Edwards, Seventeenth Indiana Volunteers took command and did good work till all support left them and the enemy were within a few yards of his pieces, when he succeeded in escaping with three of his pieces and the limber of the other. Either of these men would do honor to the commissions of the miserable shoulder-strapped poltroons who allowed the support to run away from the pieces in the hour of danger." (Captain Eli Lilly, in *O.R.*, vol. 30, pt. 1, 467.)

Teaching Points: Strength of the defensive, rapid task organizing.

Stand 20
Johnson's (Fulton's) Brigade

(Johnson's Brigade plaque, south edge of Brotherton Field [see map 3])

Situation: 19 September 1863, p.m. Around 1600, Colonel John S. Fulton's Brigade, the right of Johnson's Division, crossed LaFayette Road south of Stewart's attack, then swung north and struck the right flank of Van Cleve's position on the Brotherton ridge. Stewart's and Johnson's attacks were not coordinated but, luckily, complemented each other. Part of Brigadier General Thomas J. Wood's Federal division, moving north in turn, now struck Johnson's exposed left (southern) flank. In this movement, two regiments of Colonel Charles G. Harker's brigade of Wood's division came up LaFayette Road from the vicinity of Viniard Field, fired into Fulton's rear, and drove him back across LaFayette Road in disarray.

Vignette: "When we had gone about half way we discovered a line of troops moving by the flank in the direction of the left wing of my regiment. Before we could determine who they were the commands 'halt,' 'front,' were given by the commander of the leading regiment, and they immediately discharged a volley at our men. A general stampede of our men ensued. So sudden and unexpected was the attack from our rear that every man seemed to act for himself, regardless of orders. I was too far from my regiment to give any directions or render any assistance at the time. Major Davis was lying down behind the left of the regiment, but gave no commands of any kind. Doubtless he thought it was folly to attempt to do anything when the enemy was within 30 yards of him and in his rear. Some of the company officers ordered their men to face about and fire. A number of the men fired on the enemy. Some of them fired two or three rounds before they got out of reach.

"Immediately after the discharge of the first volley from the enemy I turned to look at the fate of my regiment. I saw that a number of the men were making their way out in the only direction by which they could possibly escape, and I saw at once that if I could get back to the line at all, the men who were left there would be prisoners before I could reach them. All of my regiment that escaped moved by the right flank about 200 yards, and then filed to the rear and came out at the right of the brigade." (Lieutenant Colonel Watt W. Floyd, 17th Tennessee Infantry Regiment [Fulton's left unit], in *O.R.*, vol. 30, pt. 2, 481.)

Teaching Points: Coordination between units, command and control, nonlinear battlefield.

Stand 21
McNair's Brigade

(39th North Carolina marker, Glenn Field [see map 4])

Situation: 19 September 1863, p.m. When Bushrod Johnson's Division advanced around 1500, Brigadier General John Gregg's Brigade was on the left of the first line, with McNair's Brigade in support. In the process of defeating part of Brigadier General Jefferson C. Davis' division, Gregg's troops became scattered. The 39th North Carolina and 25th Arkansas Infantry Regiments of McNair's Brigade passed over the left of Gregg's Brigade and continued their advance 200 yards to this point. Here, the advance was halted and forced back by enfilading fire from Wilder's mounted infantry brigade and a section of the 18th Indiana Battery on the south side of the field and the arrival of Wood's division from Lee and Gordon's Mill.

Vignette: "Moved rapidly forward, and getting near Gregg's brigade (then under a terrific fire) [we] charged impetuously with loud cheers, passing over the left of Gregg's brigade, and drove the enemy in rapid flight through the thick woods, across the Chattanooga road, past the small house 100 yards on, and into the cornfields beyond, making a distance altogether of about three-quarters of a mile. In the last advance Lieutenant-Colonel Hufstedler fell wounded with five balls.

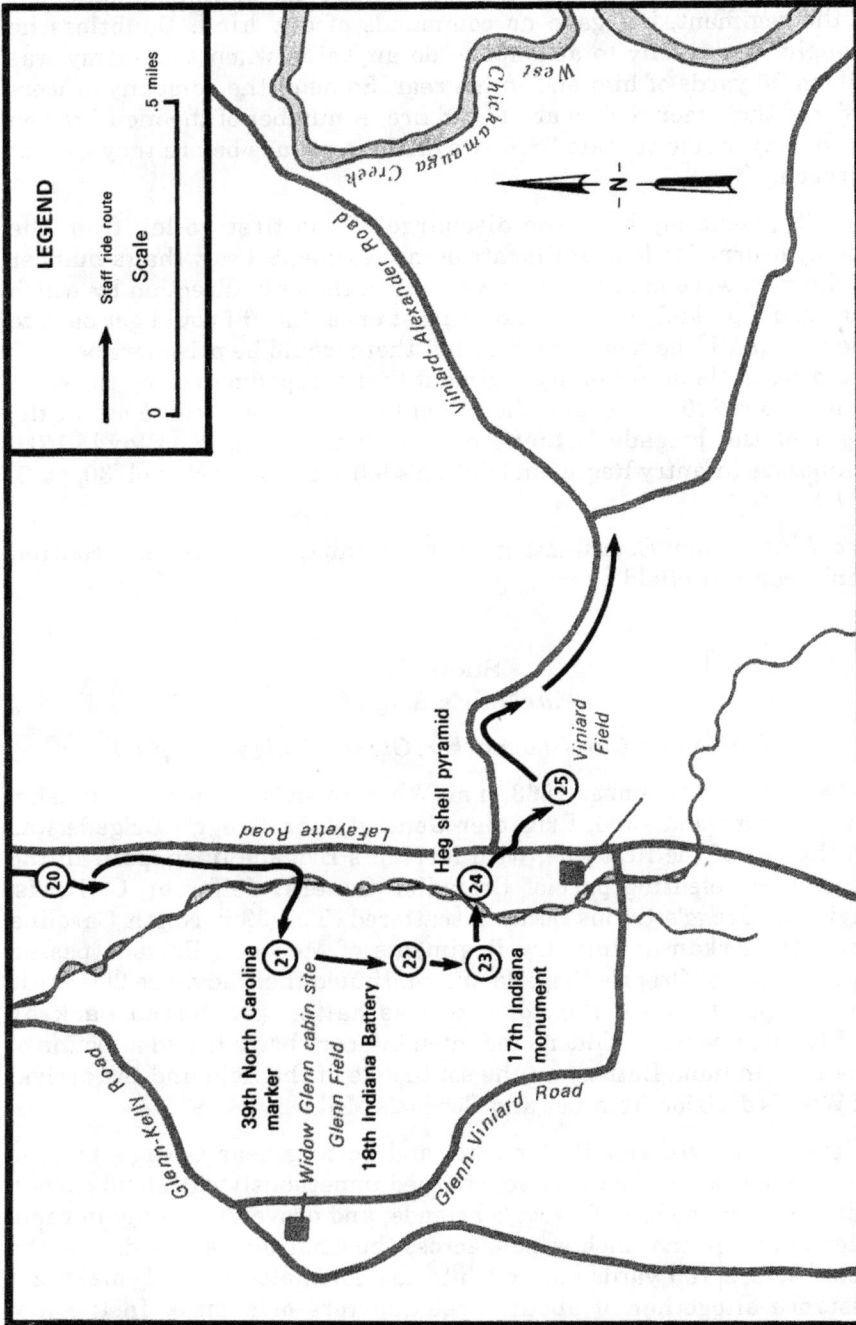

LEGEND

Staff ride route

Scale

0   .5 miles

West Chickamauga Creek

Viniard-Alexander Road

Lafayette Road

Heg shell pyramid

Viniard Field

Glenn-Kelly Road

39th North Carolina marker

Widow Glenn cabin site

Glenn Field

18th Indiana Battery

17th Indiana monument

Glenn-Viniard Road

Map 4. Day 1, stands 21 through 25

Here, though the enemy to whom we had been opposed in front were in flight, broken, and in confusion, having sustained a heavy loss in killed, the two regiments, finding their tired and weakened line exposed to a fatal flanking fire, especially on the left, unsupported on account of the rapidity of their advance, with an enemy's battery near on the left, and a strong enemy re-enforcement approaching, and our ammunition nearly exhausted, the impracticability of longer holding this advanced and exposed position was immediately manifest and the force was ordered back to the woods." (Colonel David Coleman, 39th North Carolina Infantry Regiment, in *O.R.*, vol. 30, pt. 2, 499—500.)

Teaching Points: Width of a division front, initiative, unsupported attack.

Stand 22
18th Indiana Battery

*(Edge of Glenn Field and astride ditch,
north of Viniard Field [see map 4])*

Situation: 19 September 1863, p.m. Early on this morning, Wilder's mounted infantry brigade withdrew to a defensive position at the far western edge of Viniard Field. When Davis' division and part of Wood's division were routed from Viniard Field and the woods, they passed through Wilder's line. Armed with seven-shot Spencer repeating rifles, Wilder's men halted the charge of Brigadier General Jerome B. Robertson's and Brigadier General Henry L. Benning's Brigades of Hood's Division. The Confederates then took refuge in this ditch or gully, which curved around in front of Wilder's position. Today (1992), the ditch is clogged with vegetation, but in 1863, it was open. Captain Eli Lilly positioned two of his six 3-inch rifles to cover the ditch by firing down its long axis. The effect of the canister fire was devastating on the trapped Confederates.

Vignette: "At 4:00 p.m., Major General John B. Hood's Confederate division attacked Davis' division in an assault that drove it back to the west of the road and to Wilder's line. Lieutenant Scott's guns fired canister at the advancing line, and the four guns on the left fired obliquely into the Rebels. The Johnnies reached the ravine in front of the position, in which they took shelter from the firing of Wilder's seven shooters.

"Captain Lilly understated the effect of his guns in this situation, with his report saying that his guns fired 'until they reached the ravine when they fell back in disorder except a few who laid down in the ravine and were captured.' Henry Campbell wrote, 'Capt. Lilly moved forward two guns on the left to a position where he could rake the ditch from end to end, opened out with thrible [*sic*] charges of canister down the ditch which compelled the rebels to retreat in confusion. The ditch was literally full of dead and wounded and proved to be a self made grave for hundreds of them.'

"Colonel Wilder agreed, reporting that Lilly fired 200 rounds of double-shotted canister at ranges of from 70 to 350 yards. Later he commented, 'At this point it actually seemed a pity to kill men so. They fell in heaps, and I had it in my heart to order the firing to cease, to end the awful sight.'" (John Rowell, *Yankee Artillerymen: Through the Civil War With Eli Lilly's Indiana Battery* [Knoxville: University of Tennessee Press, 1975], 117.)

Teaching Points: Analysis of terrain, initiative, combined arms, integration of fires.

Stand 23
Wilder's Brigade

(17th Indiana monument [see map 4])

Situation: 19 September 1863, p.m. As you face east, Wilder's position stretched from the gully on your left along the western and southern edges of this field. The present (1992) tree line in your front did not exist in 1863, permitting a field of fire beyond LaFayette Road and extending into Viniard Field. Leaving their horses some distance in the rear, Wilder's men fired from the protection of a rail barricade. Each man had ample ammunition for his repeating rifle (60 rounds on his person and 200 rounds in a nose bag on his saddle). Armed with a weapon of advanced technology that permitted a high rate of fire in the prone position (Spencer repeating rifle), Wilder's brigade was able to clear its front throughout the day. In addition, the brigade served as a rallying point for broken formations of Davis', Wood's, and Major General Philip H. Sheridan's divisions.

Vignette: "Suddenly I saw many of our soldiers come running out of the woods on the east side of the field, followed by more and more of them, till I could not doubt but that our men were being forced to fall back. Along the road to our right, across the open field and from all points they came running. Before they were across the field the Rebels broke out of the woods on the east side in hot pursuit of our men. We had to wait till our men were through our line as we lay behind our improvised fortifications, and then we began to shoot at the oncoming Rebels as fast as our Spencer repeating rifles would permit, while Lilly's battery was sweeping the field with canister. It was too fierce for human beings to face long, but the Rebels came on till they reached a deep ditch or gully about 15 or 20 yards in front of where we lay. Here they hesitated and our firing became so devastating they turned and fled for the protection of the woods on the far side of the field. Occasionally one would break away and make a run for the woods on the far side. One fellow carrying a flag started on a run for this place. As he came into view from behind the stable I took careful aim and fired at him, sure that I would see him fall. But what was my astonishment to see him keep right on. I had missed him. Before I could fire again he had reached the woods and was lost to sight.

"Again and again, all day each side charged back and forth across the field. Often we could not see a dozen yards in front of us for the smoke, but never did the enemy once reach us. We held our line intact. Many times during the day we had to renew our supplies of ammunition. We shot so much that before night each man had a little pile of empty shells, and I remember one time that several of the soldiers near me in a lull of the fighting compared piles to see which one had done the most shooting." (Theodore Petzoldt, 17th Indiana Mounted Infantry, in *My War Story*, Portland, OR, 1917, 103—5.)

Teaching Points: Effects of new technology, face of battle, tactics, leadership, use of terrain, fire discipline, training.

Stand 24
Heg's Brigade

(Heg shell pyramid [see map 4])

Situation: 19 September 1863, p.m. Colonel Hans C. Heg's brigade went into action in the woods east of LaFayette Road as the left of Davis' division. Around 1400, Heg became heavily engaged with Gregg's Brigade of Bushrod Johnson's Division. Heg's men were forced back across the road, rallied, attacked again, and were repulsed once more. Benning's and Robertson's Brigades eventually penetrated to this point, but when darkness fell, Federal units controlled this area. Late in the day, as he rallied his unit in a final counterattack, Heg was mortally wounded at this spot.

Vignette: Colonel Heg's last letter to his wife, Gunild, 18 September 1863: "Do not feel uneasy for me. I am well and in good spirits—and trusting to my usual good luck. I shall use all the caution and courage I am capable of and leave the rest to take care of itself. . . . I can of course say nothing about the prospects of getting home—but as soon as this present campaign is ended—I am certain of being able to come." (Theodore C. Blegen, ed., *The Civil War Letters of Colonel Hans Christian Heg* [Northfield, MN: Norwegian-American Historical Association, 1936], 245—46.)

Teaching Points: Leadership, confusion, importance of the road.

Stand 25
Viniard Field

(Line of monuments east of LaFayette Road [see map 4])

Situation: 19 September 1863, p.m. This slight rise in Viniard Field was the tactical objective for both sides on this part of the field. At least seven Federal brigades and four Confederate brigades swept back and forth over this ground from 1400 to 1800 without gaining any significant advantage. After dark, both sides withdrew from the field, leaving hundreds of wounded and dead behind. In the darkness, the cries of the wounded greatly affected those who heard them, but they could do little to help.

Vignette: "When night settled down at last firing ceased on both sides. . . . From the field in front of me and I began to hear the cries of the wounded. Some in the delirium of the fever from their wounds were calling 'Father, Oh Father, come quick,' while others cried for 'Mother, Mother,' but no mother could hear. Others were calling for a brother or a sister, while some called for a wife. . . . But the cry that was incessant and which ranged from a low moan to a loud wail was 'Water-water-water!' We had orders not to move from our places, not to strike a match, not to go to sleep or to make any unnecessary noise. But after listening to that cry for 'water, water' for a little while, I could stand it no longer. As quickly as possible, I slipped out of the woods and into the field in front of us. I had no water in my canteen to give out, but I thought probably I could find some. It was now so dark that I could but dimly see the outlines of those lying on the ground. Seeing one who was making no sound I went to him and shaking him by the shoulder I whispered: 'partner.' There was no reply. He was dead. I raised his shoulders from the ground and slipped the canteen strap over his head. Good, the canteen was nearly full of water. I went to the nearest man who was calling for water and gave it to him. With eager hands he grabbed it and began to drink. No sooner did the other wounded men in the vicinity observe that some one was near with water than they all began to beg for some. I made it go as far as I could, but it was not far. When the canteen was empty I looked about for more water, but could find none. Returning to the first man to whom I [had] given water and who by his voice I had judged to be German, I spoke to him in that language. I had guessed right. He told me that he belonged to the 32d Illinois. He had been wounded in the bowels and he had no expectation that he could live. I tried to cheer him as best I could but it is little one can say at a time like this. He said that he did not mind dying, but it troubled him to think what would become of the wife and two small children that he would leave back there in Illinois. Who would look out for them after he was gone? I could only stay a few minutes with him for I wanted to get back to our lines before my absence was discovered. How horrible it all was. Some of the water I gave to a poor fellow shot through the lungs and whose blood was slowly oozing from his mouth. He had crawled into the gully to be protected from the flying bullets during the day. I would have liked to have taken both men back to our lines, but it would have done them no good for we could not have taken care of them there if I had. So I left them in their terrible pain and misery and went back to our lines. Luckily my absence had not been discovered." (Theodore Petzoldt, 17th Indiana Infantry Regiment, in *My War Story*, Portland, OR, 1917, 106—8.)

Teaching Points: Analysis of terrain, face of battle, humanity in war.

Stand 26
General Braxton Bragg's Headquarters

(Thedford's Ford [see map 5])

Situation: 19 September 1863, p.m. The headquarters and trains area of Bragg's Army of Tennessee was located in this vicinity on this night. During the evening, Bragg formed his army into two wings, Lieutenant General Leonidas Polk commanding the Right Wing and Lieutenant General James Longstreet the Left Wing. Bragg briefed Polk but left it to Polk to inform the third lieutenant general, Daniel H. Hill, of the reorganization. After arriving at Catoosa Station around 1400, Longstreet made his way to Bragg's headquarters by 2300, was briefed on the plan for the next day, and retired for the night. Bragg's plan differed little from his earlier efforts. Once again, he proposed to turn the Federal left. The attack was to be executed in echelon by divisions from right to left.

Vignette: "In the evening, according to my custom in Virginia under General Lee, I rode back to Army headquarters to report to the Commander-in-Chief the result of the day upon my part of the line. I there met for the first time several of the principal officers of the Army of Tennessee, and, to my surprise, not one spoke in a sanguine tone regarding the result of the battle in which we were then engaged. I found the gallant Breckinridge, whom I had known from early youth, seated by the root of a tree, with a heavy slouch hat upon his head. When, in the course of brief conversation, I stated that we would rout the enemy the following day, he sprang to his feet, exclaiming, 'My

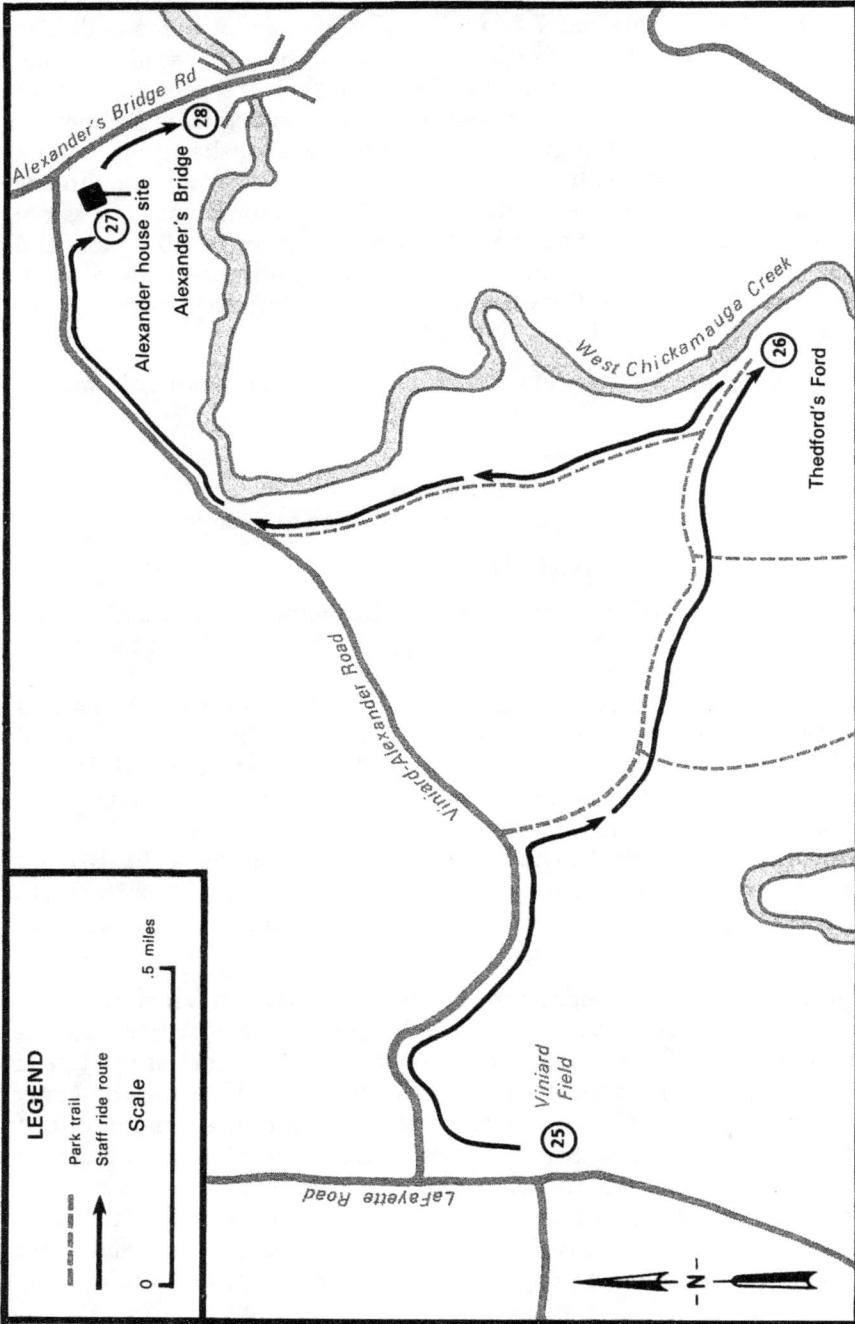

Map 5. Day 1, stands 26 through 28

dear Hood, I am delighted to hear you say so. You give me renewed hope; God grant it may be so.'

"After receiving orders from General Bragg to advance the next morning as soon as the troops on my right moved to the attack, I returned to the position occupied by my forces, and camped the remainder of the night with General Buckner, as I had nothing with me save that which I had brought from the train upon my horse. Nor did my men have a single wagon, or even ambulance in which to convey the wounded. They were destitute of almost everything, I might say, except pride, spirit, and forty rounds of ammunition to the man." (John Bell Hood, *Advance and Retreat* [Philadelphia, PA: Burke and M'Fetridge, 1880], 62.)

Teaching Points: Command post locations, commander's intent, reorganization during battle.

Stand 27
18th Indiana Battery

(Alexander house site [see map 5])

Situation: 18 September 1863, a.m. As part of the mounted forces screening the left of the Army of the Cumberland, Wilder's brigade took a position at Alexander's Bridge. Captain Eli Lilly's 18th Indiana Battery was positioned here on this slight rise overlooking the bridge. In 1863, the ground between this position and the bridge consisted of open fields and pasture, giving Lilly's guns a clear field of fire. At 0930, Lilly detached his four mountain howitzers to accompany the 72d Indiana and 123d Illinois Regiments to reinforce Minty at Reed's Bridge. At about 1230, skirmishers from Brigadier General Edward C. Walthall's Brigade of Liddell's Division appeared beyond the creek. Lilly opened fire with four of his 3-inch rifles. Covered by Lilly, Wilder's men managed to dismantle the bridge despite Walthall's vigorous attack. Blocked at Alexander's Bridge, Liddell's Division continued downsteam and crossed at Byram's Ford.

Vignette: "Soon after the line had been formed a column of Confederate Infantry issued from the woods, passed across the fields on our front, and formed line of Battle reaching from the road on the left to the woods on the right. We opened out on them with considerable effect, sending percussion Shell right through their line. Soon after, they placed a Bat. of 2 guns on a slight hill directly opposite—they only fired 4 times, we made it so hot for them that they left in a hurry. Their first shell came very close to gun No. 2—it struck the ground out in front—ricocheted and struck the corner of the log house, in front of which the gun was standing—falling down among the cannoneers with the fuze still burning. Sidney Speed seeing the danger—with great coolness, picked the shell up and threw it away before it exploded. I don't think I will ever forget the awful, unearthly screeching—that shell made—as it approached us. It seemed as if it never would strike it was so long coming. I was standing near gun No. 2 and with four or five of the boys doubled down behind a little bit of a sapling not big enough to stop a small bullet. We all knew, from the sound of it, that it would strike some place close by, and it was a great relief when it crashed in the logs above our heads." (Henry Chambers, 18th Indiana Battery, Journal, Unit Files, Chickamauga and Chattanooga National Military Park, Fort Oglethorpe, GA.)

Teaching Points: Combined arms, integrating of supporting fires, delay, bridge defense.

Stand 28
Leonidas Polk's Headquarters

(Alexander's Bridge [see map 5])

Situation: 19 September 1863, p.m. Polk's headquarters was located in the vicinity of Alexander's Bridge, probably about 500 yards to the south. After receiving his orders from Bragg, Polk returned to his headquarters; issued written orders to Hill, Walker, and Cheatham; and then went to bed. The only person left on duty at the command post was a clerk. Walker and Cheatham received their orders, but the messenger failed to find Hill. Meanwhile, Hill tried to find Bragg's headquarters but was unsuccessful. When Polk's messenger returned to Alexander's Bridge and reported his inability to find Hill, he was told not to disturb Polk or the senior staff. Because Hill also proved unable to locate Polk's headquarters, he did not learn that his corps had been ordered to initiate the attack at dawn. Because of this and other reasons, the scheduled 0530 attack did not begin until four hours later.

Vignette: "On the night of September 19, I was on duty at headquarters as courier. About 12 o'clock a dispatch was handed me to be carried to Lieutenant-General Hill. I left immediately in search of General Hill, having been informed that General Hill was near Thedford's Ford. I was unable to find General Hill after searching for him for about four hours. In my search I came up with General Cheatham and made inquiry of him for General Hill. He informed me that he knew nothing of his whereabouts. I also met with General Breckinridge and made of him the same inquiry and received of him the same answer. After going in every direction and inquiring of all the soldiers I met of his and other commands I returned to headquarters, after a search of about four hours, unable to find General Hill. Upon my return I did not report to Colonel Jack, as I understood from his clerk (Mr. McReady) that I was not to disturb him upon my return." (Private John H. Fisher, in *O.R.*, vol. 30, pt. 2, 57—58.)

Teaching Points: Command responsibility, command post operations.

———————————————

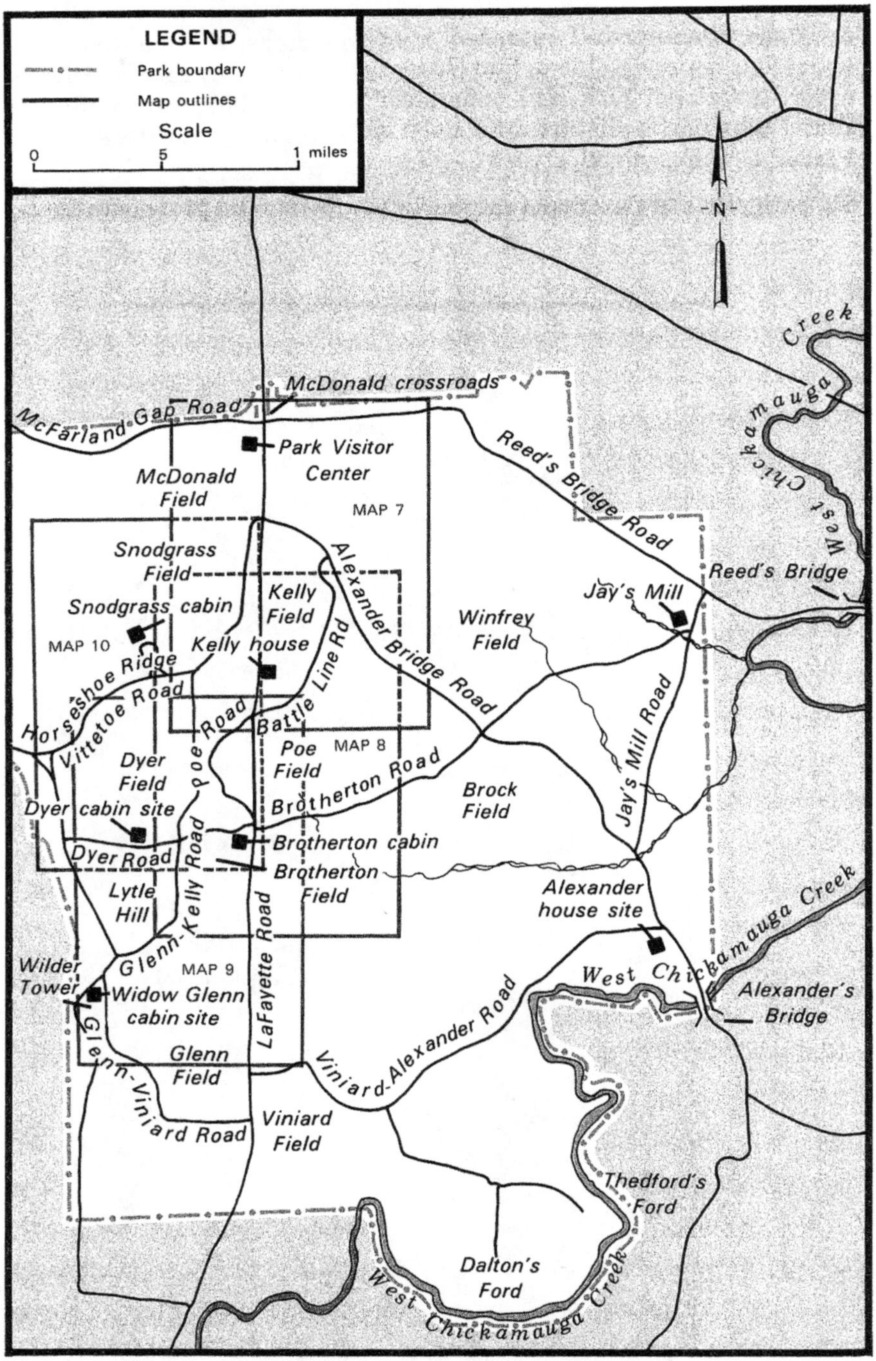

Map 6. Sites of maps 7 through 10 in relation to the Chickamauga and Chattanooga National Military Park for day 2

DAY 2 (20 SEPTEMBER 1863)

Stand 1
Breckinridge's Division

(Tennessee Artillery monument [see map 7])

Situation: 20 September 1863, a.m. The battle on 19 September had been a meeting engagement. After a night of planning and reorganization, Rosecrans chose to conduct a coordinated defense on 20 September, and Bragg proposed to launch a deliberate attack at daylight. Major General John C. Breckinridge's Division of Hill's Corps, on the Confederate right flank, was to initiate the attack for the entire army. Divisions south of Breckinridge were to join the attack successively until the entire line was engaged. Bragg had ordered the attack to commence at "day dawn," which was shortly before sunrise (0547), but a series of difficulties and subsequent decisions prevented Breckinridge from moving before 0930. His troops had little or no knowledge of the location of the Federal line.

Breckinridge formed his division with his three brigades on line: Major General Daniel W. Adams' Brigade on the right, Brigadier General Marcellus Stovall's Brigade in the center, and Brigadier General Benjamin H. Helm's Brigade on the left. This position was on the axis of advance of Adams' Brigade, about 300 yards forward (west) of the division's line of departure.

Vignette: "At 7.25 a.m. an order was shown me (just received) from Lieutenant-General Polk and addressed to my division commanders, and directing them to advance at once upon the enemy. The reason given for the issue of the order directly to them was that he (General Polk) had not been able to find the corps commander. I immediately replied to the note, saying that Brigadier-General Jackson's brigade, of his corps, was at right angles to my line; that my men were getting their rations, and that they could finish eating while we were adjusting the line of battle. General Polk soon after came on the field and made no objection to this delay. At 8 o'clock General Bragg himself came on the field, and I then learned for the first time that an attack had been ordered at daylight. However, the essential preparations for battle had not been made up to this hour, and, in fact, could not be made without the presence of the commander-in-chief. The position of the Yankees had not been reconnoitered. Our own line of battle had not been adjusted, and part of it was at right angles to the rest. There was no cavalry on our flanks, and no orders had fixed the strength or position of the reserves. My own line had been arranged north and south to correspond to the position of the enemy and be

98

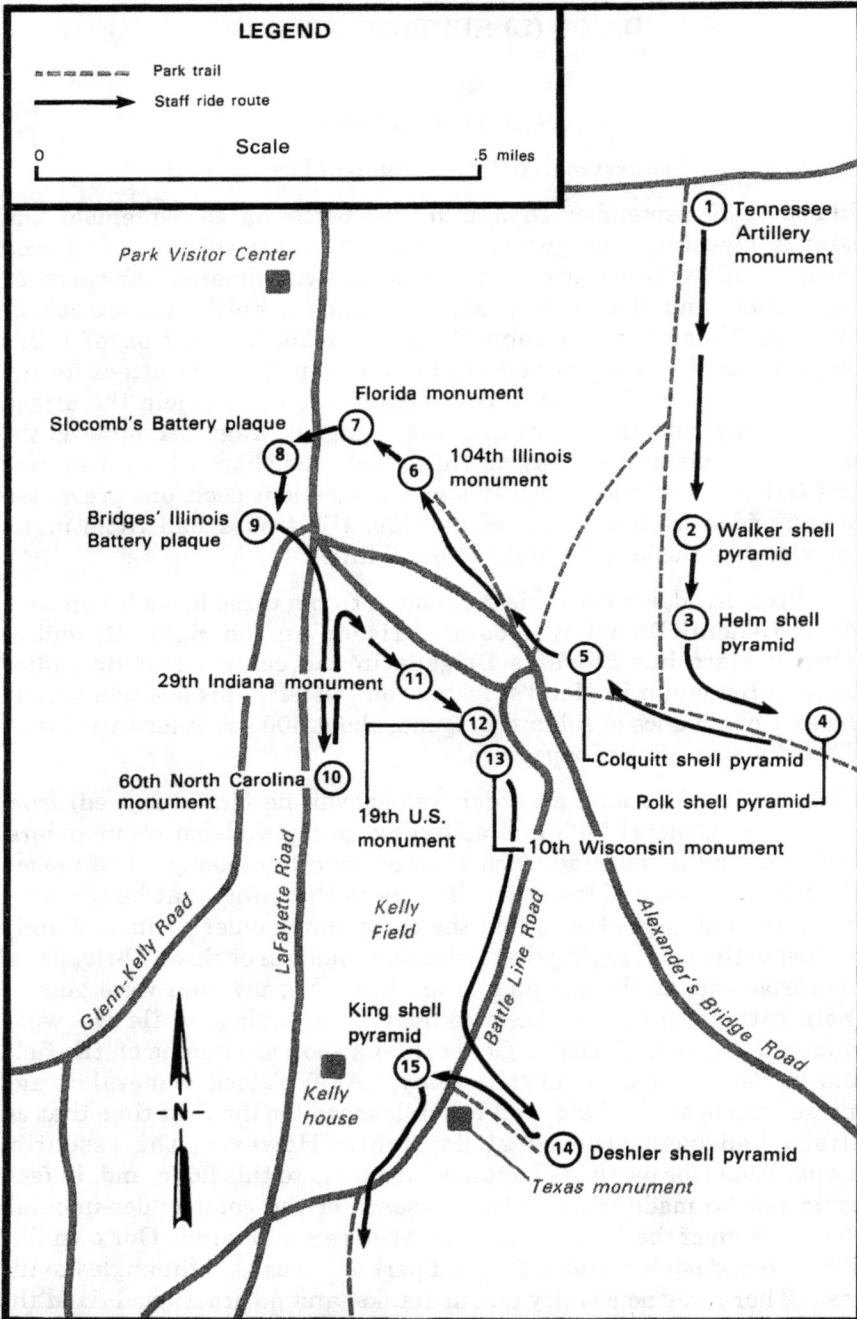

LEGEND

Park trail

Staff ride route

Scale

0   .5 miles

Park Visitor Center

Florida monument

Slocomb's Battery plaque

104th Illinois
monument

Bridges' Illinois
Battery plaque

29th Indiana monument

60th North Carolina
monument

19th U.S.
monument

10th Wisconsin monument

Colquitt shell pyramid

Polk shell pyramid

Tennessee
Artillery
monument

Walker shell
pyramid

Helm shell
pyramid

Kelly
Field

King shell
pyramid

Kelly
house

-N-

Texas monument

Deshler shell pyramid

Glenn-Kelly Road

LaFayette Road

Battle Line Road

Alexander's Bridge Road

Map 7. Day 2, stands 1 through 15

parallel to it." (Lieutenant General Daniel H. Hill, in *O.R.*, vol. 30, pt. 2, 141.)

Teaching Points: Orientation, reconnaissance.

Stand 2
Headquarters, Major General W. H. T. Walker's Reserve Corps

(Walker shell pyramid [see map 7])

Situation: 20 September 1863, a.m. Initially, Walker's Corps, consisting of Brigadier General States R. Gist's and Liddell's Divisions, was in reserve on Polk's left flank, formed and centered behind Cheatham's Division. During the delay in the Confederate attack, Polk moved Walker's Corps behind Hill's Corps. After Breckinridge's withdrawal around 1100, Walker's troops were ordered forward separately. About noon, Gist's Division attacked Thomas' fortified position northeast of Kelly Field. Instead of exploiting the partial success achieved by Breckinridge, Hill deployed Walker's units into the fight piecemeal. As a result, they were defeated in detail.

Vignette: "Before I got into my position, and while marching by the flank to gain the ground to the right, I was sent for by General Hill to [go to] his support. General Polk was with my command when I received the order. I marched rapidly forward in line of battle, part of the time in double-quick, and reported to General Hill. General Polk was with me. General Hill informed me on my arrival that he wanted a brigade. I told him there was one immediately behind him. He remarked he wanted Gist's brigade. I informed him that it was to the left and had just come up. (General Gist had a few minutes before been put in command by me of General Ector's and Colonel Wilson's brigades, and Colonel Colquitt had command of Gist's brigade.) He ordered General Gist's brigade immediately into the fight in rear of Breckinridge, a part of whose division had fallen back and the whole of which was hard pressed. I refer you to General Gist's report for the performance of his command.

"General Walthall was detached to the left to the support of Brigadier-General Polk by Hill or Polk. My command being thus disposed of, brigades being sent in to take the places of divisions, my only occupation was to help form the detached portions of my command as they came out from a position I felt certain they would have to leave when they were sent in. My division commanders received their orders direct from General Hill, and I refer you to their reports. Breckinridge's division having fallen back, General Hill having reported Cleburne's division on Breckinridge's left routed, my Reserve Corps having fallen back in the detachments in which they were sent in, and a column having been observed marching down the Chattanooga road on our right, I was compelled to insist on having something to do with my own command." (Major General William H. T. Walker, in *O.R.*, vol. 30, pt. 2, 241.)

Teaching Points: Unity of command, role of the reserve.

Stand 3
Helm's Brigade (the "Orphan Brigade")

(Helm shell pyramid [see map 7])

Situation: 20 September 1863, a.m. Helm's Brigade was the left unit of Breckinridge's Division. As Helm's men advanced westward through the woods, his three left regiments passed just to the north of the Federal breastworks and were devastated by enfilading fire from Baird's division posted northeast of Kelly Field. Helm rode to the left to rally his shattered regiments and was mortally wounded. The right side of his brigade continued forward with Stovall's Brigade, but most of Helm's unit was destroyed.

Vignette: "General Breckinridge, whose presence was inspiration, rode frequently along the line. General Helm was moving about quietly and infusing courage into the eager command. It was a picture of 'Just Before the Battle,' that can not be put on canvas. Helm's Brigade was about to commence the greatest engagement of the war. About half past nine o'clock the Fourth regiment was deployed in front of the brigade, and commanded by the fearless Nuckols, set about feeling for the enemy. It was short work, for he gave the command forward, and soon our Enfields rang out lustily through the forest. The Fourth lost severely in the charge, but the enemy was developed and formed behind breastworks covering part of a brigade front. The command now moved forward and as soon as we felt the fire of the enemy we charged, and the second day's battle began in earnest. The Second and Ninth and a small portion of the Forty-First Alabama struck their fortifications and suffered terrible slaughter. General Helm was mortally wounded. Major Rice F. Graves, the great artillery chief, was also mortally wounded, besides very many of our brave officers and men were shot down during repeated attempts to storm the works." (Fred Joyce, "Orphan Brigade at Chickamauga," *The Southern Bivouac* 3 [September 1884]:31.)

Teaching Points: Security, reconnaissance, effect of mass casualties.

Stand 4
Lieutenant General Leonidas Polk's Headquarters

(Polk shell pyramid [see map 7])

Situation: 20 September 1863, a.m. Polk's battle headquarters was located behind the center of Hill's Corps and near Hill's headquarters. Because of a series of errors, Hill did not learn of the attack order until his subordinate commanders received their orders directly from Polk around 0630. Although Breckinridge had begun his movement from Alexander's Bridge at about 0300 and was in his attack position around sunrise, the troops had not been fed, and other units to his left were not ready. Hill decided to bring up rations and modify his troops' positions, a decision reluctantly approved by Polk. Delays incident to this decision prevented the "day dawn" attack from beginning until 0930. Bragg was outraged.

Vignette 1: "About 11 o'clock on the night of the 19th, General Polk reached his headquarters near Alexander's Bridge, and stated to me that he was to attack the enemy at daylight the next morning. He instructed me to issue orders at once to Lieutenant-General Hill and Major-General Cheatham to make the attack at that time, directing me to send General Hill's orders to him at Thedford's Ford, where, as he had heard, General Hill's headquarters were established that night. These orders were accordingly issued at 11.30 p.m. General Walker's corps was to be held in reserve. A copy of the orders was handed to him on the spot. During the night the courier who bore General Cheatham's orders returned, bringing back the envelope and reporting that he had delivered the orders. The courier bearing orders to General Hill was directed to Thedford's Ford, and ordered to inquire for and find the general. He failed to deliver his orders. . . . Shortly after daylight (perhaps before sunrise) General Polk instructed me to issue orders directly to Generals Breckinridge and Cleburne to make the attack, notifying them that General Hill could not be found. These orders were prepared and placed in the hands of a staff officer, who was ordered to proceed in haste and deliver them. . . . Immediately afterward another staff officer was dispatched with verbal orders to the same officers and to the same effect. The general then rode to the front accompanied by his staff." (Lieutenant Colonel Thomas M. Jack, Polk's assistant adjutant general, in *O.R.*, vol. 30, pt. 2, 58.)

Vignette 2: "I could find no courier at Alexander's Bridge, and therefore could not find you. My divisions are getting their rations and will not be ready to move for an hour or more. Breckinridge's wagons seem to have got lost between Thedford's Ford and this place. It will be well for you to examine the line from one end to the other before starting.

Brigadier-General Jackson is running from east to west. My line is from north to south. General Cleburne reports that the Yankees were felling trees all night, and consequently now occupy a position too strong to be taken by assault. What shall be done when this point is reached?" (Lieutenant General Daniel H. Hill to Lieutenant General Leonidas Polk, 20 September 1863, in *O.R.*, vol. 30, pt. 2, 53.)

Teaching Points: Command post location, actions prior to an attack, role of personality, relationship among senior commanders.

Stand 5
Colquitt's (Gist's) Brigade

(Colquitt shell pyramid [see map 7])

Situation: 20 September 1863, a.m. Gist's Brigade of Walker's Division arrived at Catoosa Station from Rome, Georgia, during the night of 19—20 September. It then spent the predawn hours escorting an ordnance train to Alexander's Bridge. On arriving at the field, Gist found that Walker wanted him to assume command of the division so that Walker could concentrate on commanding the Reserve Corps. In turn, Colonel Peyton Colquitt moved up to command Gist's Brigade. As the morning attack developed, a gap appeared between Breckinridge's and Cleburne's Divisions. To fill the gap, Hill requested Colquitt's Brigade. Ordered to support Breckinridge, Colquitt formed in battle line, but without skirmishers, and prepared to catch up with Breckinridge. Passing almost through the exact area where Helm's Brigade had met destruction, Colquitt's troops stumbled into the same situation and were enfiladed by Federals behind breastworks just across Battle Line Road. Mortally wounded, Colquitt had only been in command approximately thirty minutes. The shattered command withdrew under covering fire from the remainder of the division and remained in reserve for the rest of the battle. The gap that had dominated Hill's thinking was never fully closed. Casualties in Colquitt's Brigade were 49 killed, 251 wounded, and 36 missing; the percentage of loss was 34.28.

Vignette: "About 11 or 12 we catch it. [Adjutant] Palmer & I were riding together in front of left center, [Colonel] Stevens up on right of Regt, [Major] Jones in front of left, when a tremendous fire opens, right on our left and down our line! [Colonel] Stevens gallops down on his blooded stallion, sword in hand, and sings out 'Change front forward on 10th Co., by companies left half wheel.' The command was given as if he was on parade. While [Adjutant] Palmer, [Major] Jones, and I were getting the left co. into the new line, Palmer was killed & Jones wounded. I got the two left companies in line & got them to lie down &

take shelter as well as they could. They opened a splendid fire. Then men crowded around me in some confusion, and while [Colonel] Stevens and I were bringing up the other companies, every officer behaving splendidly, Stevens' horse was shot, and as he mounted [Adjutant] Palmer's mare, he was badly shot. My heart sank, but the men & officers were true as steel, & I got the 24th pretty well in the new line, all lying down, firing. I did not know Colquitt had been mortally wounded, and wondered why the other regiments did not come up. Riding to the right of the 24th [my horse] got a shot through his neck, and my sword was shot out of my hand. One of Co. 'I' handed it to me, and as I sheathed it a canister shot struck it mid-way up the scabbard, and in a moment more I got a bad wound in my left thigh. I turned the command over to [Captain] Hill, was soon unconscious from loss of blood. . . . Never was a regiment subjected to a severer trial of its discipline than was our gallant regiment when it changed its front under that never to be forgotten flank fire. Here we are, Col., Lieut. Col., & Major, unable to do anything for the comfort of our noble command. Stevens has just said, 'Well, Capers, the men have been taught obedience, & the captains that are left are equal to their duties and responsibilities, & I have no fears for the Regiment.'" (Lieutenant Colonel Ellison Capers, 24th South Carolina Infantry Regiment [Colquitt's left regiment], Unit Files, Chickamauga and Chattanooga National Military Park, Fort Oglethorpe, GA.)

Teaching Points: Lack of security, fog and friction of war, face of battle.

Stand 6
John Beatty's Brigade

(104th Illinois monument [see map 7])

Situation: 20 September 1863, a.m. At dawn on 20 September, the northern (left) flank of the Federal army (Baird's division) ended in the woods south of this field. Recognizing the need to control the road junction at the McDonald house (present Park Visitor Center), Thomas requested the return of Negley's division, which was in line near the Brotherton cabin several division sectors to the south. Rosecrans ordered Negley to move at 0630, but Negley was unable to leave his position until relieved. He immediately dispatched his reserve brigade, Brigadier General John Beatty's unit. The remainder of Negley's division waited until it was relieved by Wood's division. Meanwhile, Beatty moved his brigade into position north of Baird's left and spread his regiments to cover the division sector until the rest of the division arrived. To accomplish this, he deployed two regiments on either side of the ravine between this point and the road junction near the

McDonald house. The 104th Illinois Infantry Regiment was the right-center regiment. At approximately 0930, Beatty's thinly held position was hit by Breckinridge's attack, which routed and scattered the brigade.

Vignette: "Captain Gaw, of General Thomas' staff, brought an order to advance my line to a ridge or low hill (McDonald's house) fully one-quarter of a mile distant. I represented to him that my line was long; that in advancing it I would necessarily leave a long interval between my right and General Baird's left, and also that I was already in the position indicated to me by General Thomas. He replied that the order to advance was imperative; that I would be supported by General Negley. I could not urge objections further, and advanced my line as rapidly as possible toward the point indicated.

"The Eighty-eighth Indiana (Colonel Humphrey), on the left, moved into position without difficulty. The Forty-second Indiana (Lieutenant-Colonel McIntire), on its right, met with considerable opposition in advancing through the woods, but finally reached the ridge. The One hundred and fourth Illinois (Lieutenant-Colonel Hapeman) and the Fifteenth Kentucky (Colonel Taylor), on the right, became engaged almost immediately, and being obstinately opposed, advanced slowly. The enemy, in strong force, pressed them heavily in front and on the right flank, preventing them from connecting with the regiments on their left.

"At this time I sent an aide to request General Baird or General King to throw in a force to cover the interval between their left and my right, and dispatched Captain Wilson, my assistant adjutant-general, to the rear to hasten forward General Negley to my support. The two regiments forming the right of my brigade were confronted by so large a force that they were compelled to halt, and ultimately to fall back, which they did in good order, contesting the ground stoutly as they retired." (Brigadier General John Beatty, in *O.R.*, vol. 30, pt. 1, 368.)

Teaching Points: Key terrain (road junction), hasty defense, extended frontage.

Stand 7
Reserve Corps

(Florida monument [see map 7])

Situation: 20 September 1863, a.m.—p.m. Granger's Reserve Corps began the day at McAfee's Church, guarding the route to Rossville, several miles north of this point. Granger had been told to be prepared to support Thomas. At approximately 1030, Granger heard the sounds of the fight in this vicinity. Within an hour, he placed Brigadier General James B. Steedman's division in motion toward the sound of the guns. While en route, it was forced to deploy out of march column by Forrest's cavalry guarding the Confederate right. Although Whitaker's brigade repulsed Forrest's skirmishers, Forrest effectively used artillery to interdict continued Federal movement down LaFayette Road. Granger and Steedman were then forced to take an alternate route west of the road to join Thomas. This swing to the west ultimately brought Steedman and his two brigades to Snodgrass Hill.

Teaching Points: Initiative, role of reserves.

Stand 8
Slocomb's Battery

(Slocomb's Battery plaque, west of LaFayette Road [see map 7])

Situation: 20 September 1863, a.m. Captain Charles H. Slocomb's Battery (four Napoleons and two 6-pounder James rifles) supported Adams' Brigade in its advance to LaFayette Road. When Adams' regiments turned southward, Slocomb had to decide whether to bring his guns across the ravine in the rear of this position. Disdaining the safety to be found in the rear, Slocomb crossed the ravine and took position here, while Adams' Brigade continued its drive southward behind the Federal flank. After the brigade entered the woods, the Confederate attack stalled when Adams was wounded. As the infantrymen hastily withdrew, Slocomb's Battery covered their retreat.

Vignette: "I was engaged in reforming my regiment when informed that, Brig. Gen. D. W. Adams having been disabled by a wound, the command of the brigade devolved upon me. I at once ascertained that there was no support on the left of the brigade, and ordered the command to form on the rear slope of the hill upon which Capt. C. H. Slocomb's battery, Washington Artillery, was posted. This having been accomplished, I left the line in charge of Col. Daniel Gober, Sixteenth and Twenty-fifth Louisiana Volunteers, and hastened to the left, where I observed several regiments falling back. One of these I at once moved to the support of the line on the left, and directed Captain Labouisse, assistant inspector-general, to bring up another retreating through the woods to the same position. With Captain Slocomb's assistance, he succeeded in placing two regiments in position. They were believed to belong to the brigade on our left. The Thirty-second Alabama Volunteers and Austin's battalion, which had not participated in the charge, but had been ordered to oppose the advance of a column of the enemy's infantry reported on our right and rear, were called in and directed to join the brigade on the right of the battery. It was deemed best to occupy ourselves with the enemy in sight, leaving the cavalry reports for after-consideration. These dispositions had just been made when Major-General Breckinridge reached us and approved them." (Colonel Randall L. Gibson, 13th Louisiana Infantry Regiment, Adams' Brigade, in *O.R.*, vol. 30, pt. 2, 216—17.)

Teaching Points: Command and control, confusion, exploiting success, acceptance of risk.

Stand 9
Bridges' Illinois Battery

(Bridges' Illinois Battery plaque, west of LaFayette Road [see map 7])

Situation: 20 September 1863, a.m. Captain Lyman Bridges' Battery (two Napoleons and four 3-inch rifles) supported Beatty's brigade from this position. At 0930, it fired on Confederates attacking from the northeast. When Beatty's troops were driven back in disorder, Bridges' Battery covered their withdrawal. The battery was then attacked by two brigades on its front and flank. Bridges lost two guns but saved the others and rejoined Negley on Snodgrass Hill.

Vignette: "The enemy were now pouring out of the woods into the field 400 yards in our front and right, being the ground over which our line had advanced but half an hour previously.

"As soon as the battle-flags of the enemy emerged from the woods and there was no doubt about its being the enemy, I opened fire with my full battery, the first rounds with case-shot, afterward with canister.

"His advance was checked for an instant, when, having formed his line again, he steadily advanced upon me.

"While my guns were being worked under the fire of the enemy in our front, some of my men and horses were disabled by a musketry fire from the woods upon my right. While under this fire General Beatty ordered me to retire. I gave the order and found all of the horses of two pieces were either killed or disabled; 5 cannoneers of one of these detachments and 3 cannoneers of the other were disabled.

"The enemy was each moment closing his infantry in upon my front and right, firing as they advanced, and there being no possible chance of getting these pieces off through the woods and brush, I ordered the remnant of my men still at the guns to fall back.

"At this moment my senior first lieutenant, William Bishop, was killed while endeavoring to remove his section from the field, and my horse was killed under me.

"I deem it my duty to state that during this action I had no infantry support whatever. I wish further to state that it was not from any fault of Brigadier-General Beatty, however." (Captain Lyman Bridges, in *O.R.*, vol. 30, pt. 1, 374—75.)

Teaching Points: Initiative, fighting unsupported.

Stand 10
Stovall's Brigade

(60th North Carolina monument, north end of Kelly Field [see map 7])

Situation: When Breckinridge's Division turned south through McDonald Field, Adams' Brigade was west of LaFayette Road and Stovall's Brigade was east of it. Adams' Brigade was met and halted by Colonel Timothy R. Stanley's brigade from Negley's division. Stovall's Brigade brushed past the Federal left flank and reached the northern edge of Kelly Field. Just as Stovall entered the field, which was filled with resting units, trains, and artillery teams, he encountered Van Derveer's brigade of Brannan's division. Van Derveer had been ordered forward from a reserve position farther south and just happened to enter Kelly Field at the same time as Stovall. The movement brought Van Derveer out of the woods north of the Kelly house, facing westward. Finding Confederates on his left flank, Van Derveer wheeled his brigade to the left at the same time that Stovall attacked out of the woods.

Vignette: "Our brigade moved by the left flank northward until opposite Kelly's Field, and then facing eastward, marched through a strip of thick woods and underbrush to the main road, and crossing it, into the field. Here we stood for a moment, the brigade in two lines in rear of and facing east towards, our main line of battle, which, in the woods, was not to be seen from our position. . . . Along the north end of the field, and perhaps 50 yards from the left of our left regiments was a thick woods with underbrush, into which nothing could be seen from our position. We had hardly halted, when, with a crash of musketry and a cloud of gray smoke from the edge of the woods on our left, the air was filled with bullets, and our men began to fall. A change of front to face this attack was instantly commenced, and was executed on the run; but before it brought us face to face with our enemy a good many of our men, and nearly all of the horses in the brigade were killed or wounded. As our men came into line the 2d Minnesota and 87th Indiana rushed down to the edge of the woods, and for a few minutes the opposing lines fired into each others faces, at less than thirty yards distance. But we were at a disadvantage, standing in the open field, while the enemy were protected in the woods, and moreover, the two regiments behind us were fully exposed to the enemy's fire, and unable to return it—so the second line, with guns all loaded, was ordered to pass the first, and then both lines joined in the charge into the woods. The enemy promptly gave up their position at the end of the field and retired back among the trees and brush, where, for a time, they stubbornly resisted our further advance; but after a hot contest of perhaps fifteen or twenty minutes, they withdrew altogether." (Lieutenant Colonel J. W. Bishop, 2d Minnesota Infantry Regiment, "Van Derveer's Brigade at Chickamauga," *Glimpses of the Nation's Struggle* [Minneapolis, MN: Aug. Davis, Publisher, 1909]6:12—13.)

Teaching Points: Use of reserves, initiative, luck, missed opportunity.

Stand 11
Dodge's Brigade

(29th Indiana monument [see map 7])

Situation: 20 September 1863, a.m. Dodge's brigade of Johnson's division had suffered heavily on the previous day and was initially positioned as Johnson's reserve brigade. Early on the morning of 20 September, it was sent to extend the left of Baird's division toward LaFayette Road. Shortly after Dodge reached his position, Breckinridge's attack swept forward. Although one regiment was stopped in front of Dodge, most of Stovall's Brigade passed Dodge's left and headed for the Federal trains area at Kelly Field. Dodge had three options: charge into Stovall's flank, fire into Stovall's flank, or tuck in his own left flank and hope that someone else would deal with Stovall. He chose the third option. Was he right? What would you do?

Teaching Points: Commander's intent, mission, tactical dilemma.

Stand 12
John King's Brigade

(19th U.S. monument [see map 7])

Situation: 20 September 1863, a.m.—p.m. King's brigade held the left of Baird's division and, for a time, represented the Federal army's left flank. King deployed his regiments in four lines behind low breastworks of felled trees. Initially, the 1st Battalion, 18th Infantry, was sent forward to a slight rise just beyond the open space opposite this position. From there, the Regulars enfiladed Helm's Brigade when it advanced westward across their front and mortally wounded Helm.

The regiment then rejoined King's brigade behind the breastworks and participated in the destruction of Colquitt's Brigade late in the morning. King's brigade held this position easily until late afternoon.

King's brigade consisted entirely of Regular regiments. Because of its stand here, the 19th Infantry took the name "Rock of Chickamauga," a name that remains part of its proud heritage today.

Teaching Points: Unit history, strength of the defense, tactical agility, withdrawal under pressure.

Stand 13
Thomas' Defensive Line

(10th Wisconsin monument [see map 7])

Situation: 20 September 1863, a.m.—p.m. While fighting raged east of this location on 19 September, Thomas surveyed the terrain to his rear and selected a defensive position for the next day. The new line ran roughly in a semicircle around the northern, eastern, and southern perimeter of Kelly Field, a few yards into the woods. Most of the eastern face of the line was on rising ground. During the night of 19–20 September, Thomas' men hastily fortified their positions with rocks, logs, and felled trees. Four divisions, each with local reserves, held this line, making it virtually impregnable from the front. For most of 20 September, Baird's, Johnson's, Palmer's, and Reynolds' divisions experienced no difficulty in holding this position, but when the Federal army's right flank collapsed, the Kelly Field line became untenable and had to be evacuated. The evacuation was orderly at first but soon became disorderly, especially at this end of the line.

Vignette: "As soon as it was light we were marched to the front in line with the rest of our brigade, the 15th U.S. Regulars on our left. By this time we were in good fighting condition, everybody was anxious to go ahead and do something. We were about out of provisions too, even water was scarce with us. All the forenoon we were moved around in the woods without seeing the enemy, though bullets came by our heads and several were hit. About noon we were ordered to lay up logs for a breastworks and get behind it quick. The Rebels frequently advanced on our left, while we were rolling logs together, and were repulsed by the regulars. Later the attack became general along our line and we had to work on our breastworks at intervals when we were not being attacked. Gradually we put in logs crosswise to protect ourselves from a flanking fire and by three o'clock we had entrenched ourselves so well that we had no trouble to drive them back. We began to let them get quite near to us before firing and in that way did great execution. We could see the line come up through the underbrush in good order, then waver and a number would fall, the rest would turn and be out of sight in a minute. . . . Our colonel was killed during the afternoon. We were only a handful left of my company. I had sent one man in search of water and he never showed up again. Another had deliberately run away and there were about fifteen men left at dark, or about sun down. It became evident to us early in the afternoon that we were holding an important point which the enemy was determined to take. About this time shells were dropping just in front of us, evidently fired from behind us, then we could see troops marching rapidly behind us, going to our left. We still held the fort when suddenly we were charged from the left, where we supposed our own troops were, and not being sufficiently strong there our fire did not check them and we gave away and made as best we could for our rear, only to find that we were completely surrounded. It was everyone for himself by this time, and I ran to where our flag was held up and supposed that I had escaped when I found that all there were prisoners already, flag and all. Several more of my company were hit running across the field. One of our men was shot dead just as we both raised up to leave the works. He turned to fire once more as we ran but fell dead, struck in the breast. I saw him fall and when we returned after being taken I saw him again, bent over him and found he had never moved." (August Bratnober, 10th Wisconsin Infantry Regiment, Diary, Unit Files, Chickamauga and Chattanooga National Military Park, Fort Oglethorpe, GA.)

Teaching Points: Terrain analysis, strength of position, density of units, planning ahead.

Stand 14
Deshler's Brigade

(Deshler shell pyramid [see map 7])

Situation: 20 September 1863, a.m. Cleburne's Division of Hill's Corps advanced to the attack with Polk's Brigade on the right, Wood's Brigade in the center, and Deshler's Brigade on the left. After being pinched out of line by Stewart's Division, Deshler's Brigade replaced Wood's men on this ridge around midmorning. Taken under heavy fire from the Federal breastworks (Johnson's and Palmer's divisions), Deshler's Brigade could advance no farther and quickly expended most of its ammunition. Coming forward to check his men's ammunition supply, Deshler was hit in the chest by an artillery round and killed instantly. Colonel Roger Q. Mills immediately assumed command of the brigade and held the position, although he was unable to advance.

Vignette: "About 12 m. our supply of ammunition began to give out, and I sent a courier to Brigadier General Deshler to inform him of the fact, and to ask where we could get more. A few minutes after, I saw him coming toward my right, some 40 paces from me, when he was struck by a shell in the chest and his heart literally torn from his bosom. I may pause here and pay a passing tribute to the memory of our fallen chief. He was brave, generous, and kind even to a fault. Ever watchful and careful for the safety of any member of his command, he was ever ready to peril his own. Refusing to permit a staff officer to endanger his life in going to examine the cartridge boxes to see what amount of ammunition his men had, he cheerfully started himself to brave the tempest of death that raged on the crest of the hill. He had gone but little way when he fell—fell as he would wish to fall—in the very center of his brigade, in the midst of the line, between the ranks, and surrounded by the bodies of his fallen comrades. He poured out his own blood upon the spot watered by the best blood of his brigade. . . .

"A messenger from Colonel Wilkes' regiment informed me of the fact soon after General Deshler fell; also that Colonel Wilkes was wounded and not with the regiment. Just at this critical juncture our ammunition was exhausted, and no one knew where to get more. I assumed command, and supposing that the enemy would advance as soon as the firing ceased, I ordered bayonets fixed and the cartridge boxes of the wounded and dead to be gathered, and one round from them to be given to each man to load his gun with, and hold his fire in reserve to repel an assault. While this order was being executed Lieutenant-Colonel Anderson, who was on the left of my regiment, sent Lieutenant Graham to inform me that the four left companies had not been firing. Being at too great a distance from the enemy, he had the good sense to prevent them from wasting their ammunition unnecessarily. I immediately ordered those four companies to the front on the hill, where the fire was hottest, and ordered Lieutenant-Colonel Anderson to take command of them, and hold the hill at every hazard till I could get ammunition and have it distributed. I soon procured the ammunition and refilled my cartridge boxes.

"At this time one of the major-general's staff came to me and informed me that I was ordered to hold the hill on which the brigade was formed; that I was not permitted to advance, and must not retire if it were possible to hold my position. I therefore moved my command at once some 20 or 30 paces to the rear of the crest and on the side of the hill, for cover, leaving a body of sharpshooters behind trees on the top of the hill to keep up a fire with the enemy. . . .

"The troops of my command, both officers and men, behaved with the greatest bravery, coolness, and self-possession during the whole engagement. They advanced with a steady step, under heavy fire of shell, canister, and musketry, to their position, and held it with firmness and unwavering fortitude throughout the fight. Texans vied with each other to prove themselves worthy of the fame won by their brothers on other fields, and the little handful of Arkansas troops showed themselves worthy to have their names enrolled among the noblest, bravest, and best of their State. It is scarcely possible for them to exhibit higher evidences of courage, patriotism, and pride on any other field. They were not permitted to advance and would not retire, but as brave men and good soldiers they obeyed the orders of their general and held the hill. . . .

"I feel it my duty . . . to record here the name of . . . Private William C. McCann, of Company A, Fifteenth Texas Regiment, as worthy of honorable mention for conduct more than ordinarily gallant on the field. . . . Private McCann was under my own eye. He stood upright, cheerful, and self-possessed in the very hail of deadly missiles; cheered up his comrades around him, and after he had expended all his ammunition, gathered up the cartridge boxes of the dead and wounded and distributed them to his comrades. He bore himself like a hero through the entire contest, and fell mortally wounded by the last volleys of the enemy. I promised him during the engagement that I would mention his good conduct, and as he was borne dying from the field he turned his boyish face upon me and, with a light and pleasant smile, reminded me of my promise." (Colonel Roger Q. Mills, 10th Texas Infantry, in *O.R.*, vol. 30, pt. 2, 188—90.

Teaching Points: Face of battle, leadership, coolness under fire.

Stand 15
Edward King's Brigade

(King shell pyramid [see map 7])

Situation: 20 September 1863, a.m.—p.m. The strength of Thomas' line around Kelly Field is clearly apparent, especially when the density of units and availability of local reserves is considered. Facing the four Federal divisions (eleven brigades) were five Confederate divisions (sixteen brigades), but the Confederates never attacked with more than two divisions at a time. Nevertheless, rather than thin his line by extending it to the critical McDonald crossroads, Thomas elected to remain strong in the center and call on Rosecrans for reinforcements. This calculated decision ultimately led to the crisis of the day. When the Federal army's right collapsed, Thomas' line became unhinged from the units beyond the right of Reynolds' division. In response, Reynolds withdrew Edward King's brigade behind his other brigade and placed it in this vacated position. King, a Regular officer commanding a volunteer brigade, was noted for his bravery under fire.

Late in the afternoon, while on horseback supervising his troops, King was struck by a bullet and killed instantly. Soon after this, the troops evacuated the Kelly Field line, taking King's body with them. Reynolds' division left first, with a wild charge to the northwest, followed by Palmer, Johnson, and Baird, in that order.

Vignette: "While we were lying behind our hastily built breastworks, lying as flat upon the earth as we could flatten ourselves, to avoid the fire from the enemy's musketry which was turned upon us, I saw some fine looking man, clad in a large blue overcoat and cape, walk cooly and slowly down our line, as composed as if he was in a parlor. When he came to my company I said to him, 'I would like to know who you are?' He said, 'Col. King of Reynolds' Division.' He stopped and looked toward the enemy, telling us how they were moving, which he could see as he was standing up, and leisurely passed on. It was a great wonder to me he was not killed instantly but I think it worried me more than it seemed to worry him." (Captain Orville T. Chamberlain, 74th Indiana Infantry Regiment, Medal of Honor winner, in a letter to Henry Boynton, 26 November 1895, Chickamauga and Chattanooga National Military Park, Fort Oglethorpe, GA.)

Teaching Points: Terrain analysis, leadership, withdrawal under pressure.

Stand 16
S. A. M. Wood's Brigade

(Alabama monument [see map 8])

Situation: 20 September 1863, a.m. This monument, commemorating the participation of Alabama troops, is near the dividing line between the two wings of Bragg's army. Cleburne's Division of the Right Wing and Stewart's Division of the Left Wing overlapped in this vicinity. Cheatham's Division, the army's largest, was pinched out of the line entirely. No coordination took place between the wings during the night and little during the morning of 20 September. As a result, the Confederates wasted a great deal of combat power when six brigades were unable to join the fight at this point.

Teaching Points: Coordination, boundaries.

Stand 17
Longstreet's "Grand Column"

(Bushrod Johnson monument [see map 8])

Situation: 20 September 1863, a.m. During the morning, Longstreet rearranged his lines slightly while waiting for Polk's Right Wing to

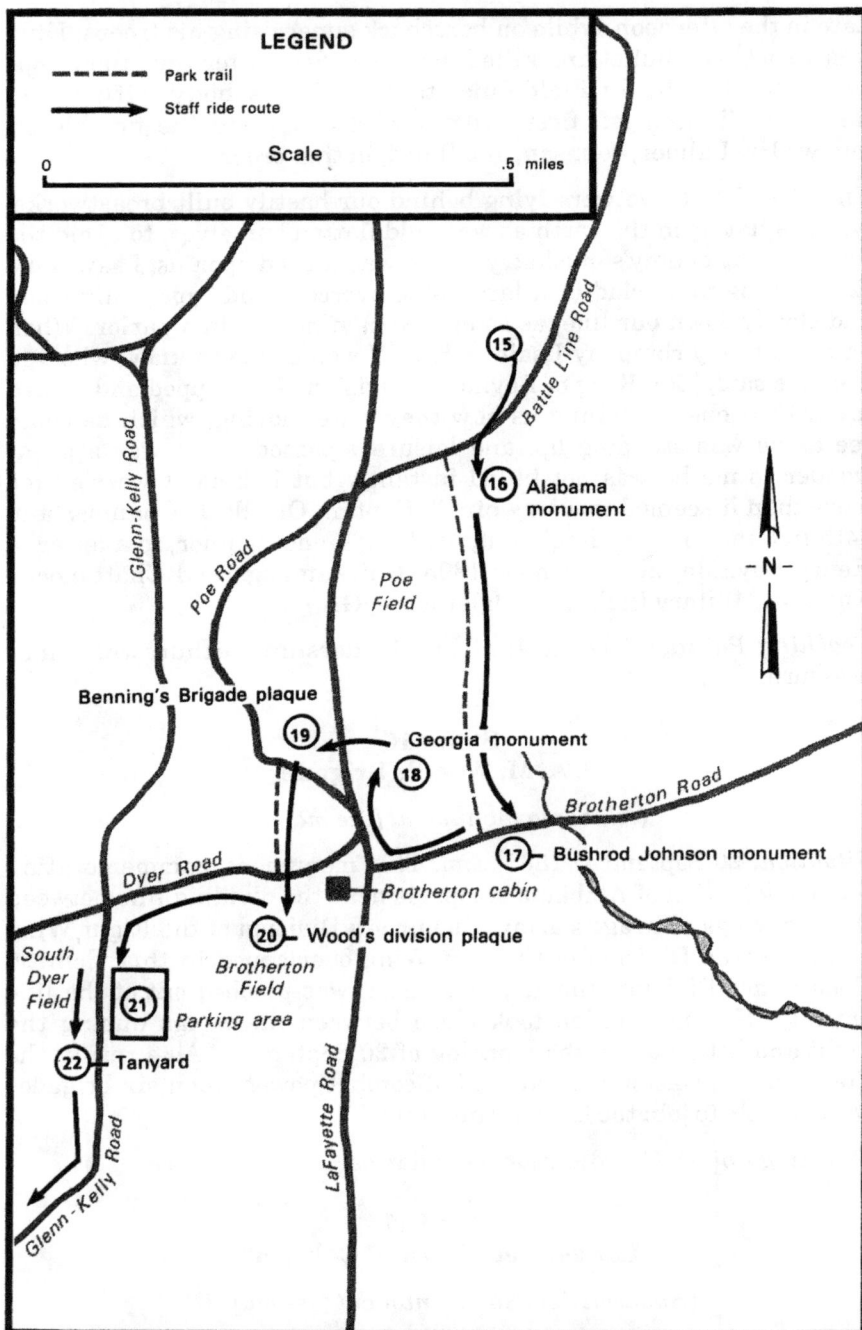

LEGEND

- - - - - Park trail

———▶ Staff ride route

Scale

0 _____ .5 miles

Map 8. Day 2, stands 16 through 22

begin the attack. When it proved impossible to get Hood's Division into the front line, this part of Longstreet's wing became a "grand column" of three divisions. As acting corps commander, Hood commanded this 11,000-man column, with Bushrod Johnson's Division at the head. Northern born and of Quaker heritage, Johnson had been a division commander for less than a week. His division began moving forward at 1110. Figure 6 shows what the column looked like when it was finally formed.

Teaching Points: Coordinated attack, assault column versus linear attack, commander's intent, mission, objective.

Stand 18
Stewart's Division and Benning's Brigade

(Georgia monument [see map 8])

Situation: 20 September 1863, a.m. Although part of Longstreet's Left Wing, Stewart's Division responded to a direct order from Bragg and began its attack prematurely. Entering Poe Field, Stewart found himself caught within an angle of the Federal line. The division was bloodily repulsed but not before Stewart's left briefly crossed LaFayette Road. By the time Longstreet's column began its attack, Stewart's Division was in retreat. When the column moved forward, fire from Brannan's Federal division caused part of Hood's second echelon, Benning's Brigade, to veer northward to take Brannan's line in flank. Benning gained the southern end of Poe Field and stalled there. Beyond supporting some artillery batteries that fired on the Federals in Kelly Field, Benning's Brigade participated no further in the battle.

Vignette 1: Stewart's attack. "In about fifteen minutes after I took command, the regiments still being shielded by rudely constructed breastworks of logs and bushes hastily thrown up, an order came to forward from the brigadier-general commanding. I repeated the command, and my boys moved with alacrity over our works. Having gained some 60 or 70 yards, I ordered double-quick with the yell, which was obeyed to a man, the men almost assuming the run, still keeping an unbroken line. Firing from the enemy's sharpshooters and batteries was constant in our front, but more injury was inflicted upon us from the left flank, there seeming to be no support on the left of Bate's brigade. On emerging [from the] woods in[to] an open, shrubby field we could see our stubborn foe definitely resisting our march across this field. Grape, canister, and musket-shot here greatly decimated my command, but swerving not it bore steadily onward. Near the center of

N

Brotherton cabin

LaFayette Road

Approximately 700 yards

Johnson's Division
2,950 men

50/1 TN   7 TX   17 TN   23 TN   25 TN   44 TN   39 NC   25 AR   4/31/4 AR   2 AR   1 AR
Johnson (Fulton)   McNair

Gregg (Sugg) (-)
30 TN   10 TN   3 TN   41 TN

Hood's (Law's) Division
3,900 men

3 AR   1 TX   4 TX   5 TX   15 AL   4 AL   47 AL   48 AL   44 AL
Robertson   Law (Perry)

15 GA   20 GA   17 GA   2 GA
Benning

McLaws'
(Kershaw's)
Division
3,700 men
Total—10,550 men

13 MS   18 MS   21 MS   17 MS   2 SC   3 SC   3 SC   15 GA   3 SC   7 SC   15 SC   8 SC
Humphreys   Kershaw

Two-letter state abbreviations are used in unit designations.

Not to scale.

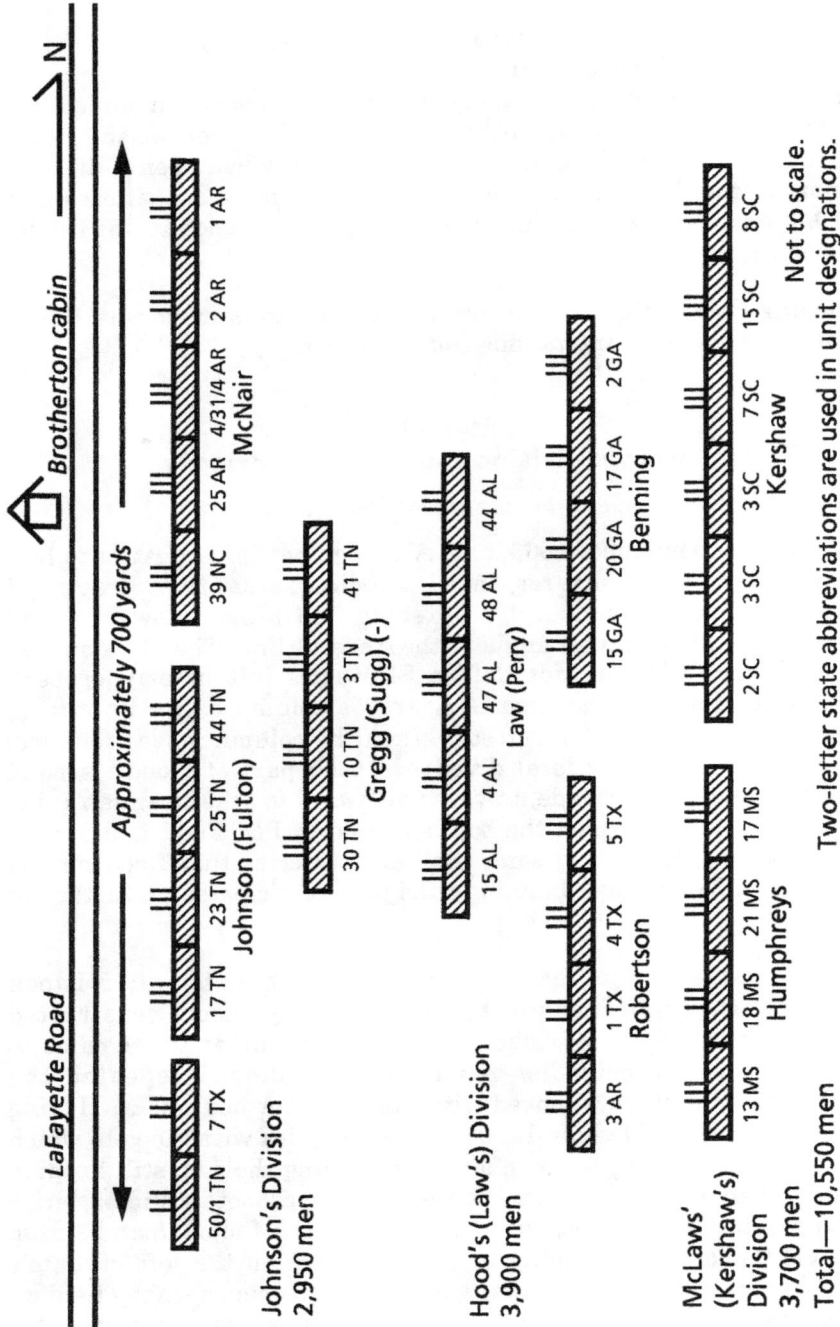

Figure 6. The grand column

this field I was disabled and fell from a wound received just below the knee, which for many minutes paralyzed my left leg. I observed as I fell that both colors were steadily moving forward through this dreadful ordeal of shell, shot and fire. I lay here many minutes entirely conscious, but unable to rise. Many of my companions lay wounded and dead around me. Upon seeing some of my command returning through this same field and reporting orders having been issued to fall back, I, with their assistance, reached the position the regiment formerly held before this murderous charge. . . . After some little time I sent forward a party to bring or to assist in bringing the wounded from the field. I feared they would burn, as the grass and bushes were on fire." (Lieutenant Colonel R. Dudley Frayser, 15/37th Tennessee Infantry Regiment, in *O.R.*, vol. 30, pt. 2, 397.)

Vignette 2: Benning's attack. "Shouts began to go up from the right, and we knew it was our boys. It soon spread along the whole line. The enemy was firing away all along the line. On the left, musketry was heavy but retiring, the cannon seeming to play a small part in it. The yell of victory became louder and fiercer as the sun declined. There seemed to be no enemy in our front. General Benning ordered me to go forward a short distance to see what was in front. We had become afraid of firing into our own men and being fired into by them. I went as ordered and came to the Chattanooga road. I was sure I saw the enemy sending men across attempting to reinforce their left. I rode back and told what I had seen. General Benning suggested artillery and sent a courier to the division commander for it. In a few minutes a number of pieces were sending shell down that road like lightning. I watched . . . the shot as it would rise, curve over and explode at the very spot aimed among the demoralized Federals. Why were we not pressed forward then? Evidently they were broken and would leave the field, perhaps were leaving then. Incompetent fools were allowing the fruits of a great victory to fly from us. I can see now how we idled and waited." (Benjamin Abbott, Benning's adjutant and inspector general, to Green Haygood, 26 September 1863, quoted in Mills Lane, ed., *"Dear Mother Don't Grieve About Me. If I Get Killed, I'll Only Be Dead." Letters From Georgia Soldiers in the Civil War* [Savannah, GA: Beehive Press, 1977], 275.)

Teaching Points: Coordination, timing of attacks, leadership, face of battle.

Stand 19
Brannan's Division

(Benning's Brigade plaque, west edge of Poe Field [see map 8])

Situation: 20 September 1863, a.m. During the night of 19—20 September, Brannan was ordered to put two brigades into line between Reynolds' and Negley's divisions. About 1100, Stewart's attack hit Brannan's right brigade (Connell's) but was repulsed. Shortly thereafter, Benning's attack struck Connell's brigade on the front and right flank. By 1130, the head of the Confederate column had outflanked Brannan's position and begun to attack it in the flank and rear. Brannan's division attempted to reorient its line to face this new threat but was soon forced to withdraw. Benning's Brigade then occupied this ground.

Vignette: "I came upon a young officer and found he was mortally wounded and suffering very much. I saw at once he would die & asked if I could do anything for him. He replied, 'I am dying. Wash me clean and bury me decently.' I promised him all I could under the circumstances. . . . I had him moved in the hut and in less than an hour he died. As far as I could I complied with his request and marked his grave with a board on which I carved his name [Lieutenant Colonel D. J. Hall] with my knife. . . . As soon as I found Hall suffering so much, I took from my pocket a small vial of morphia and gave him about half a grain, and he was relieved very soon of pain and died easily and rationally. I had carried this little vial during all my service, fearing I might be wounded and left suffering on the field. It had never served me, but it was now to relieve an enemy.

"These little incidents . . . serve to show . . . that we cannot yet be barbarians. In my own heart before the battle I felt very bitter against these men who had invaded our soil . . . and yet in the hour of victory we soldiers were touched with pity for these wounded and dying enemies. It was not the place to discuss right and wrong; it was simply a question of humanity." (Benjamin Abbott to Green Haygood, 26 September 1863, quoted in Mills Lane, ed., *"Dear Mother Don't Grieve About Me. If I Get Killed, I'll Only Be Dead." Letters From Georgia Soldiers in the Civil War* [Savannah, GA: Beehive Press, 1977], 275—76.

Teaching Points: Flank attacks, face of battle, inhumanity of war.

Stand 20
Wood's Division

(Wood's division plaque, west edge of Brotherton Field [see map 8])

Situation: 20 September 1863, a.m. Early in the morning, Wood was directed to replace Negley's division in the Federal line. Wood's division consisted of two of his own brigades (Colonel George P. Buell's and Colonel Charles G. Harker's), plus Colonel Sidney M. Barnes' brigade from Van Cleve's division. Barnes was on the left next to Brannan's division, Harker in the center, and Buell on the right. At 1045, Wood received a message from Rosecrans ordering him to close up on Reynolds as fast as possible and support him. The message assumed that Brannan's division was not in line and that a gap existed between Wood and Reynolds. Brannan, however, remained in place, forcing Wood to move to the rear first, then pass behind Brannan before joining Reynolds. Although Rosecrans was only 600 yards behind him, Wood did not request clarification of the order. Assured by Major General Alexander M. McCook that the gap thus created would be filled, Wood obeyed the order at once. Barnes and Harker cleared the position safely, but Buell's brigade was caught in motion and shattered by Longstreet's advance. Hood's column then poured through the gap and split the Federal army.

Teaching Points: Clarity of orders, obedience to orders, responsibility of subordinates, coordination procedures, role of personality.

Stand 21
Bushrod Johnson's Division

(East edge of south Dyer Field [see map 8])

Situation: 20 September 1863, a.m. Beginning its advance around 1110, Bushrod Johnson's Division led Hood's Corps across LaFayette Road, past the Brotherton cabin, and into the gap left by Wood's division. Although Johnson's right brigade was slowed somewhat by fire from Brannan, the remainder of the division smashed through Buell's brigade and broke out into the broad Dyer Field. Caught while in motion, numerous Federal units scattered to the rear in panic. Bringing up his reserve brigade, Johnson pressed forward in pursuit.

Vignette: "Our lines now emerged from the forest into open ground on the border of long, open fields, over which the enemy were retreating, under cover of several batteries, which were arranged along the crest of a ridge on our right and front, running up to the corner of a stubble-field, and of one battery on our left and front posted on an elevation in the edge of the woods, just at the corner of a field near a peach orchard and southwest of Dyer's house. The scene now presented was unspeakably grand. The resolute and impetuous charge, the rush of our heavy columns sweeping out from the shadow and gloom of the forest into the open fields flooded with sunlight, the glitter of arms, and onward dash of artillery and mounted men, the retreat of the foe, the shouts of the hosts of our army, the dust, the smoke, the noise of fire-arms—of whistling balls and grape-shot and of bursting shell—made up a battle scene of unsurpassed grandeur. Here General Hood gave me the last order I received from him on the field, 'Go ahead, and keep ahead of everything.' How this order was obeyed will be best determined by those who investigate all the details of this battle." (Brigadier General Bushrod R. Johnson, in *O.R.*, vol. 30, pt. 2, 457—58.)

Teaching Points: Agility, initiative, mission-type orders.

Stand 22
Deas' Brigade

(Tanyard [see map 8])

Situation: 20 September 1863, a.m. At approximately the same time that Johnson began his attack, Major General Thomas C. Hindman, who was on Johnson's left, also began his advance. Hindman's assault caught Davis' division moving to fill the gap left by Wood. Both of Davis' brigades broke and were driven to the rear. Meanwhile, Sheridan's division, which had been ordered north to support Thomas, was moving into the southern end of Dyer Field. Although Sheridan's leading brigade was also broken, Brigadier General William H. Lytle's brigade made a stand on a hill west of the field. There, it halted the advance of Brigadier General Zachariah C. Deas' Brigade of Hindman's Division. Deas received some assistance from an unexpected source when the 15th Alabama Infantry from Brigadier General E. McIver Law's Brigade arrived in his rear.

Vignette: "At the first fire of the enemy, so unexpected and near, my regiment exhibited a momentary hesitancy and wavering, but upon my ordering 'charge,' it moved at double-quick, and, with a shout, scaled the enemy's works, and pursued their panic-stricken and shattered ranks through the woods and undergrowth until, reaching the borders of another open field, the enemy were discovered behind some houses, potash-works, and rail breastworks. At this point there was not even a momentary hesitancy, but with an increased shout and rapidity of step, we drove the enemy from these works with great slaughter, and pursued them through the open field some 250 yards to an elevated skirt of heavy open woods, where we again came upon him and drove him in utter confusion from two pieces of artillery and other breastworks. There being no horses near, we were compelled to leave the pieces of artillery on the ground. Just here, the Fifteenth Alabama Volunteers, who were to the right of my rear, began a heavy enfilading fire upon me. I immediately discovered they were friends, and ordered my colors back to the edge of the open field, and waving them, discovered to the Fifteenth Alabama their error, upon which they came up by a left-oblique march in fine order, and, joining in with my regiment, we continued to pursue the enemy for some distance across fields, woods, roads, and hills, until we passed over the telegraph road of the enemy into the hills, where we passed also other pieces of artillery, and found we had utterly cut the enemy's lines asunder." (Colonel Samuel K. McSpadden, 19th Alabama Infantry Regiment, Deas' Brigade, in *O.R.*, vol. 30, pt. 2, 334.)

Teaching Points: Confusion of battle, improvisation, leadership, amicicide.

Stand 23
Manigault's Brigade

(Large field east of Wilder Tower [see map 9])

Situation: 20 September 1863, p.m. Brigadier General Arthur M. Manigault's Brigade represented the left of Hindman's Division. Manigault's Brigade crossed LaFayette Road about 1120, advancing to the west. The three left regiments of the brigade were crossing this field when they were engaged by Wilder's brigade, assisted by the 39th Indiana Mounted Infantry. Manigault expected support on his left from Colonel Robert C. Trigg's Brigade of Brigadier General William Preston's Division, but he did not receive it. Wilder's firepower quickly decimated Manigault's regiments and forced them all the way back across LaFayette Road. After re-forming the brigade, Manigault again advanced, this time to the northwest.

Vignette: "The fire we got under when first we became engaged in the morning exceeded anything I ever before or after experienced. The air seemed alive with bullets, and an officer afterwards remarked to me, 'General, all you had to do was to hold out your hand, and catch them.' Out of about 800 men that came into the full fury of this storm, nearly 300 were shot down in a space of time certainly not exceeding three minutes." (Arthur L. Manigault, in R. L. Tower, ed., *A Carolinian Goes to War* [Columbia: University of South Carolina Press, 1983], 103.)

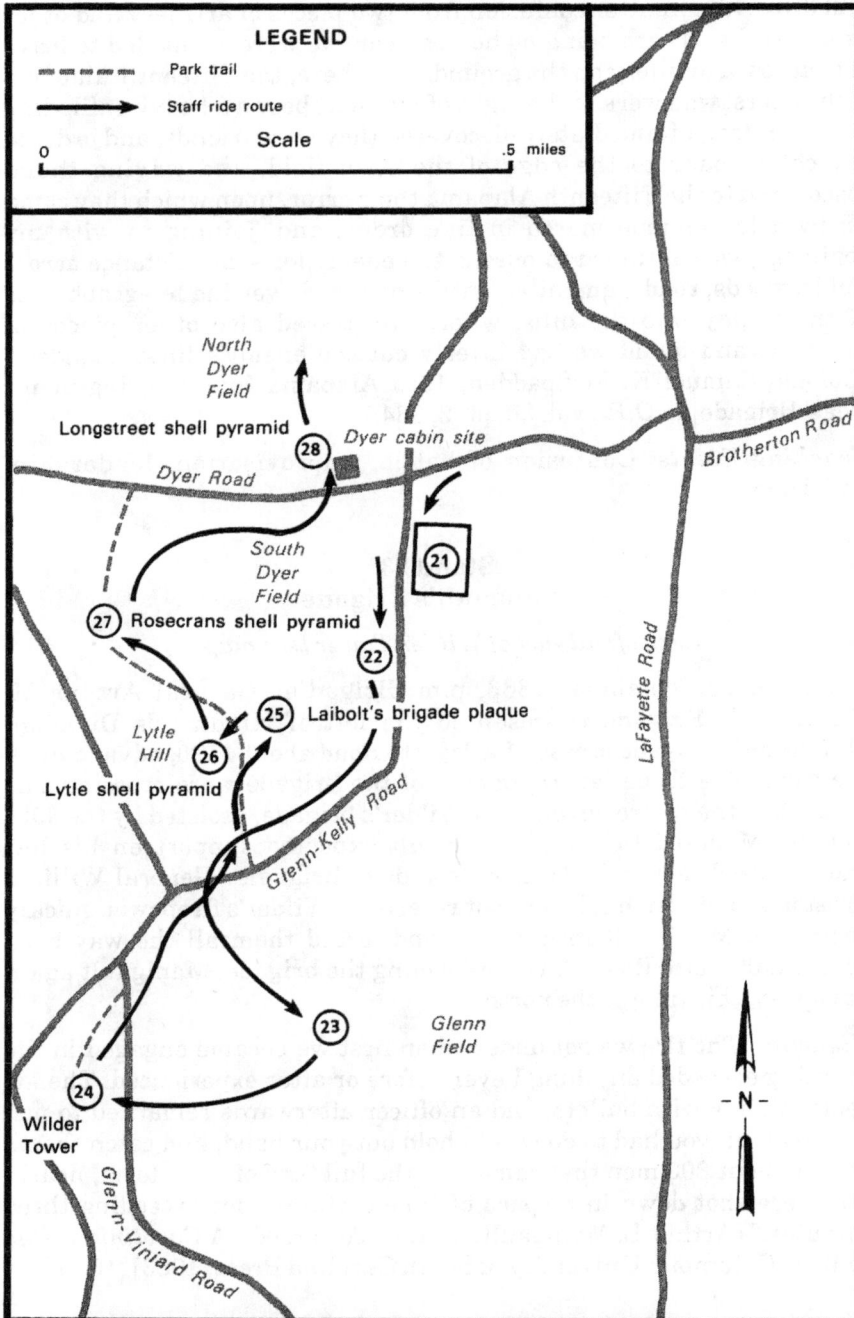

LEGEND

— — — Park trail

——→ Staff ride route

Scale

0   .5   miles

Map 9. Day 2, stands 23 through 28

Teaching Points: Psychological and physical effects of massive firepower.

Stand 24
Rosecrans' Headquarters

(Wilder Tower [see map 9])

Situation 1: 19—20 September 1863. At about 1130 on 19 September, Rosecrans and his staff moved here from Crawfish Spring, accompanied by his headquarters guard, the 15th Pennsylvania Cavalry Regiment, the 10th Ohio Infantry Regiment, and the 1st Battalion Ohio Sharpshooters. Charles Dana, the assistant secretary of war, also accompanied Rosecrans. A signal corps detachment laid a telegraph wire to Rossville, with a branch to Thomas' position. From this position on the right of the army, Rosecrans atttempted to control the battle by using the sound of the guns as a guide. That night, Rosecrans assembled his commanders at the cabin of Eliza Glenn, a widow, to determine the following day's actions. Unable to mount an attack and unwilling to retreat, Rosecrans believed he still controlled the key terrain. He therefore elected to defend the same position for one more day with Thomas' XIV Corps on the left, McCook's XX Corps on the right, and Major General Thomas L. Crittenden's XXI Corps in reserve. Granger, commanding the Reserve Corps at Rossville, was unable to attend the meeting. Although those present were completely exhausted, the conference lasted into the early hours of the morning and was followed by impromptu entertainment. Early on the morning of 20 September, Rosecrans rode north to inspect his line, having left orders for his headquarters to move northward behind the right center of the army.

Vignette: "Widow Glenn's log house was, like all the houses of that kind, provided with a large fire-place, in which a bright fire was burning—perhaps the only fire within 15 square miles, on account of the order given not to light fires on that night for any purpose. The remains of a candle were stuck into a reversed bayonet, lighting up dimly the battle map, which was spread out upon a cartridge box. The fire in the large chimney place flared up from time to time, illuminating the faces of those who took part in the council of war. There was Major-General Rosecrans, sitting, in full uniform and sword, on the edge of a rustic bed frame, bending toward the center of the scantily furnished room, listening and sometimes talking to General Thomas, who sat near the fire, occupying the only chair which had been left by the widow Glenn. There were other generals, commanding corps, divisions and brigades, some sitting on the rough-hewn barren floor, with their backs against the walls, while others stood up. It was a picture well worth painting—this the last council of war on the field of battle—the dim, flaring light, the faces of the men who directed the battles, the bright metallic shine of the swords and uniforms, when the fire flared up in the chimney." (Captain W. C. Margedant, topographical engineer, in L. W. Mulhane, *Memorial of Major-General William Stark Rosecrans*, Mount Vernon, OH, 1898, 68—69.)

Teaching Points: Headquarters location, command style, commander's intent, sleep plan.

Situation 2: 20 September 1863, a.m. After Rosecrans' departure, Sheridan's division occupied this position with Wilder's brigade in reserve on its right rear. Sheridan's troops remained here fortifying the position until about 1130, when they were ordered to move to the northeast to assist Davis' division. As Manigault's Brigade advanced across Glenn Field, Wilder's brigade, which occupied the hill, easily repulsed the attack. Wilder then prepared to attack northward into the flank of Longstreet's Left Wing. He was prevented from doing so by the arrival of Assistant Secretary of War Dana, who demanded to be taken to Chattanooga. By the time Dana was disposed of, the opportunity to attack the Confederate flank was past, and Wilder's brigade withdrew from the field.

Vignette: "Lieutenant-Colonel Thruston, chief of General McCook's staff, soon appeared and notified me that the line to my left was driven back and dispersed, and advised that I had better fall back to Lookout Mountain. I determined, however, to attempt to cut my way to join General Thomas at Rossville, and was arranging my line for that purpose when General Dana, Assistant Secretary of War, came up and said that 'our troops had fled in utter panic; that it was a worse rout than Bull Run; that General Rosecrans was probably killed or captured;' and strongly advised me to fall back and occupy the passes over Lookout Mountain to prevent the rebel occupancy of it. One of my staff officers now came up and reported that he had found General Sheridan a mile and a half to the rear and left, who sent advice to me that he 'was trying to collect his men and join General Thomas at Rossville, and that I had better fall back to the Chattanooga Valley.' I now, at 4 p.m., did so with great reluctance, bringing off with me a number of wagons loaded with ammunition, a great many ambulances, a number of caissons, a great many stragglers, and quite a number of straying beef-cattle." (Colonel John T. Wilder, in *O.R.*, vol. 30, pt. 1, 449.)

Teaching Points: Flexibility, audacity, leadership.

Stand 25
Laiboldt's Brigade

(Laiboldt's brigade plaque, east edge of Lytle Hill [see map 9])

Situation: 20 September 1863, a.m. Colonel Bernard Laiboldt's brigade of Sheridan's division was the first unit to support Davis' division. As Laiboldt moved behind Davis, his regiments found themselves in the path of Davis' troops as they were driven back in disorder. Davis' panic spread to Laiboldt's brigade and threatened the remainder of Sheridan's division as well. Only Lytle's brigade stood firmly; then, when its commander was killed and its flanks turned, it too withdrew to the west.

Vignette 1: "Our position was in an open field, about thirty rods wide; then came a pine thicket, furnishing a fine protection for the rebs to advance through. At twelve o'clock M. [noon] we were ordered to fix bayonets and charge across the field and meet the advancing foe, coming eight lines deep toward us. On reaching the edge of pine-grove, orders came for us to halt and fire. This was amid a shower of balls flying from our front, right, and left. Sergeant Lewis, regimental color-bearer, fell just before we halted, wounded in the leg. I sent Sergeants Newlin and Brown to carry him from the field. Neither of the three was heard of after the battle. Art. Terrell fell dead within a yard of me, pierced through the temples by a ball. Enoch Smith thought to be killed, and John Bostwick wounded; I ordered Sam Boen to carry him off, but he did not get him, for before reaching him Boen had to leave to save his own life. The flag was taken up by one of the color guard, immediately after Lewis fell; he soon fell; taken up by another; he fell. Then a retreat was ordered. I grasped the colors and carried them off the field. I was not struck, only by a buckshot, and that lodged in my haversack, checked by striking my tin cup. The regiment retreated 'pell mell;' could not be rallied to be effective again during the charge." (Captain Tilmon D. Kyger, Company C, 73d Illinois Infantry, Laiboldt's brigade, in W. H. Newlin, *A History of the Seventy-Third Regiment of Illinois Infantry Volunteers*, Springfield, IL, 1890, 225.)

Vignette 2: "Our brigade now wheeled into line. As we advanced up the hill, we met the 2d brig. [Laiboldt's] coming back in confusion. Gen. Sheridan spoke cheerfully telling us to keep cool and we would surely check them but I am almost ashamed to own that I thought far different. We gained the crest of the hill and layed down. On come the Rebs yelling like demons. We received them coolly and our fire soon checked them in front, but soon a more serious difficulty arose. They were flanking us and we had nothing to oppose to them. Slowly we fell back to the foot of the hill, we then rallied and charged up the hill but were again flanked and forced by the mere power of numbers to fall back. This time they planted their colors on a line in rear of our regt. Six times in succession did our regt rally and charge up the hill and was as often compelled to fall back by their flanking us. Oh if we had but a single Div to protect our flanks we could hold them. We find no trouble in forcing them back in our front. When we were rallying the sixth time Old Rossie, McCook & Sheridan rode up in our rear and Rosecrans said charge them once for Old Rossie boys, but it was of no use, we had done all that could be done without support." (John Ely, Private, 36th Illinois Infantry Regiment, Lytle's brigade, Diary, Unit Files, Chickamauga and Chattanooga National Military Park, Fort Oglethorpe, GA.)

Teaching Points: Confusion, panic.

Stand 26
Lytle's Brigade

(Lytle shell pyramid [see map 9])

Situation: 20 September 1863, a.m. Lytle's brigade of Sheridan's division moved from the Widow Glenn's cabin and occupied this position about 1130. The brigade was following Laiboldt's brigade, also of Sheridan's division, which advanced into the southern end of Dyer Field to support Davis' division. When the Confederate attack crushed Davis and Laiboldt, Lytle tried to rally his brigade on this ridge. For a brief time, he was successful, until he was hit three times (in the spine, foot, and mouth) and killed. When the brigade was driven from the field, Lytle's body was left behind. The Confederates who occupied the ground recognized Lytle, a well-known poet from Cincinnati, and placed a guard over the body. Eventually, Lytle's remains were returned to the Federals for burial.

Vignette: "While riding through the woods yesterday I came upon the dead body of General Lytle, of Cincinnati, Ohio. I recognized him at once. We had been friends in the old days, as our fathers were before us. A Confederate soldier was standing guard over the body. From what I learned from the guard it appeared that a brigade of Alabama troops, under command of General Zach. Deas, while advancing in the charge Longstreet made, had struck Lytle's brigade. The latter was behind rude entrenchments of logs and rails. These had been swept by Deas's men, driving Lytle's back. About this time Lytle was struck, and his men, retreating, left his body where he fell. He was recognized by his uniform as a general officer, and Captain West, of General Deas's staff, took charge of his watch and papers, and placed the sentinel on guard over the body. Dismounting, I asked the man his instructions, and he replied, 'I am here to take care of this body and to allow no one to touch it.' 'All right,' I said. 'I hope you will do it.' I then looked to see where Lytle had been struck, and found that one ball had entered his right instep, and another his mouth, knocking out some teeth, and making its exit in the back of the neck. When he was killed he was smoking a cigar. He was dressed in fatigue uniform. His shoulder-straps—one star—indicated the rank of brigadier-general. He wore high riding-boots, a regulation overcoat, dark kid gloves. While standing beside the body, General Preston rode up, and asked, 'Who have you there?' I replied, 'General Lytle, of Cincinnati.'—'Ah!' said General Preston, 'General Lytle, the son of my old friend, Bob Lytle! I am very sorry indeed it is so;' and he dismounted and was much affected. After asking the sentinel his instructions, and receiving the same answer I had obtained, he said to him, 'See that you do it, my man.' We then mounted and rejoined the division, which had halted on the road.

"Lytle's body was returned in an ambulance to his friends, under flag of truce, and, as he was known to the gentlemen of the Southern army to be a gallant and chivalrous soldier, as well as the author of the beautiful poem entitled, 'Anthony and Cleopatra,' all were sincerely grieved at his taking off. As the ambulance containing the remains passed on its way to the enemy's lines the road was lined with officers and men, who testified their respect for the dead General by removing their hats and looking on silently." (William Miller Owen, *In Camp and Battle With the Washington Artillery* [Boston, MA: Tichnor and Co., 1885], 286—87.)

Teaching Point: Humanity in war.

Stand 27
Field Headquarters, Army of the Cumberland

*(Rosecrans shell pyramid,
knoll at west edge of south Dyer Field [see map 9])*

Situation: 20 September 1863, a.m. On returning from riding the lines, Rosecrans established his field command post on this ridge by midmorning. The position was hardly vacant: the 15th Pennsylvania Cavalry waited behind the ridge, a large ordnance train was parked in the rear, Van Cleve's division and Crittenden were on the ridge to the north. As the battle grew in intensity, Rosecrans ordered Van Cleve to move and support Thomas. Crittenden asked and received permission to accompany his last division, and he followed it eastward. At this point, Wood's division began to pull out of line in response to the infamous order, while Davis and Sheridan also put their commands in motion. When Hood's Corps raced through the gap, Rosecrans quickly rode to rally Sheridan's division, but when that attempt failed, he lost heart and left the field, eventually following Dry Valley Road to McFarland's Gap.

Vignette: "From an elevation overlooking that part of the field, the Cincinnati Gazette reporter watched the remnants of the Union right and center—five brigades all told—heading for McFarland's Gap, completely disorganized. Said a reporter for a Louisville newspaper: The scenes I witnessed here were such as can be but poorly comprehended from description. . . . Men came madly dashing on, careless of curses and entreaties, consternation pictured in their every feature. . . . Guns, knapsacks, blankets, cartridge-boxes, everything that could impede the flight were cast away." (J. Cutler Andrews, *The North Reports the Civil War* [Pittsburgh, PA: University of Pittsburgh Press, 1955], 455—56.)

Teaching Points: Command post location, leadership, psychological impact of unexpected events.

Stand 28
Longstreet's Left Wing

(Longstreet shell pyramid [see map 9])

Situation: 20 September 1863, p.m. By early afternoon, Longstreet's Left Wing, especially Hood's massive column, had achieved far greater success than could have been expected. Moving forward in the track of Johnson's brigades, Longstreet and his small staff established a headquarters at this spot. While Longstreet watched, Confederate units pursued fleeing Federals in all directions. Gradually, a center of Federal resistance began to grow on Snodgrass Hill. About 1400, while his units paused to reorganize, Longstreet, Major General Simon B. Buckner, and their staffs ate lunch. During the meal, a messenger from Bragg called Longstreet to army headquarters to report on his situation. Longstreet rode to Bragg's headquarters in the woods a mile away, reported his success, and asked for reinforcements, even though the wing reserve, Preston's Division, was uncommitted. Bragg refused the request for reinforcements, so Longstreet returned to his headquarters around 1500 and ordered Preston forward. Confederate units had already begun to assault Snodgrass Hill, and Longstreet did not change their focus. The result was a series of uncoordinated and unsuccessful frontal assaults. No effort was made to outflank either end of the Snodgrass Hill line, although both flanks were open.

Vignette: "3 p.m. While our division was resting at a halt, under an occasional fire of a battery posted on Horseshoe Ridge, I rode to the right and rear of our line, and there saw Gens. Longstreet and Buckner, seated on a log, eating their lunch, which their boy had brought to them. General Longstreet hailed me, and asked for a pipeful of tobacco. I produced my little bag, and he filled his meerschaum pipe. I then asked him what he thought of the battle; was the enemy beaten or not?

"'Yes,' he said, 'all along his line; a few are holding out upon the ridge yonder, not many though. If we had had our Virginia army here, we could have whipped them in half the time. By the by,' he added, 'don't you want some guns for your command? I think my men must have captured fifty to-day.'

"I told him I did, and would like to make a change for better ones, those we have being very indifferent.

"'Well,' he said, 'you can have as many as you want.'

"'General, hadn't you better put that in writing?'

"He laughed, and instructed Latrobe to write an order for the guns." (William Miller Owen, Preston's staff, *In Camp and Battle With the Washington Artillery* [Boston, MA: Tichnor and Co., 1885], 281.)

Teaching Points: Branches and sequels, seeing the battlefield.

Stand 29
Harker' Brigade

(North end of north Dyer Field [see map 10])

Situation: 20 September 1863, a.m.—p.m. Harker's brigade was the second of Wood's units to move out of line after Wood received the order to move north and support Reynolds. The brigade marched behind Brannan's division northward through Dyer Field. Just as Harker left the field, he was halted by Wood and reoriented, first east and then south. Quickly changing front, the brigade formed in line of battle across the northern end of Dyer Field. From this position, Harker directed a local counterattack that routed parts of Law's and Johnson's Divisions. While the Confederates were rallying in the woods east of the field, Hood rode to assist them and was seriously wounded. The counterattack advanced to about this position. Brigadier General Joseph B. Kershaw's Division then charged Harker, forcing him back over the crest of the hill northwest of Dyer Field and, finally, to Snodgrass Hill.

Vignette 1: "The enemy fled in confusion, and disappeared for a time. We pursued 400 yards and lay down behind a prostrate fence, which was upon another less tenable, but parallel ridge to the first one. This

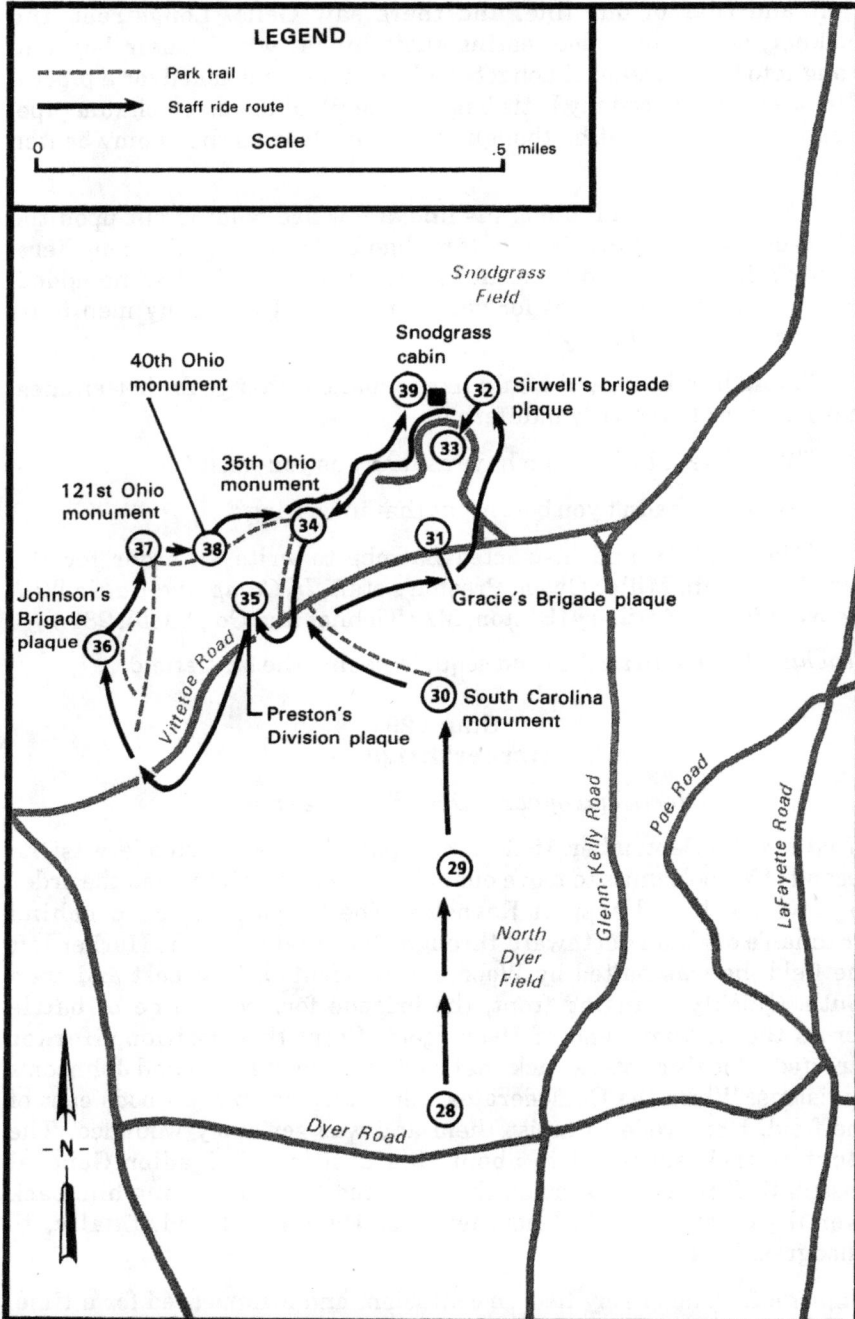

Map 10. Day 2, stands 29 through 39

ridge also rose into a wooded hill 150 yards to our right. The other regiments of the brigade soon prolonged my line to the right and left. Another line of the enemy, more formidable than the first, appeared in the distance, moving upon us. The terrible splendor of this advance is beyond the reach of my pen. The whole line seemed perfect and as if moved by a single mind. The musketry soon became severe and my losses heavy; the color-sergeant severely wounded, the standard shot in two the second time, and the colors riddled with balls. The regiment to my left gave way, and then that upon my right. My Company A, thinking this meant for all to retire, arose and faced to the rear, but almost instantly resumed their position. The enemy came on and themselves prolonged my line to the right, occupied the wooded hill there, and enfiladed my line with a destructive fire. Lieutenant King, commanding Company C, fell dead, when Sergt. Alson C. Dilley assumed command of his company. Lieutenant Barnes, commanding Company E, went down with a broken thigh, and Lieut. E. P. Evans was placed in command. Captain Yeomans carried off a ball in his upper leg, but he remained with his company during the battle under severe pain. Numbers fell dead and more were seriously wounded, but the line was firmly maintained. Lieutenant Clark coolly remarked, 'They can kill us, but whip us never.' Seeing no relief, I retired the regiment to the ridge in rear. In doing so, some troops passed obliquely through my right wing, which caused a little confusion there, but the ranks were closed immediately, and the crest occupied where ordered by General Wood." (Colonel Emerson Opdycke, 125th Ohio Infantry Regiment, in *O.R.*, vol. 30, pt. 1, 708.)

Vignette 2: "We wrestled with the resolute foe till about 2:30 p.m., when, from a skirt of timber to our left, a body of Federals rushed down upon the immediate flank and rear of the Texas brigade, which was forced to suddenly change front. Some confusion necessarily arose. I was at the time on my horse, upon a slight ridge about three hundred yards distant, and galloped down the slope, in the midst of the men, who speedily corrected their alignment. At this moment Kershaw's splendid division, led by its gallant commander, came forward. . . . Kershaw's line formed . . . an angle with that of the Federal line, then in full view in an open space near the wood. I rode rapidly to his command, ordered a change of front forward on his right, which was promptly executed under a galling fire. With a shout along my entire front, the Confederates rushed forward. . . . About this time I was pierced with a Minie ball in the upper third of the right leg; I turned from my horse upon the side of the crushed limb and fell—strange to say. . .—into the arms of some of the troops of my old brigade, which I had directed so long a period, and upon so many fields of battle." (John

Bell Hood, *Advance and Retreat* [Philadelphia, PA: Press of Burke & M'Fetridge, 1880], 63—64.)

Teaching Points: Use of terrain, confusion, initiative, importance and timing, loss of commander.

Stand 30
Kershaw's Brigade

(South Carolina monument [see map 10])

Situation: 20 September 1863, p.m. Kershaw, commanding McLaws' Division (Kershaw's and Brigadier General Benjamin G. Humphreys' Brigades) forced Harker's brigade back from Dyer Field and advanced over this hill into the ravine to the north. From there, Kershaw's Brigade unsuccessfully assaulted the Federal troops on Snodgrass Hill and were driven back to cover in the ravine. Kershaw, who was on foot, and his men were pinned in the ravine. Humphreys' Brigade briefly moved into position on the Federal flank but did not recognize its opportunity and was permitted by Longstreet to withdraw a short distance. Kershaw's men kept up the fire against Snodgrass Hill, but Humphreys' troops remained inactive for the remainder of the day.

Vignette: "In our first general advance. . . as the regiment reached the brow of the hill, just before striking the enemy's breastworks, my company and the other color company, being crowded together by the pressure of the flanks on either side, became for the moment a tangled, disorganized mass. A sudden discharge of grape from the enemy's batteries, as well as from their sharpshooters posted behind trees, threw us in greater confusion, and many men were shot down unexpectedly. A Sergeant in my company, T. C. Nunamaker, received a fearful wound in the abdomen. Catching my hand while falling, he begged to be carried off. 'Oh! for God's sake, don't leave me here to bleed to death or have my life trampled out! Do have me carried off!' But the laws of war are inexorable, and none could leave the ranks to care for the wounded, and those whose duty it was to attend to such matters were unfortunately too often far in the rear, seeking places of safety for themselves, to give much thought or concern to the bleeding soldiers. Before our lines were properly adjusted, the gallant Sergeant was beyond the aid of anyone. He had died from internal hemorrhage." (D. Augustus Dickert, 3d South Carolina Infantry Regiment, Kershaw's Brigade, in *History of Kershaw's Brigade* [Newberry, SC: Elbert H. Aull Co., 1899; reprint, Dayton, OH: Press of Morningside Bookshop, 1976], 279.)

Teaching Points: Terrain appreciation, location of commander, face of battle.

Stand 31
Gracie's Brigade

(Gracie's Brigade plaque, foot of Snodgrass Hill [see map 10])

Situation: 20 September 1863, p.m. When Kershaw's attack stalled in the ravine south of Vittetoe Road, Preston's Division was ordered forward from the vicinity of the Brotherton cabin at about 1600. With Brigadier General Archibald Gracie's Brigade on the right and Colonel John H. Kelly's on the left, the division assaulted Snodgrass Hill at about 1630. The attacks continued for more than one and one-half hours. By sundown, Gracie's Brigade had gained a toehold on the crest of the hill but could advance no farther. Of the 2,003 officers and men Gracie carried into action, 725 became casualties (90 killed, 608 wounded, and 27 missing)—36 percent casualties in 1 1/2 hours.

Vignette: "In order to reach the breastworks where the Federals were posted we had to pass over the top of a ridge several hundred yards from their position, then go down a slope into a ravine, and up the steep side of Snodgrass Hill. The moment we appeared on this ridge we were greeted by a ferocious volley of musketry. We had advanced only a few steps when Lieutenant Colonel Holt was mortally wounded. I ordered him carried to the rear. A few minutes later I was struck by a glancing ball on the inside of my left ankle. . . . We had not advanced to the bottom of the ravine before many of our men had fallen, some killed outright, more wounded. . . . When I saw how we were being butchered and discovered no ranking officer of the battalion taking charge, I endeavored to get the men to move forward without waiting to fire and reload. I saw General Gracie coming along in the rear of the line on foot. I ran to him and asked what orders he wished me to carry. He said: 'Tell the men for God's sake to go forward.' I then ran along the line repeating the General's order. The roar of the guns was so deafening that the men could scarcely hear me. While we were moving up the hill toward the breastworks and the battalion was not moving rapidly enough, I went in front of the line and motioned the men to come on faster. It occurred to me that I did not want to be shot in the back. Just after I had turned to face the enemy a Minie ball struck my left breast a little below the collar bone. . . . Lieutenant Joe Barker and one or two others ran to me and asked what they could do for me. I answered: 'Never mind me. Go on faster!'" (John Massey, Adjutant, 1st Battalion, Alabama Legion, *Reminiscences* [Nashville, TN: Publishing House of the M.E. Church, South, 1916], 186—87.) (John Massey was nineteen years old at Chickamauga. When his unit was consolidated with another after the battle, he lost his position and returned to college.)

Teaching Points: Courage, leadership, effect of mass casualties.

Stand 32
Thomas' Headquarters and Negley's Mission

(Sirwell's brigade plaque, east end of Snodgrass Hill [see map 10])

Situation: 20 September 1863, p.m. Thomas' field headquarters was at the foot of the reverse slope of this hill. During the second day of the battle, Thomas rode back and forth between this point and his Kelly Field positions issuing orders and inspiring confidence by his presence. During one of Thomas' absences, he diverted Negley and his remaining brigade to this vicinity. In a verbal message delivered by Captain Gaw, one of Thomas' aides, the corps commander ordered Negley to gather all available artillery and orient it toward the house near McDonald crossroads to cover the corps' left flank. Negley eventually gathered at this point approximately 50 guns, 50 limbers, 50 caissons, 600 horses, plus 2 infantry regiments and 4 companies (700 to 800 men). In addition, he gathered many of the ammunition wagons that had been withdrawn to the rear as the battle progressed. Negley quickly discovered that, from this point, the guns could fire into the fields near the McDonald house but could not control the crossroads. Fearing the loss of the artillery and ammunition because of the collapse of the Federal right, Negley made a fateful decision to save the guns. Around 1330, he and his remaining infantry left the field with the guns just before Brigadier General James B. Steedman arrived with two fresh brigades of troops and 95,000 rounds of ammunition. Although he saved the artillery, Negley ultimately lost his command because of his actions.

Vignette: "On the evening of the 12th I prescribed for Maj. Gen. James S. Negley; also on the two days following, which days he was on duty; the 15th and 16th he was confined to his bed, having a severe attack of diarrhea. On the 17th the command moved, he riding his horse, with the precaution to have an ambulance near to use if necessary. He arrived at camp very much exhausted. The evening of the 18th the command moved; he was up and on duty most of the night. The 19th he was busy with the command all the day, it being engaged in battle at morning and evening. This night he was much worn down from exposure, want of sleep, rest, and sickness, and was obliged to get what rest he could that night to enable him to be on duty the day following; he slept in bivouac this night with the command. I think he had labored during the day and evening all that he was physically able to endure. He arose on the morning of the 20th feeling very unwell, but was on duty all the day until late at night. On the 21st and 22d he was on duty with the command, but not really able to be so. During the whole time he was really unable to be on duty, being a fitter case for a bed patient than one being under treatment and yet laboring." (Surgeon R. G. Bogue, Negley's surgeon, in *O.R.*, vol. 30, pt. 1, 343.)

Teaching Points: Command post location, improvisation, command decisions.

Stand 33
Defense of Snodgrass Hill

(Yard of Snodgrass cabin [see map 10])

Situation: 20 September 1863, p.m. Harker's brigade reorganized here on the eastern end of Snodgrass Hill after being driven from Dyer Field. Harker took advantage of the strongest position available and deployed his four regiments in two lines. On Harker's right, remnants from Brannan's, Negley's, Van Cleve's, and Wood's divisions gradually extended the Federal line to the west. Harker's men and the associated fragments fended off the initial assaults of Kershaw and later attacks by Hindman's and Preston's Divisions. Eventually, other troops extended the Federal line even farther westward.

Vignette 1: "General Brannan, having rallied a part of his command, it, together with fragments of other commands, formed on the hill at my right, while my brigade formed in two lines to the left of Brannan, fronting to the south and nearly perpendicular to Reynolds' division, then on my left.

"It will be seen that the right and a part of the center and Van Cleve's division being completely swept away, our line now reduced and in the form of a crochet [hook], must resist nearly the whole rebel force in our front, or itself be swept away, and the great Army of the Cumberland—the pride of the nation—be utterly routed. Our brave troops, appreciating the importance of their position, promised to hold to the last. Nobly did they redeem their promise. From about 1 p.m. until nightfall this line was repeatedly attacked, but remained unbroken. . . . It affords me great pleasure to refer to the grand volley firing of the regiments of my brigade on the afternoon of the 20th. I have remarked before that while occupying a part of the 'key of the position' they were formed in two lines.

"They were lying a little below the northern or eastern crest of the hill; the front line firing by volley would retire, when the rear would move forward and execute the same movement. Thus a continuous volley fire was kept up for some length of time. This system was resumed whenever the rebels made their appearance in force, and repulsed them on every occasion. It had never before been my fortune to witness so grand an example of effective musket firing." (Colonel Charles G. Harker, in *O.R.*, vol. 30, pt. 1, 695.)

Teaching Points: Terrain appreciation, rallying of broken units.

Note: A wide variety of evidence indicates that Federal plaques and monuments in the vicinity of Snodgrass Hill (Horseshoe Ridge) are incorrectly located. While correct placement is difficult to determine, it appears that most Federal markers should be shifted approximately one brigade front to the west.

Stand 34
Van Derveer's Brigade

(35th Ohio monument [see map 10])

Situation: 20 September 1863, p.m. On this knob, fragments from several brigades made their stand. Anchoring their right in the saddle to the west was another relatively intact brigade, Van Derveer's brigade of Brannan's division. Although Confederate forces made repeated assaults, this position was also held until after sunset. Monuments to Confederate units on the forward slope of the hill just below the crest indicate how near the Confederates came to breaching the Federal line.

Vignette: "The slope in our front was now well cleared of underbrush, and we could see the gray legs of the front line, as, in regular step, they crossed the road at the foot and commenced the ascent, a second line following, each containing more men than were in the thin, single line of defenders. 'Don't waste any cartridges now, boys,' was the only instruction given, (and this was quite unnecessary) as our line commenced firing—and the men in gray commenced falling; but they seemed to bow their heads to the storm of bullets, and picking their way among and over their fallen comrades who already encumbered the slope by hundreds, they came bravely and steadily on; as however they approached nearer, and the firing in their faces grew hotter and more deadly, they seemed to lose the assuring touch of elbows, and as the vacancies rapidly increased, they began to hesitate—'Now we've got'em, see'em wabble' were the first words that passed in our lines since the firing had begun—then they halted and commenced firing wildly into the tree tops, then turned and rushed madly down the slope, carrying the second line with them." (Lieutenant Colonel J. W.

Bishop, 2d Minnesota Infantry Regiment, "Van Derveer's Brigade at Chickamauga," *Glimpses of the Nation's Struggle* [Minneapolis, MN: Aug. Davis, Publisher, 1909] 6:17.)

Teaching Points: Defense, individual bravery.

Stand 35
Preston's Division

(Preston's Division plaque, foot of Snodgrass Hill [see map 10])

Situation: 20 September 1863, p.m. After Longstreet failed to receive reinforcements from Bragg, he committed his own reserve, Preston's Division, to the assault on Snodgrass Hill (Horseshoe Ridge). Gracie's Brigade attacked the eastern end of the ridge, while Kelly's Brigade assaulted the sector west of this position. On being repulsed, Kelly's and Gracie's men rallied under the slight protection provided by the road at the foot of the ridge. Initially, Trigg's Brigade was held in reserve, but it eventually joined the battle west of Kelly around sunset. Preston's Division carried into action 4,078 officers and men, most of them untested in battle. The division suffered a total of 1,338 casualties, a loss of 33 percent in 1 1/2 hours.

Vignette: "The position held by the enemy is a very Gibraltar, its sides precipitous, and difficult to climb, but the day is wearing away, and no time should be lost. Longstreet determines to put in his Tenth legion, Preston's 5,000, and sends for the General, and orders an immediate advance. 'It shall be done,' replies Preston, and the command Attention! is given down the lines of the three brigades. The young troops spring to their arms; it is their first baptism of fire, and if they are whipped they won't know it.

"The lines are dressed, and at the commands, Forward! forward! the 5,000 move on in beautiful order. The enemy opens a terrific fire; but up the hill our men advance; now the enemy's bullets begin to tell upon the lines, and men fall to the right and left, dead and wounded; but the rest move on undismayed, firing rapidly as they advance; but the artillery and infantry fire is too hot for them, although they have fought most gallantly, and, halting under the crest where some protection is had, the lines are dressed, and General Preston, reassuring them by his presence, rides down the lines and coolly examines each man's cartridge-box, and says, 'Men, we must use the bayonet,—the bayonet,—we will give them the bayonet!' The men, one and all cry out, 'Go ahead, General! we are not whipped yet!' Confidence restored by the General's cool demeanor, and with the enthusiasm of the troops raised to the highest pitch, Preston rides to the front and centre of his line, and leads the way with splendid dash and bravery, waving his cap above his head, his gray hair floating in the breeze.

"With fierce yells and shouts the troops advance." (William Miller Owen, *In Camp and Battle With the Washington Artillery* [Boston, MA: Tichnor and Co., 1885], 282—83.)

Teaching Points: Attack over difficult terrain, effect of heavy losses, leadership.

Stand 36
Johnson's (Fulton's) Brigade

(Johnson's Brigade plaque [see map 10])

Situation: 20 September 1863, p.m. At about 1400, Bushrod Johnson's Division advanced toward the western end of Horseshoe Ridge. Gregg's Brigade was on the right and Johnson's (Fulton's) Brigade on the left, with Dent's and York's Batteries in support. Fulton gained the ridge and was turning Brannan's flank when he was struck and repulsed by the advance of Steedman's fresh division. After falling back to reorganize, Fulton and Gregg assaulted again, this time supported by McNair's Brigade and part of Manigault's Brigade of Hindman's Division. The fighting continued until Steedman withdrew around sunset.

Vignette: "My line was again ordered forward, the enemy being within 50 yards of the batteries and but one piece firing. Here commenced a most desperate struggle for the possession of this ground—[Horseshoe] Ridge. The battle raged furiously and the tide of success wavered in the balance. Charge after charge was repulsed, only to rally and charge again. Again our line fell back, and the untiring, indomitable, and determined officers rallied again their fast thinning ranks and again moved forward. Here officers and men behaved most gallantly. Appeals to love of home and wounded comrades and the peril of the moment were made, and never did men rush forward more eager, daring, desperate, and defiant. The enemy's treble lines now began to show that our fire was terribly effective upon them. Our cartridge boxes had been replenished as required, and still we were nearly out. Again more ammunition was supplied and the conflict continued hot and heavy. The enemy was now slowly giving back, hard pressed by our now shattered remnants. Another charge, with the yells of the men and cheers of the officers, and forward we pressed, only to discover the victory was ours and the enemy in full retreat. This series of engagements lasted four long hours, during which Johnson's brigade won many laurels and an imperishable name." (Colonel John S. Fulton, commanding Johnson's Brigade, in *O.R.*, vol. 30, pt. 2, 476.)

Teaching Points: Difficulty of terrain, offensive spirit, initiative, leadership.

Stand 37
Steedman's Division

(121st Ohio monument [see map 10])

Situation: 20 September 1863, p.m. Late in the morning, Granger, commanding the Reserve Corps near Rossville, decided to move with three brigades toward the sounds of battle. Granger and two brigades under Steedman reached the vicinity of the Snodgrass cabin around 1400. Their timely arrival was one of the most dramatic moments of the battle. Thomas first considered placing Steedman on the Federal left but quickly changed his mind and sent the two brigades to the right of Van Derveer's brigade. Steedman's brigades, led by Brigadier General Walter C. Whitaker and Colonel John G. Mitchell, raced up the reverse slope of the ridge and ran headlong into Bushrod Johnson's Confederate troops advancing up the other side. After a severe struggle, Steedman's troops held the crest of the ridge for the remainder of the afternoon. Around sunset, the two Federal brigades quietly withdrew northward and joined the retreating Army of the Cumberland.

Vignette: "My men fought them by firing until out of ammunition and when I sent to Colonel Mitchell for orders and was directed to hold the hill at the point of the bayonet, I bid farewell to home and friends and the 113th. I gave the order and the men obeyed with spirit, and over the hill we went, but the Rebels seemed not very anxious, and willing to stay back, and I let the men fall back over the crest and lie down and with the few men from the cover of trees who had supplied themselves with cartridges from the boxes of their dead and wounded comrades, we kept the hill until night when we received orders to fall back. I went into the fight with 345 men and officers, counting myself, and lost in the fight 127 killed, wounded and missing as follows—killed 22, wounded 95, missing 10. No comment is necessary on these figures and no one can begin to realize what it required for men to withstand it." (Colonel Darius B. Warner, 113th Ohio Infantry Regiment, Mitchell's brigade, in a letter home, 27 September 1863, Unit Files, Chickamauga and Chattanooga National Military Park, Fort Oglethorpe, GA.)

Teaching Points: Timing, luck, leadership.

Stand 38
The "Lost Regiments"

(40th Ohio monument [see map 10])

Situation: 20 September 1863, p.m. Late in the day, when Thomas left Snodgrass Hill (Horseshoe Ridge) to supervise the Federal withdrawal from Kelly Field, he left Granger in charge of the troops on Snodgrass Hill. Granger, who had spent most of the afternoon serving as a cannoneer in the yard of the Snodgrass cabin, departed the field not long after Thomas, leaving subordinate commanders to their own devices. By nightfall, Wood, Brannan, and Steedman all had withdrawn their commands from the ridge safely. Left behind, probably inadvertently, were three regiments, the 22d Michigan, 21st Ohio, and 89th Ohio. All three had been detached from their parent commands earlier and had been serving temporarily with unfamiliar units. As their ammunition ran out, the regiments received orders to hold their position with bayonets. The withdrawal of Federal forces on the flanks of these regiments permitted Kelly's and Trigg's Brigades of Preston's Division to surround the three regiments and eventually capture them in the darkness.

Vignette: "I was unable to communicate with General Negley, and no general officer was designated to whom I might report. But we continued to hold our position. The cartridge-boxes of our killed and wounded were carefully searched, also the hospitals for any ammunition that might be carried there in the cartridge-boxes of our wounded, and by this means obtained sufficient ammunition to meet the enemy in their assault upon our position about 5 o'clock.

"In this assault the enemy crossed the ravine in our front and carried his banners up the hill to with[in] 20 yards of our line. He was repulsed, and did not retire in good order. During the afternoon a battery had range upon our position, inflicting some damage upon us, also setting fire to the leaves and brush in our front, and the enemy advanced under cover of the smoke. The wounded, under cover of our fire, were removed.

"A heavy line of skirmishers continued to annoy us, and a sharp fire upon this line exhausted our ammunition a short time before sundown, at which time the Second Regiment Minnesota Volunteers relieved us. A further search for ammunition resulted in finding one round each for the men composing my command, which had now become very much reduced in numbers.

"At this time Colonel Van Derveer (who assumed command) ordered me to occupy a position on the extreme right, from which a part of our line had just been driven by the enemy. In obedience to the order we occupied the position and captured 9 prisoners. A sharp fire from the enemy forced us back, but we regained our position and held it until dark, at which time a brigade of four regiments, under Colonel Trigg, moved upon us and overwhelmed us.

"Simultaneous with this movement of the enemy, which was upon our right flank and rear, we received a fire from the enemy, who had also opened upon our left, which took effect both upon the enemy on our right and ourselves. During the misunderstanding thus occasioned, a part of my men escaped under cover of the night. Colonel Van Derveer having withdrawn the troops under his command, my command was unsupported, and both flanks were exposed. Thus we lost our stand of colors, which were made sacred to us by the blood of many comrades who fell in their defense and for their honor on other fields as well as on the unfortunate field of Chickamauga." (Major Arnold McMahan, 21st Ohio Infantry Regiment, in *O.R.*, vol. 30, pt. 1, 389.)

Teaching Points: Fate of attached units, leadership.

Stand 39
End of the Battle

(Snodgrass cabin [see map 10])

Situation: 20 September 1863, p.m. As darkness fell on Snodgrass Hill, Federal units withdrew quietly northward, leaving the battlefield to the Confederates. Too exhausted to mount a meaningful pursuit, the Army of Tennessee halted where it had fought. Most soldiers tried to sleep, but many attempted to aid the wounded or sought lost comrades. Losses on both sides were appalling.

Vignette: "Night finally put an end to the outrageous havoc. So thorough was the exhaustion of the troops from long continued battle, that at the close of this day there was indeed a cessation of the storm. Gracie's brigade having been so terribly shattered, was relieved at dark. The troops constituting the relief occupied the position, laid down upon their arms, and slept amid the dead. It was scarcely possible to distinguish the living from the dead, so profound was the slumber of the former. Silence reigned upon the battle-field!— comparative silence. An attentive ear would have caught, here and there, a low plaintive wail, sob or sigh, from the countless wounded. Being one of the few survivors of the 1st Battalion who escaped unharmed, the writer was called upon to go with a squad to search out and convey to the field-hospital the wounded of the command. This task occupied until past midnight. The appearance of that battle-ground by moonlight is never to be forgotten.

"At about midnight the last of the wounded of the 1st Battalion was being carried from the battleground, and the writer accompanied the litter to the field-hospital. Here was presented a scene which surpassed in horror, if possible, the battlefield itself. At this point was congregated the wounded who had covered a large area of the field. A lurid glare was cast by scores of flaming rail fires upon the pale, agonized features of the many victims of the battle. There was no canopy for the sufferers save the heavens—no couch save the uneven earth—and no pillows save billets of wood—.... I stood in one spot and witnessed many death scenes occurring simultaneously. From the field hospital we hurried, sick at heart, to the rendezvous of the command. After much difficulty, we found the remnant of the 1st Battalion [62 left of 230]—now a mere squad—huddled around a single fire. Each face was powder stained and haggard to the last degree. There was but little talking; our thoughts were of our fallen comrades. As a specimen of what was spoken around that fire that night, I give the following: 'Jim, poor fellow, was shot down at the first volley; he fell forward on his face and never spoke.' 'Bird, they say, is mortally wounded; he was a good boy.' 'During the fight I passed brother Archy lying on his side, wounded. I could not stop to help him. The poor fellow smiled faintly on me, and summoning all his strength, waived his hand towards the enemy.'" (Lewellyn A. Shaver, 1st Battalion, Alabama Legion, Gracie's Brigade, *A History of the Sixtieth Alabama Regiment, Gracie's Alabama Brigade* [Montgomery, AL: Barrett & Brown, Publishers, 1867], 17—19.)

Teaching Point: Cost of the battle.

IV. SUPPORT FOR A STAFF RIDE TO CHICKAMAUGA

1. Information and Assistance.

a. The Staff Ride Team of the Combat Studies Institute at Fort Leavenworth has conducted the Chickamauga Staff Ride as an elective for the Command and General Staff Officer Course for a number of years. The Staff Ride Team has designed Staff Rides for numerous military units and groups and can provide advice and assistance on every aspect of the Chickamauga campaign. The committee's resources include extensive files, detailed knowledge of the campaign and battle, and familiarity with the Chickamauga and Chattanooga National Military Park and surrounding area.

Address: U.S. Army Command and General Staff College
Combat Studies Institute
ATTN: ATZL-SWI
Fort Leavenworth, Kansas 66027-6900

Telephone: AUTOVON 552-3414/3831
Commercial (913) 684-3414/3831

b. The National Park Service maintains the Chickamauga and Chattanooga National Military Park, which includes Visitor Centers at Chickamauga and Lookout Mountain. The National Park Service staff can provide advice and assistance to any group desiring to visit the park. The Visitor Center at Chickamauga includes a museum with an impressive collection of shoulder arms and a book store. Several picnic areas are located throughout the park, but restroom facilities are located only at the Visitor Center. Because some restrictions on the use of the park exist, any military group should coordinate its plans with the park headquarters before the actual battlefield visit.

Address: Superintendent
Chickamauga and Chattanooga National Military
Park
P.O. Box 2126
Fort Oglethorpe, Georgia 30742

Telephone: (404) 866-9241

2. Logistics.

a. Meals.

(1) No facilities exist within the park itself, but numerous restaurants, grocery stores, and fast-food establishments can be found in Fort Oglethorpe, which is within minutes of the park Visitor Center.

Although the park prohibits a private business from catering within the park, it is permissible for a group to purchase and bring in food. The park requires visitors to use one of the existing picnic areas unless they otherwise arrange with the park headquarters.

(2) Military groups should consider offering morning and afternoon coffee or soda breaks and eating the noon meal in the park. It is possible to bus participants to Fort Oglethorpe for lunch, but this practice can be time consuming. In addition, leaving the battlefield for lunch tends to break the participants' concentration on the battlefield study.

(3) One person with a car or van can easily support any planned breaks or meals. Most of the fast-food restaurants in Fort Oglethorpe offer take-out service and hot or cold drinks (make arrangements a day in advance for large groups). Consider bringing such items as insulated beverage jugs. Also, soft drinks and snacks can be purchased more cheaply at a home station commissary than in local stores. Do not forget standard items such as trash bags.

b. Lodging.

(1) Numerous motels can be found in the surrounding area. Perhaps the largest concentration is near the East Ridge Exit on Interstate 75, east of Chattanooga. Many motels offer reduced rates for large groups.

(2) For military groups, the National Guard Training Center at Catoosa, Georgia, can provide billeting, based on training commitments.

Address: Catoosa Area Training Center
Route 1, Box 1836
Tunnel Hill, Georgia 30755-9998

Telephone: (404) 935-4897

3. Medical.

The nearest civilian hospital is in Fort Oglethorpe, within minutes of the Visitor Center. No military medical facilities exist in the immediate area.

4. Other Considerations.

a. Ensure that the group has proper clothing, including raincoats, gloves, etc., for inclement weather. Because the trails are often wet and muddy, comfortable boots or hiking shoes are best.

b. Make provisions for fluids because drinking water is available only at the Visitor Center. Supplies to treat blisters might also prove useful, even for groups accustomed to walking.

c. Check with the park headquarters on the condition of trails immediately prior to the visit. Recent rains may have flooded trails or washed out small foot bridges, requiring a modified route.

d. Maintain good relations with the park officials by coordinating unusual requirements well in advance. Be sure to obey the rules.

e. Traffic along roads in the park is often heavy. Stress safety in crossing roads, and walk along the shoulders whenever possible.

APPENDIX A
Order of Battle: Army of the Cumberland

Organization of the Army of the Cumberland, commanded by Maj. Gen. William S. Rosecrans at the Battle of Chickamauga, Georgia, 19—20 September 1863.

General Headquarters
1st Battalion Ohio Sharpshooters, Capt. Gershom M. Barber
10th Ohio Infantry, Lt. Col. William M. Ward
15th Pennsylvania Cavalry, Col. William J. Palmer

XIV ARMY CORPS
Maj. Gen. George H. Thomas

General Headquarters

Provost Guard
9th Michigan Infantry, Col. John G. Parkhurst (Not engaged; guarding trains and performing provost duty)

Escort
1st Ohio Cavalry, Company L, Capt. John D. Barker

1ST DIVISION
Brig. Gen. Absalom Baird

1st Brigade
Col. Benjamin F. Scribner

38th Indiana, Lt. Col. Daniel F. Griffin
2d Ohio, Lt. Col. Obadiah C. Maxwell, Maj. William T. Beatty, Capt. James Warnock
33d Ohio, Col. Oscar F. Moore
94th Ohio, Maj. Rue P. Hutchins
10th Wisconsin, Lt. Col. John H. Ely, Capt. Jacob W. Roby

2d Brigade
Brig. Gen. John C. Starkweather

24th Illinois, Col. Geza Mihalotzy, Capt. August Mauff
79th Pennsylvania, Col. Henry A. Hambright
1st Wisconsin, Lt. Col. George B. Bingham
21st Wisconsin, Lt. Col. Harrison C. Hobart, Capt. Charles H. Walker

3d Brigade
Brig. Gen. John H. King

15th United States, 1st Battalion, Capt. Albert B. Dod
16th United States, 1st Battalion, Maj. Sidney Coolidge, Capt. R. E. A. Crofton
18th United States, 1st Battalion, Capt. George W. Smith
18th United States, 2d Battalion, Capt. Henry Haymond
19th United States, 1st Battalion, Maj. Samuel K. Dawson, Capt. Edmund L. Smith

Artillery
Indiana Light, 4th Battery (2d Brigade), Lt. David Flansburg, Lt. Henry J. Willits

1st Michigan Light, Battery A (1st Brigade), Lt. George W. Van Pelt, Lt. Almerick W. Wilbur

5th United States, Battery H (3d Brigade), Lt. Howard M. Burnham, Lt. Joshua A. Fessenden

2D DIVISION
Maj. Gen. James S. Negley

1st Brigade
Brig. Gen. John Beatty

104th Illinois, Lt. Col. Douglas Hapeman
42d Indiana, Lt. Col. William T. B. McIntire
88th Indiana, Col. George Humphrey
15th Kentucky, Col. Marion C. Taylor

2d Brigade
Col. Timothy R. Stanley
Col. William L. Stoughton

19th Illinois, Lt. Col. Alexander W. Raffen
11th Michigan, Col. William L. Stoughton, Lt. Col. Melvin Mudge
18th Ohio, Lt. Col. Charles H. Grosvenor

3d Brigade
Col. William Sirwell

37th Indiana, Lt. Col. William D. Ward
21st Ohio, Lt. Col. Dwella M. Stoughton, Maj. Arnold McMahan, Capt. Charles H. Vantine
74th Ohio, Capt. Joseph Fisher
78th Pennsylvania, Lt. Col. Archibald Blakeley

Artillery
Illinois Light, Bridges' Battery (1st Brigade), Capt. Lyman Bridges
1st Ohio Light, Battery G (3d Brigade), Capt. Alexander Marshall
1st Ohio Light, Battery M (2d Brigade), Capt. Frederick Schultz

3D DIVISION
Brig. Gen. John M. Brannan

1st Brigade
Col. John M. Connell

82d Indiana, Col. Morton C. Hunter
17th Ohio, Lt. Col. Durbin Ward
31st Ohio, Lt. Col. Frederick W. Lister
38th Ohio, Col. Edward H. Phelps (Not engaged; train guard)

2d Brigade
Col. John T. Croxton
Col. William H. Hays

10th Indiana, Col. William B. Carroll, Lt. Col. Marsh B. Taylor
74th Indiana, Col. Charles W. Chapman, Lt. Col. Myron Baker

4th Kentucky, Lt. Col. P. Burgess Hunt, Maj. Robert M. Kelly
10th Kentucky, Col. William H. Hays, Lt. Col. Gabriel C. Wharton
14th Ohio, Lt. Col. Henry D. Kingsbury

3d Brigade
Col. Ferdinand Van Derveer

87th Indiana, Col. Newell Gleason
2d Minnesota, Col. James George
9th Ohio, Col. Gustave Kammerling
35th Ohio, Lt. Col. Henry V. N. Boynton

Artillery

1st Michigan Light, Battery D (1st Brigade), Capt. Josiah W. Church
1st Ohio Light, Battery C (2d Brigade), Lt. Marco B. Gary
4th United States, Battery I (3d Brigade), Lt. Frank G. Smith

4TH DIVISION
Maj. Gen. Joseph J. Reynolds

1st Brigade
(Detached from its division and serving as mounted infantry.)
Col. John T. Wilder

92d Illinois, Col. Smith D. Atkins
98th Illinois, Col. John J. Funkhouser, Lt. Col. Edward Kitchell
ⁿ123d Illinois, Col. James Monroe
17th Indiana, Maj. William T. Jones
72d Indiana, Col. Abram O. Miller

2d Brigade
Col. Edward A. King
Col. Milton S. Robinson

68th Indiana, Capt. Harvey J. Espy
75th Indiana, Col. Milton S. Robinson, Lt. Col. William O'Brien
101st Indiana, Lt. Col. Thomas Doan
105th Ohio, Maj. George T. Perkins

3d Brigade
Brig. Gen. John B. Turchin

18th Kentucky, Lt. Col. Hubbard K. Milward, Capt. John B. Heltemes
11th Ohio, Col. Philander P. Lane
36th Ohio, Col. William G. Jones, Lt. Col. Hiram F. Devol
92d Ohio, Col. Benjamin D. Fearing, Lt. Col. Douglas Putnam Jr.

Artillery
Indiana Light, 18th Battery (1st Brigade), Capt. Eli Lilly
Indiana Light, 19th Battery (2d Brigade), Capt. Samuel J. Harris, Lt. Robert S. Lackey
Indiana Light, 21st Battery (3d Brigade), Capt. William W. Andrew

XX ARMY CORPS

Maj. Gen. Alexander M. McCook

General Headquarters

Provost Guard

81st Indiana Infantry, Company H, Capt. William J. Richards

Escort

2d Kentucky Cavalry, Company I, Lt. George W. L. Batman

1ST DIVISION

Brig. Gen. Jefferson C. Davis

1st Brigade

(Not engaged; guarding supply train.)

Col. P. Sidney Post

59th Illinois, Lt. Col. Joshua C. Winters
74th Illinois, Col. Jason Marsh
75th Illinois, Col. John E. Bennett
22d Indiana, Col. Michael Gooding
Wisconsin Light Artillery, 5th Battery, Capt. George Q. Gardner

2d Brigade

Brig. Gen. William P. Carlin

21st Illinois, Col. John W. S. Alexander, Capt. Chester K. Knight
38th Illinois, Lt. Col. Daniel H. Gilmer, Capt. Willis G. Whitehurst
81st Indiana, Capt. Nevil B. Boone, Maj. James E. Calloway
101st Ohio, Lt. Col. John Messer, Maj. Bedan B. McDanald, Capt. Leonard D. Smith
Minnesota Light Artillery, 2d Battery (Capt. William A. Hotchkiss, chief of division artillery), Lt. Albert Woodbury, Lt. Richard L. Dawley

3d Brigade

Col. Hans C. Heg

Col. John A. Martin

25th Illinois, Maj. Samuel D. Wall, Capt. Wesford Taggart
35th Illinois, Lt. Col. William P. Chandler
8th Kansas, Col. John A. Martin, Lt. Col. James L. Abernathy
15th Wisconsin, Lt. Col. Ole C. Johnson
Wisconsin Light Artillery, 8th Battery, Lt. John D. McLean

2D DIVISION

Brig. Gen. Richard W. Johnson

1st Brigade

Brig. Gen. August Willich

89th Illinois, Lt. Col. Duncan J. Hall, Maj. William D. Williams
32d Indiana, Lt. Col. Frank Erdelmeyer
39th Indiana (detached from its brigade and serving as mounted infantry),Col. Thomas J. Harrison
15th Ohio, Lt. Col. Frank Askew

49th Ohio, Maj. Samuel F. Gray, Capt. Luther M. Strong
1st Ohio Light Artillery, Battery A, Capt. Wilbur F. Goodspeed

2d Brigade
Col. Joseph B. Dodge

79th Illinois, Col. Allen Buckner
29th Indiana, Lt. Col. David M. Dunn
30th Indiana, Lt. Col. Orrin D. Hurd
77th Pennsylvania, Col. Thomas E. Rose, Capt. Joseph J. Lawson
Ohio Light Artillery, 20th Battery, Capt. Edward Grosskopff

3d Brigade
Col. Philemon P. Baldwin
Col. William W. Berry

6th Indiana, Lt. Col. Hagerman Tripp, Maj. Calvin D. Campbell
5th Kentucky, Col. William W. Berry, Capt. John M. Huston
1st Ohio, Lt. Col. Bassett Langdon
93d Ohio, Col. Hiram Strong, Lt. Col. William H. Martin
Indiana Light Artillery, 5th Battery, Capt. Peter Simonson

3D DIVISION
Maj. Gen. Philip H. Sheridan

1st Brigade
Brig. Gen. William H. Lytle
Col. Silas Miller

36th Illinois, Col. Silas Miller, Lt. Col. Porter C. Olson
88th Illinois, Lt. Col. Alexander S. Chadbourne
21st Michigan, Col. William B. McCreery, Maj. Seymour Chase
24th Wisconsin, Lt. Col. Theodore S. West, Maj. Carl von Baumbach
Indiana Light Artillery, 11th Battery, Capt. Arnold Sutermeister

2d Brigade
Col. Bernard Laiboldt

44th Illinois, Col. Wallace W. Barrett
73d Illinois, Col. James F. Jaquess
2d Missouri, Maj. Arnold Beck
15th Missouri, Col. Joseph Conrad
1st Missouri Light Artillery, Battery G (Capt. Henry Hescock, chief of division artillery), Lt. Gustavus Schueler

3d Brigade
Col. Luther P. Bradley
Col. Nathan H. Walworth

22d Illinois, Lt. Col. Francis Swanwick
27th Illinois, Col. Jonathan R. Miles
42d Illinois, Col. Nathan H. Walworth, Lt. Col. John A. Hottenstein

51st Illinois, Lt. Col. Samuel B. Raymond
1st Illinois Light Artillery, Battery C, Capt. Mark H. Prescott

XXI ARMY CORPS
Maj. Gen. Thomas L. Crittenden

General Headquarters

Escort
15th Illinois Cavalry, Company K, Capt. Samuel B. Sherer

1ST DIVISION
Brig. Gen. Thomas J. Wood

1st Brigade
Col. George P. Buell

100th Illinois, Col. Frederick A. Bartleson, Maj. Charles M. Hammond
58th Indiana, Lt. Col. James T. Embree
13th Michigan, Col. Joshua B. Culver, Maj. Willard G. Eaton
26th Ohio, Lt. Col. William H. Young

2d Brigade
(Stationed at Chattanooga and not engaged.)
Brig. Gen. George D. Wagner

15th Indiana, Col. Gustavus A. Wood
40th Indiana, Col. John W. Blake
57th Indiana, Lt. Col. George W. Lennard
97th Ohio, Lt. Col. Milton Barnes

3d Brigade
Col. Charles G. Harker

3d Kentucky, Col. Henry C. Dunlap
64th Ohio, Col. Alexander McIlvain
65th Ohio, Lt. Col. Horatio N. Whitbeck, Maj. Samuel C. Brown, Capt. Thomas Powell
125th Ohio, Col. Emerson Opdycke

Artillery
Indiana Light, 8th Battery (1st Brigade), Capt. George Estep
Indiana Light, 10th Battery (2d Brigade) (stationed at Chattanooga and not engaged), Lt. William A. Naylor
Ohio Light, 6th Battery (3d Brigade), Capt. Cullen Bradley

2D DIVISION
Maj. Gen. John M. Palmer

1st Brigade
Brig. Gen. Charles Cruft

31st Indiana, Col. John T. Smith
1st Kentucky (five companies detached as wagon guard), Lt. Col. Alva R. Hadlock
2d Kentucky, Col. Thomas D. Sedgewick
90th Ohio, Col. Charles H. Rippey

2d Brigade
Brig. Gen. William B. Hazen

9th Indiana, Col. Isaac C. B. Suman
6th Kentucky, Col. George T. Shackelford, Lt. Col. Richard Rockingham, Maj. Richard T. Whitaker
41st Ohio, Col. Aquila Wiley
124th Ohio, Col. Oliver H. Payne, Maj. James B. Hampson

3d Brigade
Col. William Grose

84th Illinois, Col. Louis H. Waters
36th Indiana, Lt. Col. Oliver H. P. Carey, Maj. Gilbert Trusler
23d Kentucky, Lt. Col. James C. Foy
6th Ohio, Col. Nicholas L. Anderson and Maj. Samuel C. Erwin
24th Ohio, Col. David J. Higgins

Artillery
Capt. William E. Standart

1st Ohio Light, Battery B (1st Brigade), Lt. Norman A. Baldwin
1st Ohio Light, Battery F (2d Brigade), Lt. Giles J. Cockerill
4th United States, Battery H (3d Brigade), Lt. Harry C. Cushing
4th United States, Battery M (3d Brigade), Lt. Francis L. D. Russell

Unattached
11th Illinois (battalion) (not engaged), Capt. E. Hibbard Topping

3D DIVISION
Brig. Gen. Horatio P, Van Cleve

1st Brigade
Brig. Gen. Samuel Beatty

79th Indiana, Col. Frederick Knefler
9th Kentucky, Col. George H. Cram
17th Kentucky, Col. Alexander M. Stout
19th Ohio, Lt. Col. Henry G. Stratton

2d Brigade
Col. George F. Dick

44th Indiana, Lt. Col. Simeon C. Aldrich
86th Indiana, Maj. Jacob C. Dick
13th Ohio, Lt. Col. Elhannon M. Mast, Capt. Horatio G. Cosgrove
59th Ohio, Lt. Col. Granville A. Frambes

3d Brigade
Col. Sidney M. Barnes

35th Indiana, Maj. John P. Dufficy
8th Kentucky, Lt. Col. James D. Mayhew, Maj. John S. Clark
21st Kentucky (stationed at Whiteside's and not engaged), Col. S. Woodson Price

51st Ohio, Col. Richard W. McClain, Lt. Col. Charles H. Wood

99th Ohio, Col. Peter T. Swaine

Artillery

Indiana Light, 7th Battery, Capt. George R. Swallow

Pennsylvania Light, 26th Battery, Capt. Alanson J. Stevens, Lt. Samuel M. McDowell

Wisconsin Light, 3d Battery, Lt. Cortland Livingston

RESERVE CORPS
Maj. Gen. Gordon Granger

1ST DIVISION
Brig. Gen. James B. Steedman

1st Brigade
Brig. Gen. Walter C. Whitaker

96th Illinois, Col. Thomas E. Champion

115th Illinois, Col. Jesse H. Moore

84th Indiana, Col. Nelson Trusler

22d Michigan (temporarily attached), Col. Heber Le Favour, Lt. Col. William Sanborn, Capt. Alonzo M. Keeler

40th Ohio, Lt. Col. William Jones

89th Ohio (temporarily attached), Col. Caleb H. Carlton, Capt. Isaac C. Nelson

Ohio Light Artillery, 18th Battery, Capt. Charles C. Aleshire

2d Brigade
Col. John G. Mitchell

78th Illinois, Lt. Col. Carter Van Vleck, and Lt. George Green

98th Ohio, Capt. Moses J. Urquhart, Capt. Armstrong J. Thomas

113th Ohio, Lt. Col. Darius B. Warner

121st Ohio, Lt. Col. Henry B. Banning

1st Illinois Light Artillery, Battery M, Lt. Thomas Burton

2D DIVISION
Brig. Gen. James D. Morgan

2d Brigade
Col. Daniel McCook

85th Illinois, Col. Caleb J. Dilworth

86th Illinois, Lt. Col. David W. Magee

125th Illinois, Col. Oscar F. Harmon

52d Ohio, Maj. James T. Holmes

69th Ohio (temporarily attached), Lt. Col. Joseph H. Brigham

2d Illinois Light Artillery, Battery I, Capt. Charles M. Barnett

CAVALRY CORPS
Brig. Gen. Robert B. Mitchell

1ST DIVISION
Col. Edward M. McCook

1st Brigade
Col. Archibald P. Campbell
2d Michigan, Maj. Leonidas S. Scranton
9th Pennsylvania, Lt. Col. Roswell M. Russell
1st Tennessee, Lt. Col. James P. Brownlow

2d Brigade
Col. Daniel M. Ray
2d Indiana, Maj. Joseph B. Presdee
4th Indiana, Lt. Col. John T. Deweese
2d Tennessee, Lt. Col. William R. Cook
1st Wisconsin, Col. Oscar H. La Grange
1st Ohio Light Artillery, Battery D (section), Lt. Nathaniel M. Newell

3d Brigade
Col. Louis D. Watkins
4th Kentucky, Col. Wickliffe Cooper
5th Kentucky, Lt. Col. William T. Hoblitzell
6th Kentucky, Maj. Louis A. Gratz

2D DIVISION
Brig. Gen. George Crook

1st Brigade
Col. Robert H. G. Minty
3d Indiana (battalion), Lt. Col. Robert Klein
4th Michigan, Maj. Horace Gray
7th Pennsylvania, Lt. Col. James J. Seibert
4th United States, Capt. James B. McIntyre

2d Brigade
Col. Eli Long
2d Kentucky, Col. Thomas P. Nicholas
1st Ohio, Lt. Col. Valentine Cupp, Maj. Thomas J. Patten
3d Ohio, Lt. Col. Charles B. Seidel
4th Ohio, Lt. Col. Oliver P. Robie

Artillery
Chicago (Illinois) Board of Trade Battery, Capt. James H. Stokes

APPENDIX B
Order of Battle: Army of Tennessee

Organization of the Army of Tennessee, commanded by General Braxton Bragg, CSA, 19—20 September 1863

Headquarters

Escort

Capt. Guy Dreux

Dreux's Company Louisiana Cavalry, Lt. O. De Buis
Holloway's Company Alabama Cavalry, Capt. E. M. Holloway

RIGHT WING
Lt. Gen. Leonidas Polk

Escort

Greenleaf's Company Louisiana Cavalry, Capt. Leeds Greenleaf

CHEATHAM'S DIVISION (of Polk's Corps)
Maj. Gen. Benjamin F. Cheatham

Escort

Company G, 2d Georgia Cavalry, Capt. Thomas M. Merritt

Jackson's Brigade
Brig. Gen. John K. Jackson

1st Georgia (Confederate), 2d Battalion, Maj. James Clark Gordon
5th Georgia, Col. Charles P. Daniel
2d Georgia Battalion Sharpshooters, Maj. Richard H. Whiteley
5th Mississippi, Lt. Col. W. L. Sykes, Maj. John B. Herring
8th Mississippi, Col. John C. Wilkinson

Smith's Brigade
Brig. Gen. Preston Smith
Col. Alfred J. Vaughn Jr.

11th Tennessee, Col. George W. Gordon
12th Tennessee/47th Tennessee, Col. William M. Watkins
18th Tennessee/154th Tennessee, Col. A. J. Vaughn Jr., Lt. Col. R. W. Pitman
29th Tennessee, Col. Horace Rice
Dawson's (battalion) Sharpshooters (composed of two companies from the 11th Tennessee, two from the 12th and 47th Tennessee [consolidated], and one from the 154th Senior Tennessee), Maj. J. W. Dawson, Maj. William Green, Maj. James Purl

Maney's Brigade
Brig. Gen. George Maney

1st Tennessee/27th Tennessee, Col. Hume R. Feild
4th Tennessee (Provisional Army), Col. James A. McMurry, Lt. Col. Robert N. Lewis, Maj. Oliver A. Bradshaw, Capt. Joseph Bostick

6th Tennessee/9th Tennessee, Col. George C. Porter
24th Tennessee Battalion Sharpshooters, Maj. Frank Maney

Wright's Brigade
Brig. Gen. Marcus J. Wright

8th Tennessee, Col. John H. Anderson
16th Tennessee, Col. D. M. Donnell
28th Tennessee, Col. Sidney S. Stanton
38th Tennessee and Maj. Thomas B. Murray's (Tennessee) Battalion,Col. John C. Carter
51st Tennessee/52d Tennessee, Lt. Col. John G. Hall

Strahl's Brigade
Brig. Gen. Otho F. Strahl

4th Tennessee /5th Tennessee, Col. Jonathan J. Lamb
19th Tennessee, Col. Francis M. Walker
24th Tennessee, Col. John A. Wilson
31st Tennessee, Col. Egbert E. Tansil
33d Tennessee, Col. Warner P. Jones

Artillery
Maj. Melancthon Smith

Carnes' (Tennessee) Battery, Capt. William W. Carnes
Scogin's (Georgia) Battery, Capt. John Scogin
Scott's (Tennessee) Battery, Lt. John H. Marsh, Lt. A. T. Watson, Capt.William L. Scott
Smith's (Mississippi) Battery, Lt. William B. Turner
Stanford's (Mississippi) Battery, Capt. Thomas J. Stanford

HILL'S CORPS
Lt. Gen. Daniel H. Hill

CLEBURNE'S DIVISION
Maj. Gen. Patrick R. Cleburne

Escort
Sanders' Company Tennessee Cavalry, Capt. C. F. Sanders

Wood's Brigade
Brig. Gen. S. A. M. Wood

16th Alabama, Maj. John H. McGaughy, Capt. Frederick A. Ashford
33d Alabama, Col. Samuel Adams
45th Alabama, Col. E. B. Breedlove
18th Alabama Battalion, Maj. John H. Gibson, Col. Samuel Adams (33d Alabama)
32d Mississippi/45th Mississippi, Col. M. P. Lowrey
15th Mississippi Battalion Sharpshooters, Maj. A. T. Hawkins, Capt. Daniel Coleman

Polk's Brigade
Brig. Gen. Lucius E. Polk

1st Arkansas, Col. John W. Colquitt
3d Confederate/5th Confederate, Col. J. A. Smith

2d Tennessee, Col. William D. Robison

35th Tennessee, Col. Benjamin J. Hill

48th Tennessee, Col. George H. Nixon

Deshler's Brigade

Brig. Gen. James Deshler

Col. Roger Q. Mills

19th Arkansas/24th Arkansas, Lt. Col. A. S. Hutchison

6th Texas Infantry/10th Texas Infantry/15th Texas Cavalry (dismounted), Col. Roger Q. Mills, Lt. Col. T. Scott Anderson

17th Texas Cavalry (dismounted)/18th Texas Cavalry (dismounted)/24th Texas Cavalry (dismounted)/25th Texas Cavalry (dismounted), Col. F. C. Wilkes, Lt. Col. John T. Coit, Maj.William A. Taylor

Artillery

Maj. T. R. Hotchkiss

Capt. Henry C. Semple

Calvert's (Arkansas) Battery, Lt. Thomas J. Key

Douglas' (Texas) Battery, Capt. James P. Douglas

Semple's (Alabama) Battery, Capt. Henry C. Semple, Lt. R. W. Goldthwaite

BRECKINRIDGE'S DIVISION

Maj. Gen. John C. Breckinridge

Escort

Foules' Company Mississippi Cavalry, Capt. H. L. Foules

Helm's Brigade

Brig. Gen. Benjamin H. Helm

Col. Joseph H. Lewis

41st Alabama, Col. Martin L. Stansel

2d Kentucky, Lt. Col. James W. Hewitt, Lt. Col. James W. Moss

4th Kentucky, Col. Joseph P. Nuckols, Maj. Thomas W. Thompson

6th Kentucky, Col. Joseph H. Lewis, Lt. Col. Martin H. Cofer

9th Kentucky, Col. John W. Caldwell, Lt. Col. John C. Wickliffe

Adams' Brigade

Brig. Gen. Daniel W. Adams

Col. Randall L. Gibson

32d Alabama, Maj. John C. Kimbell

13th Louisiana/20th Louisiana, Col. Randall L. Gibson, Col. Leon von Zinken, Capt. E. M. Dubroca

16th Louisiana/25th Louisiana, Col. Daniel Gober

19th Louisiana, Lt. Col. Richard W. Turner, Maj. Loudon Butler, Capt. H. A. Kennedy

14th Louisiana Battalion, Maj. J. E. Austin

Stovall's Brigade

Brig. Gen. Marcellus A. Stovall

1st Florida/3d Florida, Col. William S. Dilworth

4th Florida, Col. W. L. L. Bowen

47th Georgia, Capt. William S. Phillips, Capt. Joseph S. Cone
60th North Carolina, Lt. Col. James M. Ray, Capt. James Thomas Weaver

Artillery
Maj. Rice E. Graves

Cobb's (Kentucky) Battery, Capt. Robert Cobb
Graves' (Kentucky) Battery, Lt. S. M. Spencer
Mebane's (Tennessee) Battery, Capt. John W. Mebane
Slocomb's (Louisiana) Battery, Capt. C. H. Slocomb

RESERVE CORPS
Maj. Gen. William H. T. Walker

WALKER'S DIVISION
Brig. Gen. States R. Gist

Gist's Brigade
Brig. Gen. States R. Gist
Col. Peyton H. Colquitt
Lt. Col. Leroy Napier

46th Georgia, Col. Peyton H. Colquitt, Maj. A. M. Speer
8th Georgia Battalion, Lt. Col. Leroy Napier, Maj. Z. L. Watters
16th South Carolina (not engaged, at Rome), Col. James McCullough
24th South Carolina, Col. Clement H. Stevens, Lt. Col. Ellison Capers

Ector's Brigade
Brig. Gen. Matthew D. Ector

Stone's (Alabama) Battalion Sharpshooters, Maj. T. O. Stone
Pound's (Mississippi) Battalion Sharpshooters, Capt. M. Pound
29th North Carolina, Col. William B. Creasman
9th Texas, Col. William H. Young
10th Texas Cavalry (serving as infantry), Lt. Col. C. R. Earp
14th Texas Cavalry (serving as infantry), Col. J. L. Camp
32d Texas Cavalry (serving as infantry), Col. Julius A. Andrews

Wilson's Brigade
Col. Claudius C. Wilson

25th Georgia, Lt. Col. A. J. Williams
29th Georgia, Lt. George R. McRae
30th Georgia, Lt. Col. James S. Boynton
1st Georgia Battalion Sharpshooters, Maj. Arthur Shaaff
4th Louisiana Battalion, Lt. Col. John McEnery

Artillery
Ferguson's (South Carolina) Battery (not engaged, at Rome),Lt. R. T. Beauregard
Howell's (Georgia) Battery (formerly Martin's), Capt. Evan P. Howell

LIDDELL'S DIVISION
Brig. Gen. St. John R. Liddell

Liddell's Brigade
Col. Daniel C. Govan

2d Arkansas/15th Arkansas, Lt. Col. Reuben F. Harvey, Capt. A. T. Meek
5th Arkansas/13th Arkansas, Col. L. Featherston, Lt. Col. John E. Murray
6th Arkansas/7th Arkansas, Col. D. A. Gillespie, Lt. Col. Peter Snyder
8th Arkansas, Lt. Col. George F. Baucum, Maj. A. Watkins
1st Louisiana (Regulars), Lt. Col. George F. Baucum (8th Arkansas), Maj. A. Watkins
   (8th Arkansas)

Walthall's Brigade
Brig. Gen. Edward C. Walthall

24th Mississippi, Lt. Col. R. P. McKelvaine, Maj. W. C. Staples, Capt. B. F. Toomer, Capt.
   J. D. Smith
27th Mississippi, Col. James A. Campbell
29th Mississippi, Col. William F. Brantly
30th Mississippi, Col. Junius I. Scales, Lt. Col. Hugh A. Reynolds, Maj. James M.
   Johnson
34th Mississippi, Maj. William G. Pegram, Capt. H. J. Bowen, Lt. Col. Hugh A. Reynolds
   (30th Mississippi)

Artillery
Capt. Charles Swett

Fowler's (Alabama) Battery, Capt. William H. Fowler
Warren Light Artillery (Mississippi Battery), Lt. H. Shannon

LEFT WING
Lt. Gen. James Longstreet

HINDMAN'S DIVISION (of Polk's Corps)
Maj. Gen. Thomas C. Hindman
Brig. Gen. Patton Anderson

Escort
Lenoir's Company Alabama Cavalry, Capt. T. M. Lenoir

Anderson's Brigade
Brig. Gen. Patton Anderson
Col. J. H. Sharp

7th Mississippi, Col. W. H. Bishop
9th Mississippi, Maj. T. H. Lynam
10th Mississippi, Lt. Col. James Barr
41st Mississippi, Col. W. F. Tucker
44th Mississippi, Col. J. H. Sharp, Lt. Col. R. G. Kelsey
9th Mississippi Battalion Sharpshooters, Maj. W. C. Richards
Garrity's (Alabama) Battery, Capt. James Garrity

Deas' Brigade
Brig. Gen. Zachariah C. Deas

19th Alabama, Col. Samuel K. McSpadden
22d Alabama, Lt. Col. John Weedon, Capt. Harry T. Toulmin
25th Alabama, Col. George D. Johnston
39th Alabama, Col. Whitfield Clark
50th Alabama, Col. J. G. Coltart
17th Alabama Battalion Sharpshooters, Capt. James F. Nabers
Dent's (Alabama) Battery (formerly Robertson's), Capt. S. H. Dent

Manigault's Brigade
Brig. Gen. Arthur M. Manigault

24th Alabama, Col. N. N. Davis
28th Alabama, Col. John C. Reid
34th Alabama, Maj. John N. Slaughter
10th South Carolina/19th South Carolina, Col. James F. Pressley
Waters' (Alabama) Battery, Lt. Charles W. Watkins

BUCKNER'S CORPS
Maj. Gen. Simon B. Buckner

Escort
Clark's Company Tennessee Cavalry, Capt. J. W. Clark

STEWART'S DIVISION
Maj. Gen. Alexander P. Stewart

Johnson's Brigade
(Part of Johnson's Provisional Division)
Brig. Gen. Bushrod R. Johnson
Col. John S. Fulton

17th Tennessee, Lt. Col. Watt W. Floyd
23d Tennessee, Col. R. H. Keeble
25th Tennessee, Lt. Col. R. B. Snowden
44th Tennessee, Lt. Col. John L. McEwen Jr., Maj. G. M. Crawford

Bate's Brigade
Brig. Gen. William B. Bate

58th Alabama, Col. Bushrod Jones
37th Georgia, Col. A. F. Rudler, Lt. Col. Joseph T. Smith
4th Georgia Battalion Sharpshooters, Maj. T. D. Caswell, Capt. B. M. Turner, Lt. Joel
Towers
15th Tennessee/37th Tennessee, Col. R. C. Tyler, Lt. Col. R. Dudley Frayser, Capt. R. M.
Tankesley
20th Tennessee, Col. Thomas B. Smith, Maj. W. M. Shy

Brown's Brigade
Brig. Gen. John C. Brown
Col. Edmund C. Cook

18th Tennessee, Col. Joseph B. Palmer, Lt. Col. William R. Butler, Capt. Gideon H. Lowe
26th Tennessee, Col. John M. Lillard, Maj. Richard M. Saffell
32d Tennessee, Col. Edmund C. Cook, Capt. Calaway G. Tucker
45th Tennessee, Col. Anderson Searcy
23d Tennessee Battalion, Maj. Tazewell W. Newman, Capt. W. P. Simpson

Clayton's Brigade
Brig. Gen. Henry D. Clayton

18th Alabama, Col. J. T. Holtzclaw, Lt. Col. R. F. Inge, Maj. P. F. Hunley
36th Alabama, Col. Lewis T. Woodruff
38th Alabama, Lt. Col. A. R. Lankford

Artillery
Maj. J. Wesley Eldridge

1st Arkansas Battery, Capt. John T. Humphreys
T. H. Dawson's (Georgia) Battery, Lt. R. W. Anderson
Eufaula Artillery (Alabama Battery), Capt. McDonald Oliver
Company E, 9th Georgia Artillery Battalion (Billington W. York's Battery), Lt. William S. Everett

PRESTON'S DIVISION
Brig. Gen. William Preston

Gracie's Brigade
Brig. Gen. Archibald Gracie Jr.

43d Alabama, Col. Young M. Moody
1st Alabama Battalion (Hilliard's Legion), Lt. Col. John H. Holt, Capt. George W. Huguley
2d Alabama Battalion (Hilliard's Legion), Lt. Col. Bolling Hall Jr., Capt. W. D. Walden
3d Alabama Battalion (Hilliard's Legion), Lt. Col. John W. A. Sanford
4th Alabama Battalion (artillery battalion, Hilliard's Legion, serving as infantry), Maj. John D. McLennan
63d Tennessee, Lt. Col. Abraham Fulkerson, Maj. John A. Aiken

Trigg's Brigade
Col. Robert C. Trigg

1st Florida Cavalry (dismounted), Col. G. Troup Maxwell
6th Florida, Col. J. J. Finley
7th Florida, Col. Robert Bullock
54th Virginia, Lt. Col. John J. Wade

3d Brigade
Col. John H. Kelly

65th Georgia, Col. R. H. Moore

5th Kentucky, Col. Hiram Hawkins
58th North Carolina, Col. John B. Palmer
63d Virginia, Maj. James M. French

Artillery Battalion
Maj. A. Leyden

Jeffress' (Virginia) Battery, Captain William C. Jeffress
Peeples (Georgia) Battery, Capt. Tyler M. Peeples
Wolihin's (Georgia) Battery, Capt. Andrew M. Wolihin

RESERVE CORPS ARTILLERY
Maj. Samuel C. Williams

Baxter's (Tennessee) Battery, Capt. Edmund D. Baxter
Darden's (Mississippi) Battery, Capt. Putnam Darden
Kolb's (Alabama) Battery, Capt. R. F. Kolb
McCants' (Florida) Battery, Capt. Robert P. McCants

JOHNSON'S DIVISION
(This division was a provisional organization embracing Johnson's and, part of the time, Robertson's, Gregg's, and McNair's Brigades. On 19 September, the division was attached to Longstreet's Corps under Maj. Gen. John B. Hood.)

Brig. Gen. Bushrod R. Johnson.

Gregg's Brigade
Brig. Gen. John Gregg
Col. Cyrus A. Sugg

3d Tennessee, Col. Calvin H. Walker
10th Tennessee, Col. William Grace
30th Tennessee, Lt. Col. James J. Turner, Capt. Charles S. Douglass
41st Tennessee, Lt. Col. James D. Tillman
50th Tennessee, Col. Cyrus A. Sugg, Lt. Col. Thomas W. Beaumont, Maj. Christopher W. Robertson, Col. Calvin H. Walker (3d Tennessee)
1st Tennessee Battalion, Maj. Stephen H. Colms, Maj. Christopher W. Robertson (50th Tennessee)
7th Texas, Col. H. B. Granbury, Maj. K. M. Vanzandt
Bledsoe's (Missouri) Battery, Lt. R. L. Wood

McNair's Brigade
Brig. Gen. Evander McNair
Col. David Coleman

1st Arkansas Mounted Rifles (dismounted), Col. Robert W. Harper
2d Arkansas Mounted Rifles (dismounted), Col. James A. Williamson
25th Arkansas, Lt. Col. Eli Hufstedler
4th/31st Arkansas and 4th Arkansas Battalion (consolidated), Maj. J. A. Ross
39th North Carolina, Col. David Coleman
Culpeper's (South Carolina) Battery, Capt. James F. Culpeper

LONGSTREET'S CORPS

(The Army of Northern Virginia. Its organization was taken from returns of that army for 31 August 1863. Pickett's Division was left in Virginia.)

Maj. Gen. John B. Hood

McLAWS' DIVISION

Brig. Gen. Joseph B. Kershaw

Maj. Gen. Lafayette McLaws

Kershaw's Brigade

Brig. Gen. Joseph B. Kershaw

2d South Carolina, Lt. Col. Franklin Gaillard
3d South Carolina, Col. James D. Nance
7th South Carolina, Lt. Col. Elbert Bland, Maj. John S. Hard, Capt. E. J. Goggans
8th South Carolina, Col. John W. Henagan
15th South Carolina, Col. Joseph F. Gist
3d South Carolina Battalion, Capt. Joshua M. Townsend

Humphreys' Brigade

Brig. Gen. Benjamin G. Humphreys

13th Mississippi, Lt. Col. Kennon McElroy
17th Mississippi, Lt. Col. John C. Fiser
18th Mississippi, Capt. W. F. Hubbard
21st Mississippi, Lt. Col. D. N. Moody

HOOD'S DIVISION

Maj. Gen. John B. Hood

Brig. Gen. E. McIver Law

Law's Brigade

Brig. Gen. E. McIver Law

Col. James L. Sheffield

Col. William F. Perry

4th Alabama, Col. Pinckney D. Bowles
15th Alabama, Col. W. C. Oates
44th Alabama, Col. William F. Perry
47th Alabama, Maj. James M. Campbell
48th Alabama, Lt. Col. William M. Hardwick

Robertson's Brigade

(Served part of the time in Johnson's Provisional Division.)

Brig. Gen. Jerome B. Robertson

Col. Van H. Manning

3d Arkansas, Col. Van H. Manning
1st Texas, Capt. R. J. Harding
4th Texas, Lt. Col. John P. Bane, Capt. R. H. Bassett
5th Texas, Maj. J. C. Rogers, Capt. J. S. Cleveland, Capt. T. T. Clay

Benning's Brigade
Brig. Gen. Henry L. Benning

2d Georgia, Lt. Col. William S. Shepherd, Maj. W. W. Charlton
15th Georgia, Col. Dudley M. Du Bose, Maj. P. J. Shannon
17th Georgia, Lt. Col. Charles W. Matthews
20th Georgia, Col. J. D. Waddell

RESERVE ARTILLERY
Maj. Felix H. Robertson

Barret's (Missouri) Battery, Capt. Overton W. Barret
Le Gardeur's (Louisiana) Battery (not mentioned in the reports but in Reserve Artillery on 31 August, and Captain Le Gardeur, etc., relieved from duty in Army of Tennessee on 1 November 1863), Capt. G. Le Gardeur Jr.
Havis' (Georgia) Battery, Capt. M. W. Havis
Lumsden's (Alabama) Battery, Capt. Charles L. Lumsden
Massenburg's (Georgia) Battery, Capt. T. L. Massenburg

CAVALRY
Maj. Gen. Joseph Wheeler

WHARTON'S DIVISION
Brig. Gen. John A. Wharton

1st Brigade
Col. C. C. Crews

Malone's (Alabama) Regiment, Col. J. C. Malone Jr.
2d Georgia, Lt. Col. F. M. Ison
3d Georgia, Col. R. Thompson
4th Georgia, Col. Isaac W. Avery

2d Brigade
Col. Thomas Harrison

3d Confederate, Col. W. N. Estes
3d Kentucky, Lt. Col. J. W. Griffith
4th Tennessee, Lt. Col. Paul F. Anderson
8th Texas, Lt. Col. Gustave Cook
11th Texas, Col. G. R. Reeves
White's (Tennessee) Battery, Capt. B. F. White Jr.

MARTIN'S DIVISION
Brig. Gen. William T. Martin

1st Brigade
Col. John T. Morgan

1st Alabama, Lt. Col. D. T. Blakey
3d Alabama, Lt. Col. T. H. Mauldin
51st Alabama, Lt. Col. M. L. Kirkpatrick
8th Confederate, Lt. Col. John S. Prather

2d Brigade
Col. A. A. Russell

4th Alabama (Russell's Regiment), Lt. Col. J. M. Hambrick
1st Confederate, Capt. C. H. Conner
J. H. Wiggins' (Arkansas) Battery, Lt. J. P. Bryant

FORREST'S CORPS
Brig. Gen. Nathan B. Forrest

Escort
Jackson's Company Tennessee Cavalry, Capt. J. C. Jackson

ARMSTRONG'S DIVISION
Brig. Gen. Frank C. Armstrong

Armstrong's Brigade
Col. James T. Wheeler

3d Arkansas, Col. A. W. Hobson
2d Kentucky, Lt. Col. Thomas G. Woodward
6th Tennessee Battalion, Lt. Col. James H. Lewis
18th Tennessee Battalion, Maj. Charles McDonald

Forrest's Brigade

Col. George G. Dibrell

4th Tennessee, Col. William S. McLemore
8th Tennessee, Capt. Hamilton McGinnis
9th Tennessee, Col. Jacob B. Biffle
10th Tennessee, Col. Nicholas Nickleby Cox
11th Tennessee, Col. Daniel Wilson Holman
Shaw's Battalion, O. P. Hamilton's Battalion, and R. D. Allison's Squadron (consolidated), Maj. Joseph Shaw
Huggins' (Tennessee) Battery (formerly Freeman's), Capt A. L. Huggins
Morton's (Tennessee) Battery, Capt. John W. Morton Jr.

PEGRAM'S DIVISION
Brig. Gen. John Pegram

Davidson's Brigade
Brig. Gen. H. B. Davidson

1st Georgia, Col. J. J. Morrison
6th Georgia, Col. John R. Hart
6th North Carolina, Col. George N. Folk
Rucker's (1st Tennessee) Legion, Col. E. W. Rucker (12th Tennessee Battalion, Maj. G. W. Day, and 16th Tennessee Battalion, Capt. John Q. Arnold [captain Company B, 12th Battalion])
Huwald's (Tennessee) Battery, Capt. Gustave A. Huwald

Scott's Brigade
Col. John S. Scott

10th Confederate, Col. C. T. Goode
Detachment of John H. Morgan's command, Lt. Col. R. M. Martin
1st Louisiana, Lt. Col. James O. Nixon
2d Tennessee, Col. H. M. Ashby
5th Tennessee, Col. George W. McKenzie
N. T. N. Robinson's (Louisiana) Battery (one section), Lt. Winslow Robinson

———————————————————————

APPENDIX C
Chickamauga Medal of Honor Recipients

Carson, William J.

Rank and Organization: Musician, Company E, 1st Battalion, 15th United States Infantry.

Place and Date: At Chickamauga, Georgia, 19 September 1863.

Entered Service at:

Birth: Washington County, Pennsylvania.

Date of Issue: 27 January 1894.

Citation: Most distinguished gallantry in battle.

Myers, George S.

Rank and Organization: Private, Company F, 101st Ohio Infantry.

Place and Date: At Chickamauga, Georgia, 19 September 1863.

Entered Service at:

Birth: Fairfield, Ohio.

Date of Issue: 9 April 1894.

Citation: Myers saved the regimental colors by greatest personal devotion and bravery.

Reed, Axel H.

Rank and Organization: Sergeant, Company K, 2d Minnesota Infantry.

Place and Date: At Chickamauga, Georgia, 19 September 1863; at Missionary Ridge, Tennessee, 25 November 1863.

Entered Service at:

Birth: Maine.

Date of Issue: 2 April 1898.

Citation: While in arrest at Chickamauga, Georgia, Reed left his place in the rear and voluntarily went to the line of battle, secured a rifle, and fought gallantly during the two-day battle; Reed was released from arrest in recognition of his bravery. At Missionary Ridge, he commanded his company and gallantly led it, being among the first to enter the enemy's works; he was severely wounded, losing an arm, but declined a discharge and remained in active service to the end of the war.

Richey, William E.

Rank and Organization: Corporal, Company A, 15th Ohio Infantry.

Place and Date: At Chickamauga, Georgia, 19 September 1863.

Entered Service at:

Birth: Athens County, Ohio.

Date of Issue: 9 November 1893.

Citation: While on the extreme front, between the lines of the combatants, Richey single-handedly captured a Confederate major who was armed and mounted.

Chamberlain, Orville T.

Rank and Organization: Second Lieutenant, Company G, 74th Indiana Infantry.

Place and Date: At Chickamauga, Georgia, 20 September 1863.

Entered Service at:

Birth: Kosciusko County, Indiana.

Date of Issue: 11 March 1896.

Citation: While exposed to a galling fire, Chamberlain went in search of another regiment, found its location, procured ammunition from the men thereof, and returned with the ammunition to his own company.

Cilley, Clinton A.

Rank and Organization: Captain, Company C, 2d Minnesota Infantry.

Place and Date: At Chickamauga, Georgia, 20 September 1863.

Entered Service at: Farmington, New Hampshire.

Birth: Rockingham County, New Hampshire.

Date of Issue: 12 June 1895.

Citation: Cilley seized the colors of a retreating regiment and led it into the thick of the attack.

Porter, Horace

Rank and Organization: Captain, Ordnance Department, United States Army.

Place and Date: At Chickamauga, Georgia, 20 September 1863.

Entered Service at: Pennsylvania.

Birth: Pennsylvania.

Date of Issue: 8 July 1902.

Citation: While acting as a volunteer aide at a critical moment when the lines were broken, Porter rallied enough fugitives to hold the ground under heavy fire long enough to effect the escape of wagon trains and batteries.

Taylor, Anthony

Rank and Organization: First Lieutenant, Company A, 15th Pennsylvania Cavalry.

Place and Date: At Chickamauga, Georgia, 20 September 1863.

Entered Service at:

Birth: Burlington, New Jersey.

Date of Issue: 4 December 1893.

Citation: Taylor held out to the last with a small force against the advance of superior numbers of the enemy.

Whitney, William G.

Rank and Organization: Sergeant, Company B, 11th Michigan Infantry.

Place and Date: At Chickamauga, Georgia, 20 September 1863.

Entered Service at:

Birth: Allen, Michigan.

Date of Issue: 21 October 1895.

Citation: As the enemy was about to charge, Whitney went outside the temporary Union works among the dead and wounded enemy soldiers, and, at great exposure to himself, cut off and removed their cartridge boxes, bringing them within the Union lines. The ammunition was then used with good effect in again repulsing the attack.

————————————

APPENDIX D
Meteorological Data Relevant to the Chickamauga Campaign

1. There had been no appreciable rainfall in the area of operations for approximately six weeks prior to the battle of 18—20 September 1863.

2. On 18 September, the sky was cloudy and the temperature at noon was 62 degrees.

3. The temperature dropped precipitously into the 30s during the night of 19 September, making the morning of 20 September very cold with a heavy frost.

4. On the morning of 20 September, a heavy fog covered the battle area, especially near Chickamauga Creek. The fog was enhanced by smoke from the burning woods. By midmorning, the fog had dissipated.

5. On 20 September, sunrise occurred at 0547, sunset at 1800, and EENT (end evening nautical twilight) at 1930.

6. The moon reached first quarter on 20 September and set at approximately midnight on that night.

BIBLIOGRAPHY

This bibliography is not intended to be comprehensive. Its focus is on general usefulness and probable availability.

I. Conducting a Staff Ride.

Robertson, William G. *The Staff Ride*. U.S. Army Center of Military History, 1987.

This pamphlet outlines the philosophy behind Staff Rides and offers suggestions on how to create one.

II. Campaign.

Cist, Henry M. *The Army of the Cumberland*. New York: Charles Scribner's, 1882.

Written by a junior staff officer, this comprehensive account is flawed by an extreme pro-Rosecrans bias.

Connelly, Thomas. *Autumn of Glory: The Army of Tennessee, 1862—1865*. Baton Rouge: Louisiana State University Press, 1971.

Although strongly anti-Bragg, the Chickamauga chapters are the best scholarly analysis of the Confederate side currently in print.

Van Horne, Thomas B. *History of the Army of the Cumberland: Its Organization, Campaigns, and Battles*. 2 vols. Cincinnati, OH: Ogden, Campbell, & Co., 1875. Reprint. Wilmington, NC: Broadfoot Publishing Co., 1988.

Written by a member of George Thomas' staff who had access to his papers, this account is especially useful on Thomas and the XIV Corps.

The War of the Rebellion: A Compilation of the Official Records of the Union and Confederate Armies. Vol. 30 (4 parts). Washington, DC: U.S. Government Printing Office, 1899. Reprint. Wilmington, NC: Broadfoot Publishing Co., 1985.

Essential for any detailed study, this work contains battle reports, correspondence, messages, and miscellaneous reports.

West Point Atlas of American Wars. Vol. 1. New York: Praeger, 1959. Also available as Griess, Thomas E., ed. *Atlas for the American Civil War*. West Point Military History Series. Wayne, NJ: Avery Publishing Group, 1986.

This useful set of campaign maps contains some minor inaccuracies regarding troop dispositions. Also, the terrain of Lookout Mountain is misrepresented; no true gaps across the mountain exist.

III. The Battle.

Tucker, Glenn. *Chickamauga: Bloody Battle in the West*. Dayton, OH: Morningside Press, 1984.

Flawed by extensive digressions and lack of analysis, this book nevertheless is the most detailed modern account of the battle.

_____. *The Battle of Chickamauga*. Philadelphia, PA: Eastern Acorn Press, 1969.

Though not without errors, this extended magazine article represents an inexpensive executive summary of the battle and includes useful battle maps.

IV. Weapons and Tactics.

Coggins, Jack. *Arms and Equipment of the Civil War*. Garden City, NY: Doubleday, 1962. Reprint. Wilmington, NC: Broadfoot Publishing Co., 1987.

This very useful primer, whose superb illustrations enhance an authoritative text, offers an excellent foundation for the study of specific battles.

Daniel, Larry J. *Cannoneers in Gray: The Field Artillery of the Army of Tennessee, 1861—1865*. Tuscaloosa: University of Alabama Press, 1984.

The Chickamauga chapter is useful more for organizational questions than for tactical details.

Griffith, Paddy. *Battle in the Civil War*. Nottinghamshire, England: Fieldbooks, 1986.

This inexpensive, highly useful primer covers a complex subject well from a modern perspective.

Morelock, Jerry. "Ride to the River of Death: Cavalry Operations in the Chickamauga Campaign." *Military Review* 64 (October 1984):2—21.

Focusing solely on operations of the opposing cavalry forces, this article analyzes that aspect of the campaign from a modern perspective.

Thomas, Dean S. *Cannons: Introduction to Civil War Artillery*. Arendtsville, PA: Thomas Publications, 1985.

This very helpful primer describes the technical characteristics of most of the field artillery weapons employed at Chickamauga.

V. Combat Support and Combat Service Support.

Brown, Joseph Willard. *The Signal Corps, U.S.A., in the War of the Rebellion*. Boston, MA: U.S. Veteran Signal Corps Association, 1896.

This book provides both general background information on Civil War Signal Corps activities and specific material on Union signal activity in the Chickamauga campaign.

Gillett, Mary C. *The Army Medical Department, 1818—1865*. Army Historical Series. Washington, DC: U.S. Army Center of Military History, 1987.

An exhaustive treatment of its subject, this work is useful for background information only.

Huston, James A. *The Sinews of War: Army Logistics, 1775—1953*. Army Historical Series. Washington, DC: Office of the Chief of Military History, United States Army, 1966.

Wide in scope and with authoritative information, Huston's work provides helpful background data on Civil War logistics.

Kyle, William. "Logistics at Chickamauga." *Army Logistician* 18 (September-October 1986):26—30.

This brief article analyzes the Chickamauga campaign from a logistical perspective.

. Lord, Francis A. *They Fought for the Union.* Harrisburg, PA: Stackpole, 1960. Reprint. Westport, CT: Greenwood Press, 1981.

This book provides data on almost every subject relating to the Union Army in the Civil War, except its campaigns.

VI. *Biographies (Federal).*

Warner, Ezra J. *Generals in Blue.* Baton Rouge: Louisiana State University Press, 1964. Reprinted 1984.

Short biographical sketches of 583 Federal general officers are in this work.

Rosecrans

Lamers, William M. *The Edge of Glory: A Biography of General William S. Rosecrans, U.S.A.* New York: Harcourt, Brace, and World, 1961.

The only modern biography of Rosecrans, this work also presents the best possible view of the man.

Thomas

Cleaves, Freeman. *Rock of Chickamauga: The Life of General George H. Thomas.* Norman: University of Oklahoma Press, 1948.

This book is a solid, though relatively general, account of Thomas' life.

McKinney, Francis F. *Education in Violence: The Life of George H. Thomas and the History of the Army of the Cumberland.* Detroit, MI: Wayne State University Press, 1961. Reprint. Chicago, IL: Americana House, 1991.

Although suffering from a pedestrian writing style, this book is the best biography of George Thomas.

VII. *Biographies (Confederate).*

Warner, Ezra J. *Generals in Gray.* Baton Rouge: Louisiana State University Press, 1959. Reprinted 1983.

This work contains short biographical sketches of all Confederate general officers.

Bragg

McWhiney, Grady. *Braxton Bragg and Confederate Defeat.* Vol. 1. *Field Command.* New York: Columbia University Press, 1969. Reprint. Tuscaloosa: University of Alabama Press, 1991.

This volume ends in 1862 but provides useful character insights.

Hallock, Judith Lee. *Braxton Bragg and Confederate Defeat.* Vol. 2. Tuscaloosa: University of Alabama Press, 1991.

More positive in tone than McWhiney's volume, Hallock's book has considerable Chickamauga utility.

Buckner

Stickles, Arndtt M. *Simon Bolivar Buckner: Borderland Knight.* Chapel Hill: University of North Carolina Press, 1940. Reprint. Wilmington, NC: Broadfoot Publishing Co., 1987.

This book is a useful but not especially perceptive biography of a minor figure at Chickamauga.

Cleburne

Purdue, Howell, and Elizabeth Purdue. *Pat Cleburne, Confederate General: A Definitive Biography.* Hillsboro, TX: Hill Junior College Press, 1973.

This work is a detailed study of one of the most competent Confederate division commanders.

Forrest

Henry, Robert Selph. *"First With the Most" Forrest.* Indianapolis, IN: Bobbs-Merrill, 1944.

Henry's work is one of the best of the many biographies of Forrest.

VIII. Films.

The Battle of Chickamauga. 60 min. Columbia, MD: Classic Images, 1988.

This film contains some excellent graphics and is the best available film overview of the battle.

U.S. Department of the Army. *.58 Rifled Musket.* TVT 21-84 (705967DA). 16 min. *12 Pounder Napoleon.* TVT 21-85 (705968DA). 16 min.

Created by the Department of History at West Point, both films feature firing demonstrations of actual weapons, as well as background information.

U.S. Department of the Army. *The Staff Ride*. TVT 20-762 (706159DA). 36 min.

This film presents an excellent overview of what a Staff Ride entails and provides advice on how to conduct one.

VIII. Maps.

U.S. Department of the Interior Geological Survey. East Ridge TN-GA 34085-H2-TM-024, 1982, DMA 3953 I NW-Series V845; Fort Oglethorpe TN-GA 34085-H3-TM-024, 1982, DMA 3953 IV NE-Series V845. For sale by U.S. Geological Survey, Reston, VA 22092; Tennessee Department of Conservation, Division of Geology, Nashville, TN 37219; U.S. Tennessee Valley Authority, Chattanooga, TN 37401 or Knoxville, TN 37902.

These two 1:24,000 modern topographic map sheets cover the battlefield and surrounding area from Rossville to the town of Chickamauga (Crawfish Spring in 1863).

"Chickamauga Battlefield Location Map for Monuments, Markers, and Plaques." Reproduced from U.S. Geological Survey, 1934, Chickamauga and Chattanooga National Military Park, GA (Chickamauga Battlefield), Scale 1:9,600. Eastern National Park and Monument Association, 1986.

This map, available in a waterproofed version, covers the battlefield and contains an order of battle and alphabetical listing of monuments, markers, and tablets on the back. It is available through the park bookstore.

THE AUTHORS OF THE HANDBOOK

Dr. William Glenn Robertson

Dr. William Glenn Robertson is chief, Instructor Team III, at the Combat Studies Institute, U.S. Army Command and General Staff College. A graduate of the University of Richmond, he received his M.A. and Ph.D. degrees in history from the University of Virginia. He is the author of *Back Door to Richmond: The Bermuda Hundred Campaign; The Petersburg Campaign: The Battle of Old Men and Young Boys;* the Bull Run chapter in *America's First Battles, 1776—1965;* Leavenworth Paper No. 13, *Counterattack on the Naktong, 1950;* and Center of Military History Pamphlet 70-21, *The Staff Ride.* Dr. Robertson currently directs Staff Rides to all the major western-theater Civil War battlefields.

**Lieutenant Colonel
Edward P. Shanahan**

Lieutenant Colonel Edward P. Shanahan is a military history instructor and member of the Staff Ride Team at the Combat Studies Institute, U.S. Army Command and General Staff College. He received his commission in Armor from Eastern Kentucky University, Richmond, Kentucky, and his M.S. in geography from The Pennsylvania State University, University Park, Pennsylvania. He has served as a scout pilot in Vietnam and as an S3 and executive officer of an armor battalion in Germany. He has also been an instructor in geography and assistant professor of history at the U.S. Military Academy.

Lieutenant Colonel John I. Boxberger

Lieutenant Colonel John I. Boxberger is currently the senior brigade trainer for the National Training Center, Fort Irwin, California. He received a B.S. degree from the U.S. Military Academy and an M.A. in history from the University of North Carolina at Chapel Hill. An Armor officer, he has served with the 11th Armored Cavalry Regiment, 9th Infantry Division, and the 1st Armored Division. He has taught history at the U.S. Military Academy and at the U.S. Army Command and General Staff College (CGSC). As part of the Staff Ride Team at CGSC, he helped lead Staff Rides of all the major western-theater Civil War battlefields.

**Major
George E. Knapp**

Major George E. Knapp is a history instructor at the Combat Studies Institute, U.S. Army Command and General Staff College. He is a graduate of Spring Hill College in Mobile, Alabama; has an M.A. degree in history from the University of Missouri at Kansas City; and is a USACGSC graduate. He served in Vietnam as an enlisted man and received his commission in the Infantry from Officer Candidate School in 1978. He commanded infantry companies in the 2d Armored Division (Forward). Other assignments at Fort Leavenworth include service at the TRADOC Analysis Command and the School of Advanced Military Studies.